CHRISTIAN PHILOSOPHY

**University of Notre Dame Studies
in the Philosophy of Religion**

Number 6

Christian Philosophy

edited by Thomas P. Flint

University of Notre Dame Press • Notre Dame, Indiana

Library of Congress Cataloging-in-Publication Data

Christian philosophy / edited by Thomas P. Flint.
        p.   cm. — (University of Notre Dame studies in the
philosophy of religion ; no. 6)
    Papers presented at the Conference on Christian and
Theistic Philosophy held Feb. 25–27, 1988, at the
University of Notre Dame.
    Contents: Faith seeks, understanding finds—
Augustine's charter for Christian philosophy / Norman
Kretzmann—Justice, mercy, supererogation, and
atonement / Richard L. Purtill—Providence and the
problem of evil / Eleonore Stump—Can anybody in a
post-Christian culture rationally believe in the Nicene
Creed? / Alan Donagan—The remembrance of things
(not) past—philosophical reflections on Christian liturgy /
Nicholas Wolterstorff—Love and absolutes in Christian
ethics / J. L. A. Garcia—Taking St. Paul seriously—sin as
an epistemological category / Merold Westphal.
    ISBN 0–268–00776–4
    1. Christianity—Philosophy—Congresses.   I. Flint,
Thomas P. II. Conference on Christian and Theistic
Philosophy (1988 : University of Notre Dame)
III. Series.
BR100.C53   1990
190—dc20   89–40388

To

ELLEN AND PAUL FLINT

AND

HELEN AND JOSEPH DELLANEVA

Contents

Contributors   ix

Introduction   xi

Faith Seeks, Understanding Finds: Augustine's Charter
for Christian Philosophy • *Norman Kretzmann*   1

Justice, Mercy, Supererogation, and
Atonement • *Richard L. Purtill*   37

Providence and the Problem of Evil • *Eleonore Stump*   51

Can Anybody in a Post-Christian Culture Rationally
Believe the Nicene Creed? • *Alan Donagan*   92

The Remembrance of Things (Not) Past: Philosophical
Reflections on Christian Liturgy • *Nicholas Wolterstorff*   118

Love and Absolutes in Christian Ethics • *J. L. A. Garcia*   162

Taking St. Paul Seriously: Sin as an
Epistemological Category • *Merold Westphal*   200

Contributors

ALAN DONAGAN is professor of philosophy at California Institute of Technology. He is the author of numerous works on ethics, the history of philosophy, and action theory, including *The Theory of Morality* and *Choice: The Essential Element in Human Action.*

J. L. A. GARCIA is associate professor in Georgetown University's philosophy department as well as senior research fellow at Georgetown's Kennedy Institute of Ethics. He has written about two dozen essays on value theory, deontic logic, desert, and other topics in theoretical ethics, philosophy of action, and the theory of rules.

NORMAN KRETZMANN is Susan Linn Sage Professor of Philosophy at Cornell University. The principal editor of *The Cambridge History of Later Medieval Philosophy*, he has authored, co-authored or edited eight other books in medieval philosophy, and has published many articles and reviews in medieval philosophy and philosophy of religion.

RICHARD PURTILL is professor of philosophy at Western Washington University. He has published work in philosophy of religion, logic, metaphysics, and ethics.

ELEONORE STUMP is professor of philosophy at Virginia Polytechnic Institute. Her research interests lie in medieval philosophy, philosophy of religion, and philosophy of mind. Her recent publications include *Dialectic in the Development of Medieval Logic.*

MEROLD WESTPHAL is professor of philosophy at Fordham University. The author of *History and Truth in Hegel's Phenomenology, God, Guilt, and Death: An Existential-Phenomenology of Religion,* and *Kierkegaard's Critique of Reason and Society,* he is currently working on the hermeneutics of suspicion in Marx, Nietzsche, Freud, and Kierkegaard.

NICHOLAS WOLTERSTORFF is professor of philosophical theology at the Divinity School of Yale University, having taught for many years at Calvin College and at the Free University of Amsterdam. He has published work in metaphysics, aesthetics, social philosophy, and epistemology, and is presently working on two books (one on John Locke, one on Thomas Reid) exploring the emergence of modern notions of rationality.

Introduction

In recent years, a major change has occurred among those scholars who take both their Christianity and their philosophy seriously. Gone, it seems, are the days when Christians engaged in philosophy were tacitly expected to bracket their religious beliefs when exploring philosophical topics other than, perhaps, those in the philosophy of religion. Gone, too, are the days when the philosophy of religion itself was broadly viewed as involving little more than recapitulations of timeworn arguments for and against the existence of God and lengthy (some might say interminable) discussions of the nature of religious language. By and large, Christians who are also philosophers have come to view these distinctively modern restrictions upon investigating the relations between their religious and philosophical beliefs as both artificial and detrimental to their attempt to fashion a unified picture of the world. They have come to see themselves as, perhaps even primarily as, engaged in what can most properly be called *Christian philosophy*.

What exactly *is* Christian philosophy? While there is no consensus among those who consider themselves Christian philosophers concerning the right answer to this question, most (though not all) Christian philosophers would probably agree that we could properly think of Christian philosophy as consisting of two major divisions. On the one hand, there are those projects which consist of attempts to *reflect philosophically upon Christian belief*—by, for example, providing arguments for that belief, offering apologetical responses to attacks upon it, suggesting elucidations of the concepts inherent in that belief, investigating the presuppositions of the practices by which that belief is made manifest, and the like. On the other hand, efforts at offering *Christian reflections upon philosophical issues*—i.e., explorations of the ways in which one's Christian commitment might affect one's views in epistemology, ethics, or other areas of philosophy—are also widely viewed as being part of Christian philosophy. Understood as incorporating both of these two dimensions, Christian philosophy would clearly comprise an exceedingly large number and variety of potential investigations.

The seven essays contained in this volume provide ample evidence of the diversity of subjects properly considered part of Christian philosophy. Originally presented at a Conference on Christian and Theistic Philosophy (sponsored by the Notre Dame Center for Philosophy of Religion and held at Notre Dame on February 25–27, 1988), these essays represent the efforts of seven of the finest participants in the field to reflect upon and/or exhibit what they take to be Christian philosophy. Though an attempt to pigeonhole their contributions into one of the two dimensions of Christian philosophy delineated above runs the risk of imposing too arbitrary and unyielding an order upon them, it may nevertheless be helpful to view the first five essays as instances of the first type of Christian philosophy (philosophical reflection upon Christian belief), while the last two essays fit more readily into the second category (Christian reflection upon philosophical issues).

The first essay, Norman Kretzmann's "Faith Seeks, Understanding Finds: Augustine's Charter for Christian Philosophy," focuses on the defensibility of a Christian's engaging in what we have called Christian philosophy. Kretzmann notes that Christian philosophy, if understood as incorporating only the first of our two dimensions, has often been looked upon as an impious attempt to demystify the mysteries of faith. Augustine flatly rejected this anti-intellectualism and insisted, on the contrary, that engaging in Christian philosophy was, at least in a limited sense, a duty for every mature Christian.

Though Kretzmann's goal is to defend Augustine's apologia for Christian philosophy, he contends that Augustine's remarks on the relation between faith and reason seem to lead to three significant problems. Augustine says that understanding supplements but does not supplant faith; he maintains that faith precedes understanding; and he views faith as a means to understanding, a state of seeking what understanding finds. So long as we take him to be talking solely about what Kretzmann calls *propositional faith* (belief based on authority) and *propositional understanding* (knowledge based on reason), Kretzmann concedes, these problems appear insoluble. What we need to recognize, though, is that Augustine also employs notions of *religious faith* (the life or way of faith) and *religious understanding* (that granted in the beatific vision). Once we realize that Augustine's discussion of faith and understanding is centered not primarily on the relation between propositional faith and propositional understanding, but rather on that between religious faith and propositional understanding, our three difficulties disappear.

Indeed, the precedence which Augustine gives to religious faith shows why Christians are *prima facie* committed to seeking some degree of philosophical elucidation of the doctrines they profess. The union with God which the faithful hope for in the beatific vision, and the religious understanding afforded thereby, is but the perfection of the propositional understanding available to us in this life. To love and hope for that vision while "shrinking from foretaste of it" is hardly the ideal course for the Christian to follow.

If the case for Christian philosophy made by Augustine and seconded by Kretzmann is accepted, one would expect a considerable amount of effort in this area to be devoted to the philosophical elucidation of the various concepts essential to Christianity. The next two essays, Richard Purtill's "Justice, Mercy, Supererogation, and Atonement" and Eleonore Stump's "Providence and the Problem of Evil," are fully in keeping with such an expectation.

Purtill examines three objections to the Christian belief that Christ suffered and died to save us from our sins. The first objection, from *justice,* questions the fairness of both an innocent person's suffering for the guilty and a guilty person's benefiting from that suffering. The second objection, from *mercy,* suggests that the Atonement was unnecessary, for God could and should have forgiven us without anyone's suffering for our sins. The third objection, from *intelligibility,* questions the meaningfulness of the very concept of vicarious atonement.

Purtill believes that the first two objections can be answered by our giving "a more careful analysis of our intuitions about justice and mercy." The objection from justice depends upon a strict retributionist view according to which no one can justly be punished or rewarded more or less than they deserve, while the objection from mercy presupposes the weak retributionist contention that one should never punish the repentant. Purtill argues that neither strict nor weak retributionism is in line with either our everyday moral intuitions or our specifically Christian beliefs; hence, both of these objections fail.

The third objection—that it does not make sense to speak of the merits from one person's (Christ's) sufferings being transferred to others—is seen by Purtill as more formidable. After considering the ways in which various theories of the Atonement would attempt to deal with this objection, he concludes that the third objection can be answered only by our taking quite seriously ("as a genuine metaphysical fact") the idea that we are members of Christ's mystical body. As members of his body, we can make a claim upon the merits Christ accrued through his passion and death.

Suffering, evil, and sin also appear in the forefront of Stump's essay. Her focus here, though, is not on the doctrine of the Atonement, but rather on the question: Why does a good God permit undeserved suffering? As she sees it, the philosopher who is also a Christian has particularly, perhaps even uniquely, suitable means of handling this troubling question. Christians believe that we all come into the world with a fallen nature, with a will which is defective and which puts us at odds with God. Since this defect, if left unchecked, would result in our eternal misery in hell, God, whose love for his creatures is as boundless as his power and knowledge, does all that he can to heal us. An especially effective way for God to cure his children and bring them into union with him is for God to permit them to experience evil, because the suffering engendered by such experience can have a chastening effect on the human will and consequently turn us toward our Creator. This, in brief, is why God allows evil.

Stump is well aware that this general account, insofar as it is open to numerous questions and misinterpretations, is in need of explication, and she tries to provide us with such by turning to Aquinas. Building upon St. Thomas's distinction between an action's object and its end, his emphasis on the virtue of justice, his notion of providence as God's all-inclusive and never-failing plan for his creatures, and his distinction between God's antecedent and consequent will, Stump suggests that we can give a much fuller defense of the thesis that God permits a person to suffer a particular undeserved evil only if his permitting that evil is the best available means of drawing that person closer to him. Furthermore, she argues, the suffering of those who have already directed their lives toward God—e.g., of martyrs such as St. Thomas More—is also explicable given the Thomistic notion of providence she outlines.

The fourth essay, Alan Donagan's "Can Anybody in a Post-Christian Culture Rationally Believe the Nicene Creed?", incorporates not an attempt to elucidate conceptual components of Christian belief, but rather an effort in apologetics. Donagan examines three problems which he feels educated Christians who live in our current post-Christian culture are likely to encounter with regard to accepting the Nicene creed. The first centers on the development of dogma. How can the claim that what the church teaches is genuinely apostolic be maintained, given the fact that much of its teachings (including much in the creed) is not to be found in scripture? Donagan argues that development of dogma is best thought of as a matter, not of clarifying what is left vague in scripture nor of deducing conclusions contained implicitly therein, but of ruling out certain beliefs as being inconsistent with what the Apostles taught. Just as these beliefs might incorporate concepts of which the Apostles were unaware, so might we restate, say, the assertions of fourth- or sixth-century Christians by employing concepts foreign to their experience.

The second problem has to do with the way in which the credibility of an assertion varies with culture. Until the late nineteenth century, Donagan contends, the western world continued to maintain a predominantly Christian culture, a culture whose fundamental idea was that the natural universe was made by God. Such a culture made accepting the creed a far easier task than does our current post-Christian culture, which presents the natural world as a purely material system, the existence of which requires no explanation. Though Donagan is skeptical of frontal assaults (à la C. S. Lewis) on the tenability of materialism, he claims that Christians can and should question the naturalistic assumptions of current scientific culture, in particular by pointing to the failure of naturalism to provide (so far, at least) an adequate account of moral psychology.

Donagan's third problem concerns the historical claims of Christianity. Why should we accept the body of testimony about Jesus which we find in the scriptures, or believe the creed which claims to be based on that testimony? Donagan argues that one who is dissatisfied with naturalism, who sees life as radically tainted with evil, and who carefully studies the religious history of the human race can reasonably conclude that the relation between God and the people of Israel was indeed a special one, and can go on to ask whether Christianity might not be the culmination of that special relation. Though many biblical scholars would answer this last question negatively, Donagan insists that the bulk of this scholarship, beset as it is with naturalistic assumptions, leaves much to be desired. If we look at the New Testament itself, and in particular at the early letters of Paul, we can indeed find therein "the foundation of the trinitarian doctrine formulated in the Nicene creed."

In the fifth essay, Nicholas Wolterstorff's "The Remembrance of Things (Not) Past: Philosophical Reflections on Christian Liturgy," the focus is not so much upon Christian belief as it is upon Christian practice. Wolterstorff takes as his starting point the fact that so many of the hymns used liturgically are written in the present tense, even when the events being described happened in the distant past. Why, he asks, is this so? Is liturgy supposed somehow to transport us to the time of those events? Or is the suggestion rather that those events are in some sense happening now?

Wolterstorff notes that remembering what God has done for us is crucial to Christianity. Though such remembering is fostered via the story narrated in scripture and retold in the liturgy, liturgical actions and objects also play a role in commemoration. After discussing the concept of commemoration and stressing its prevalence in our lives and liturgies, Wolterstorff focuses on the Eucharist as a prime example and asks how we should understand it as commemorating Christ. Two of what Wolterstorff calls signification interpretations of the Eucharist—namely, that we view it as a dramatic representation of the story told in scripture, and that we see it as an allegory of the life of Christ—are presented and criticized. Though Wolterstorff agrees that there is indeed signification in the liturgy, he endorses something closer to what he calls a reality interpretation, according to which God himself acts by way of our liturgical actions: God speaks through his proxy's voice, and acts causally on the occasion of someone's doing something in the liturgy.

We as Christians, then, not only commemorate our theophanies and see them as relevant to all people; we commemorate them in such a way that God's special activity is as present now as it was at the time of the events we remember. Hence, Wolterstorff concludes, it is natural for us to cast our hymns in the present tense.

Wolterstorff's focusing upon this element of Christian practice should serve to remind us that Christianity has much to say about action as well as belief. Indeed, it would hardly be surprising to one approaching philosophical issues from a Christian perspective to discover that such a perspective is particularly illuminating with regard to questions concerning action in general and right or moral action in particular. Jorge Garcia's "Love and Absolutes in Christian Ethics" offers an example of how one might see Christianity as guiding moral theory. As Garcia sees it, Christianity insists that there is an intimate connection between morality and love, with the former being based upon the latter. Garcia tries to outline a moral approach which is in keeping with this insight and argues that this approach lends support to the Christian belief in moral absolutes.

Garcia contends that morality is concerned with one's roles or relationships with others—as friend, parent, spouse, and the like. Rights, duties, and virtues are relative to the roles one has. Furthermore, moral attributions are essentially linked to the will. To say that something is bad is to say that the desire (the want, the intention) for it is bad, and the desire for it *is* bad because it is malevolent. Malevolent desires tends to make us bad in our roles (bad parents, bad spouses, and the like), while benevolent desires make us good in our roles. Hence, benevo-

xviii / *Thomas P. Flint*

lence, good will, is the ultimate duty, and any failure to exhibit good will needs to be justified.

It is crucial to note, though, that there are two ways of deviating from benevolence. One may fail to will another good (which Garcia labels *inofficious* behavior), or one may actively will another evil (which Garcia calls *counter-officious* behavior). Garcia contends that counter-officious behavior is further removed from our basic obligation of benevolence than is inofficious behavior, and that this distinction allows us to defend the concept of moral absolutes. We need "a floor beneath which we will not go in our departures from goodwill," and the dividing line is roughly that between inofficious (sometimes justifiable) actions and counter-officious (never justifiable) ones. Garcia argues at length that this approach supports the traditional Christian belief that it is never morally acceptable intentionally to kill the innocent, and suggests that other moral absolutes—against mercy-killing, suicide, sterilization, adultery, and lying—can also be defended in this way.

Much as Garcia suggests that Christian ethicians should acknowledge and be guided by the primacy accorded love by their religion, so does Merold Westphal, in his "Taking St. Paul Seriously: Sin as an Epistemological Category," recommend that Christians give sin center stage in their epistemological theorizing. Taking sin to be neither particular acts nor the tendency to perform such acts but rather the self-assertive pride which lies behind them, Westphal focuses on the idea that sin (so understood) distorts not only our acting but also our thinking. This idea, he notes, goes back through Calvin, Luther, and Augustine to St. Paul and his famous allegation (in Romans) that we willfully and perversely suppress the truth about God.

Westphal contends that our view of philosophy would be radically altered if we took seriously St. Paul's intimations regarding the noetic effects of sin. After briefly noting that Augustine, Hobbes, Kant, and Fichte would count among the many philosophers who have held that desires and practices which Christians see as sinful distort our formation and retention of beliefs, Westphal focuses on the rise and fall of foundationalism. In trying to replace *doxa* with *episteme*, foundationalists saw themselves as engaging in an act of intellectual purification—of freeing the mind of the distorting effects of tradition, superstition, and the like. Foundationalism can thus be seen as inchoately aware of the noetic effects of sin. But its remedy for our plight—namely, the suggestion that we can purify our thought by our own efforts—is little more than philosophical Pelagianism, at least to one who takes St. Paul seriously; the suggested cure is but another sign of the disease of pride.

Though Westphal believes the demise of foundationalism should thus open the door to an acceptance in epistemology of the Pauline emphasis on sin, he contends that many of foundationalism's critics have unfortunately not availed themselves of this opening. Among those whom Westphal chides in this regard are such recent advocates of Calvinist epistemology as Plantinga and Wolterstorff—the former for failing to see that sin distorts the thinking of believers and non-believers alike, the latter for naively (from a Pauline perspective) supposing that Christians have a large stock of innocently produced beliefs which they have the right to accept in the absence of disproof. For Christian philosophers to take St. Paul seriously, then, they need to reject their inclination toward "epistemological Phariseeism" and acknowledge that they too are in need of divine help to cleanse their sin-ravaged intellects.

These seven papers, then, reflect both sides of the rather coarse-grained division within Christian philosophy suggested earlier. Though the merits of each paper individually are considerable, their collective impact is perhaps even more impressive, pointing as it does to the fertility and diversity of investigations in Christian philosophy.

In closing, it is appropriate that a word of thanks be offered to those (along with myself) who responded to these papers when they were originally presented. Commentators and panel discussants at the conference included William Alston, Frederick Crosson, Stephen Evans, William Hasker, George Mavrodes, Ralph McInerny, Thomas Morris, Alvin Plantinga, Philip Quinn, and Nicholas Rescher. Needless to say, their contributions to the essays, and hence to this volume, were both significant and appreciated.

Faith Seeks, Understanding Finds: Augustine's Charter for Christian Philosophy

Norman Kretzmann

Christian Philosophers and Christian Philosophy

European philosophy during the Middle Ages was carried on by Christian philosophers, but not all of it was Christian philosophy.[1] The achievements of the medievals in logic and natural philosophy, for instance, typically have nothing to do with Christian doctrine. Their philosophical theology, on the other hand, still deserves to be considered the most thorough and most penetrating development of systematic Christian philosophy ever produced. By systematic Christian philosophy I mean the enterprise of supporting and clarifying propositions of Christian doctrine by means of analysis and argument, building on the classical metaphysics around which Christian doctrine developed, beginning with the most fundamental doctrinal propositions and proceeding in some approximation of logical order.[2] Aquinas's two Summas are and ought to be everyone's paradigms of attempts at doing Christian philosophy in this way. Although not all medieval Christian philosophers contributed to this product, none of them, as far as I know, questioned its feasibility or desirability.[3]

Before the Middle Ages, however, Christian philosophers were anything but unanimously approving of Christian philosophy. The project of drawing on pagan philosophy or of applying philosophical methods in an attempt to support or clarify prop-

1

ositions of the faith was as repugnant to Tertullian and Hippoly-
tus as it was attractive to Justin and Clement. Since the Middle
Ages—more precisely, since the Reformation—Christian philosophers in the Protestant tradition have often opposed the application of the methods of philosophy to Christian doctrine, a
project they have associated, reasonably enough, with Catholic
scholasticism. Since Vatican II, many philosophers in the Catholic tradition seem to have joined in the repudiation of the medieval project.

The premedieval Christian opponents of Christian philosophy were motivated primarily by their observation that many of
the heresies arose out of combining philosophy and Christianity.
The Christian opposition to Christian philosophy that has developed since the Middle Ages seems to stem more often from a
failure of nerve, from a conviction that medieval philosophical
theology went too far—i.e., far enough to show that Christian
doctrine *cannot* be made acceptable, understandable, or even coherent by the standards applied to other intellectual systems. If
that is true, 'Christian philosophy' is a contradiction in terms.

In this essay I assume what I believe to be true, that Christianity has not been shown, in that way or any other, to be essentially irrational. I certainly do not think Christian doctrine
has yet been shown to be fully rational. Perhaps we never will
succeed completely in this enterprise. But we know that progress
toward that ideal is possible, because progress of that sort has
undeniably been made; and I think it may well have been slowed
because the medieval enterprise was abandoned too soon.[4]

Christian philosophers during the Middle Ages were moved
to this enterprise by two interrelated motives, both of which are
or ought to be still efficacious. In the first place, a Christian
philosopher, recognizing that many people, perhaps including
herself, view the propositions of Christian doctrine as *prima facie* unlikely or even impossible, may be motivated to employ
analysis and argument in the service of apologetics. In the second place, a Christian philosopher may engage in the intellectual
exploration and development of fundamental doctrinal propositions in the conviction that the doctrine itself is eminently understandable and acceptable, but in need of clarification of a sort
most likely to be accessible through analysis and argument.

When I use the words 'support' and 'clarification' in describing Christian philosophy, I have these two motives in mind. In Aquinas's *Summa contra gentiles,* support is paramount; in *Summa theologiae,* clarification. But for Aquinas, as for most medievals engaged in Christian philosophy, the first of these motives is merely an outgrowth of the second; and that particular ordering of motivations strikes me as constituting the only solid basis for the enterprise of Christian philosophy in any era.[5]

With the aim of supporting that enterprise generally, I am going to present and examine some of the epistemological, moral, and theological considerations that made philosophy an integral, active part of Christianity by the end of the Patristic period. Those considerations lead to the conclusion that normal, adult Christians who recognize no need to try to attain at least some clarification of the doctrines they profess (and in that way to move closer to Christian philosophy) are in a condition that is epistemologically unnatural and even morally worrisome. And those considerations strike me as no less compelling now than they were early in the fifth century when Augustine invoked them in providing Christian philosophy with its charter.[6]

I suppose there would have been Christian philosophy in the Middle Ages if Augustine had never written a word, but its actual development was so thoroughly dependent on Augustine that he deserves to be considered its founder. There are at least two respects in which he is responsible for this development. First, his treatises provided models of Christian philosophy—unsystematic in their presentation but not in the pattern of their thought, overflowing with analysis and argumentation, sometimes unstrict but almost always subtle, rich, and deep. During the formative period of the early Middle Ages, when virtually all the philosophical literature of antiquity was inaccessible, the impact and value of those models were enormous. But the second respect in which Augustine counts as the founder of Christian philosophy is the one on which I want to focus. It is Augustine's view of the relationship between Christianity and philosophy, a view which made Christian philosophy not just a permissible project but a conditional duty for Christians—and one which put Tertullian's party out of power for a thousand years. Of course I am not suggesting that Augustine was the only formidable figure on his side of the Patristic controversy over Christian philosophy. But I am suggesting that it was his formulation and treatment of the issues that carried the day for his side, partly because he lived near the end of the Patristic period and so could come close to getting the last word, but mostly because of the way he resolved those issues.

Christian Anti-Intellectualism

Everyone with any knowledge of the history of Christianity or, for that matter, anyone who reads the newspapers knows that Christianity is sometimes associated with a principled anti-intellectualism. In the Patristic period this familiar strain in Christianity manifested itself as specifically anti-philosophical, especially because pagan philosophy (the only kind there was) was justifiably considered to be a source of heresies,[7] but also because of St. Paul's warnings against the misuse of worldly wisdom, the most pertinent of which is "Beware lest any man spoil you through philosophy and vain deceit . . . " (Col. 2:8).

Tertullian provides the classic presentation of the anti-philosophical strain in Christianity. He began his intellectual life studying the Greek philosophers. Even after becoming a Christian he wrote at least one unmistakably philosophical treatise, *De anima,* so he seems to have seen nothing wrong in being both a Christian and a philosopher, despite what he says in such passages as: "But then what likeness is there between the philosopher and the Christian—the disciple of Greece and the disciple of heaven; the one concerned with reputation, the other with the life of salvation; the man of words and the man of deeds; the architect of error and its destroyer;[8] the one who corrupts the truth and the one who restores it; the thief of truth and its guardian?"[9] I think it is clear that what he is really repudiating, even in passages of that sort, is the very idea of a *Christian philosophy.* Like Augustine two hundred years after him, Tertullian discussed at length the interrelations of authority, faith, reason, and understanding; but in glaring contrast with Augustine he rejected the application of reasoning to religious truth and viewed the project of a Christian philosophy as at best a waste of time.

"After Christ Jesus, we have no need of curiosity; after the Gospel, no need of inquiry."[10]

The two passages I have quoted from Tertullian so far suggest that his anti-intellectualism was founded on moral and esthetic considerations. No doubt such considerations helped to motivate his diatribes, but he also had another, philosophically more interesting basis for repudiating the enterprise of Christian philosophy. Because he took the doctrines essential to Christianity to be absolutely inaccessible to reason, he insisted that Christians must assent to them as certain on the basis of divine authority alone, or perhaps on no basis at all. I do not know where, if anywhere, Tertullian said "*credo quia absurdum*," as he is so often said to have said, but this famous passage comes as close as any I know: "The Son of God died. This is believable, because it is ridiculous (*ineptum*). And after having been buried he rose again. This is certain, because it is impossible."[11] Since at least some of the propositions assented to in faith are, according to Tertullian, "ridiculous" and "impossible," reasoning applied to them *cannot* provide a correct interpretation of them or any support for them. And so a full-fledged Christian philosophy is out of the question. Whatever one may think of Tertullian's way of dealing with such propositions, the fact that the existence of theological "mysteries" is itself a doctrinal claim certainly does appear to raise a difficulty for the enterprise of a reasoned Christianity.[12]

Tertullian's position is worth examining in its own right, but I am only sketching it here as a reminder of Christian obstacles to a Christian philosophy as they appeared in the Patristic period. For, even setting Tertullian aside, from one undeniably orthodox point of view Augustine's project appears to distort Christianity's image of itself. If analysis and argument applied to doctrinal propositions can provide clarification and support of at least many of those propositions, the project of showing Christian doctrine to be reasonable is not hopeless. Then how, if at all, is Christ crucified a stumbling-block to the Jews and foolishness to the Greeks, as St. Paul preached?

In order to provide Christian philosophy with its charter, Augustine had to show how such an enterprise could flourish without spoiling what it was meant to serve. And even if he could show that it was not positively harmful in that way, he would also have to show why any Christian should engage in it. Finally, the project he advocated and engaged in had to satisfy certain intellectual criteria if it was going to count as philosophy. I think he achieved all those aims in his treatment of authority and faith, reason and understanding.

Propositional Faith and Propositional Understanding

It seems sensible to begin this investigation on the more recognizably philosophical side of Augustine's very full but widely scattered account of these matters, the side where faith and understanding appear to be simply propositional attitudes or, more precisely, two differently based kinds of propositional assent. Faith is assent to a proposition in virtue of its having been put forward by an authority one has accepted on rational grounds.[13] Understanding is assent to a proposition in virtue of its having been clarified or supported (or both) by one's reason on the basis of analysis and argument. To distinguish these from other Augustinian conceptions of faith and understanding to be considered, I will call them propositional faith and propositional understanding. They can be recognized in any number of passages, e.g.:

> (A1) . . . we [Augustine and Evodius] wanted to seek out the origin of evil by means of argumentation. And we argued in such a way that, if we could manage it, our carefully considered, well worked out reasoning would bring to our understanding what we believed about this matter on the basis of the available divine authority, to the extent to which we could achieve this in discussion, with God's help, (*Retractationes* I ix 1; 23.2–6)

> (A2) Authority demands faith, and prepares a person for reason. Reason leads to understanding and knowledge. Reason does not entirely desert authority, however, when we consider who is to be believed; and, of course, once the truth is known and made manifest, it has the supreme authority. (*De vera religione* xxiv 45; 215.4–8)[14]

Augustine sometimes says things that suggest that propositional faith might have foundations other than authority—miracles, for instances[15]—but the other considerations he mentions seem really to count as rational credentials for the authority itself, which appears to be the only immediate basis he recognizes for faith of any sort. Propositional faith is assent to a proposition authoritatively expressed by a human or divine person whose authority has been accepted on rational grounds.[16] The authority of the source is the immediate support of that faith, and, ideally, the rationality of the believer's acceptance of the authority provides a deeper support.[17]

Linguistic Comprehension, Correct Interpretation, and Proof

There is nothing unusual in treating faith (or belief, as Augustine often calls it) as a kind of assent, but Augustine's notion of propositional understanding may need a little explaining. His word 'intellectus', like our word 'understanding', often means mere linguistic comprehension, understanding what the words mean—a necessary precondition for both propositional faith and propositional understanding, as Augustine clearly recognizes.[18] Understanding in this sense of mere linguistic comprehension has no explicit role to play in the rest of this discussion; we can simply take it for granted.

Understanding a proposition in the related but loftier sense of interpreting it clearly and correctly is an aim of philosophical analysis and thus one of the goals of philosophy, Christian or otherwise. As support is what is primarily sought through argument, so clear, correct interpretation is what is sought through analysis in acquiring propositional understanding.[19] Of course the operations of analysis and argument are intertwined in philosophical practice, where the clarification and certification of a proposition often develop together, where argument, too, aids clarification. Augustine's usage reflects this intimate connection, and so I will use 'propositional understanding' indifferently for the results of philosophical analysis or argument.

'Knowledge' (scientia) is Augustine's other name for the full-fledged propositional understanding that typically involves both analysis and argument, and it clearly bears a strong family resemblance to the sort of knowledge Plato and Aristotle ranked above mere opinion. Full-fledged Augustinian propositional understanding might well be described in older terms as true belief accompanied by a rational account, or as involving a grasp of the causes of what the correctly interpreted proposition says.

For most Christians, having a clear, correct interpretation of a theological proposition and recognizing it as correct will be a much more important form of propositional understanding than assenting to the proposition as the conclusion of an argument:

> (A3) Love understanding deeply, for the Holy Scriptures themselves, which advocate faith before understanding where great issues are concerned, cannot be of any use to you unless you understand them correctly. All the heretics who accept the Scriptures as authoritative think they are following them while in reality they are following their own errors. And they are heretics not because they despise the Scriptures, but rather because they do not understand them. (*Epistula CXX* iii 13; 716.4–9)[20]

In Augustine's view understanding ranks above faith in that understanding is a state of seeing clearly what faith sees only unclearly, if at all.[21] Human beings seek the theoretically preferable cognitive condition naturally, simply in virtue of being rational:

> (A4) Understanding is one thing, reason another. For we have reason also before we understand, but we cannot understand unless we have reason. . . . [A human being is an animal] to whose nature reason belongs and which already has reason before it understands. It is because reason comes first that a human being wants to understand. (*Sermo XLIII* ii 3; PL 38.255)[22]

The propositional understanding of theological propositions by means of analysis and argument is what Augustinian Christian philosophy is out to achieve, directing a natural human drive in the service of religion.

Faith and Understanding in *De libero arbitrio II*

Everything we have seen so far about propositional faith and understanding is illustrated well in the situation presented in the second book of Augustine's *De libero arbitrio*. Augustine says to Evodius, "At least you're certain that God exists," and Evodius replies, "Even this I hold firmly in virtue of believing it, but not on the basis of having considered it thoughtfully." If challenged by an unbeliever, Evodius would support his faith by what he takes to be a reasonable appeal to the authority of the writers of Scripture. Well, says Augustine, "if you think the question of God's existence is satisfactorily answered on the basis of our having decided that it isn't rash to believe such men, why don't you think we should likewise believe on the basis of their authority also as regards the things we have begun to seek out as if they were uncertain and entirely unknown? In that way we would save ourselves from any further labor in investigating them." Evodius replies, "But we want to *know* and to *understand* what we believe," including the proposition that God exists, which, Evodius freely acknowledges, is *not* sufficiently proved on the basis of an appeal to Scripture.[23] And so Augustine works with Evodius through most of Book Two, employing a great deal of analysis and argumentation, to develop a proof of that proposition, concluding with

> (A5) God exists, and he exists truly and in the highest possible degree. This, I think, we now not only hold by faith, as undoubted, but we also arrive at it with a form of knowledge that is certain even though still very narrow. (II xv 39; 264.13–16)

To this conclusion Evodius responds, "I accept these things with an altogether incredible joy that I cannot express to you in words, and I declare them to be absolutely certain."[24]

The Augustinian account of propositional faith and propositional understanding as presented so far looks philosophically familiar and raises no particular philosophical problems of its own, especially if we read it as an account of cognitive states more traditionally described as belief based on authority and knowledge based on reason. But philosophical problems show up in this account as it develops, at least one of them in the exemplification of it in these passages from *De libero arbitrio*. After I point out three such problems, I will try to show that there are philosophically respectable ways of dealing with them within Augustinian Christian philosophy.

The Problem of the Combination of Faith and Understanding

The exchange between Augustine and Evodius brings out a feature of Augustinian faith and understanding that casts doubt on their being easily assimilated to the older notions of opinion and knowledge.[25] In passage (A5), for instance, Augustine implies that as a result of the argument he and Evodius have just developed they now have both faith and understanding regarding one and the same proposition, that God exists. Evodius makes clear in the exchanges that precede the proof that he wants understanding where he now has only faith, just as a pagan philosopher might have wanted to replace mere opinion with knowledge. But it turns out that the cognitive state Evodius and Augustine rejoice in at the conclusion of the proof is one in which understanding has supplemented rather than supplanted faith. A cognitive state in which authority-based opinion is merely supplemented rather than supplanted by reason-based knowledge seems incoherent, however.[26] And so Augustine's conceptions of propositional faith and understanding are either different from those more familiar notions or philosophically embarrassing or both.

Although there are passages here and there in which Augustine may seem to be suggesting that faith is only a deficient cognitive state to be supplanted by understanding,[27] the prevailing tone in his pronouncements on the subject and the models provided in his contributions to Christian philosophy leave no doubt that he thinks of the combination of faith and understanding regarding some propositions as not only coherent but desirable:

> (A6) Our understanding, therefore, advances toward things that are to be understood, things it believes, and faith advances toward things that are to be believed, things it understands. (*Enarrationes in Psalmos* CXVIII, *Sermo* xviii 3; 1724.36–1725.38)

The problem of the combination of faith and understanding is only exacerbated by the natural suspicion that what leads Augustine to take this evidently peculiar, perhaps epistemologically indefensible position is his special consideration for propositional faith when its objects are propositions of Christian doctrine.

The Problem of the Precedence of Faith

When in *De libero arbitrio* Augustine helps Evodius supplement his faith by acquiring understanding of a proposition he had only believed on authority, he proceeds in accordance with familiar philosophical methods—analysis and argument. And in general Augustine's discussion of propositional understanding reflects his practice, unmistakably suggesting that propositional understanding of the sort he is seeking is acquired in the way knowledge or understanding is ordinarily acquired in philosophy. Here is part of one such discussion:

> (A7) If someone who is already a believer asks for a reason so that he may understand what he believes, his ability must be considered so that the reason provided will enable him to add to his faith as much understanding as he is capable of—more if he comprehends more, less if less—seeing to it, however, that in attaining to the fullness and completion of knowledge he does not depart from the way of faith. (*Epistula CXX* i 4; 707.12–17)

But there is one feature of these examples and discussions that is definitely not typical of the acquisition of philosophical understanding, and that is the fact that in each of them the proposition that is to become an object of a person's understanding is first an object of that person's faith. If the precedence of faith that appears in these passages is only accidental, it raises no particular problem. It happens often enough, though certainly not invariably, that a person who comes to understand how and why a given proposition is true was earlier in a state of merely believing that it was true. But in Augustine's account of faith and understanding the precedence of faith may very well appear to be essential to the acquisition of understanding. The best-known evidence that this is so is his use of (an old Latin translation of) Isaiah 7:9 as his slogan: "Unless you believe, you will not understand,"[28] but there are plenty of passages in which he makes the same point in his own voice:

> (A8) Understanding is the reward of faith. Therefore do not seek to understand in order that you may believe, but believe in order that you may understand. (*In Ioannis evangelium tractatus* xxix 6; 287.16–17)

(A9) The hidden things and secrets of the Kingdom of God first seek out believing men, that they may make them understand. For faith is understanding's ladder, and understanding is faith's reward. (*Sermo CXXVI* i 1; PL 38.698)

(A10) If a person says to me, "I want to understand in order that I may believe," I reply, "Believe in order that you may understand." (*Sermo XLIII* iii 4; PL 38.255)

(A11) If it were not one thing to believe and another to understand, and if we did not first have to believe the great, divine matter we want to understand, the Prophet would have spoken to no purpose when he said, "Unless you believe, you will not understand." (*De libero arbitrio* II ii 6;239.67–70)

If the precedence of faith in Augustine's account of faith and understanding really is essential, it seems to constitute another philosophical embarrassment for the account, independent of the first. Even if the problem of the combination of faith and understanding can be solved, it still seems plainly untrue that a person's believing a proposition on authority is a necessary precondition of her coming to have the correct interpretation or argumentational support of that proposition.

And this problem carries with it a practical embarrassment as well. The application of philosophical reasoning to doctrinal propositions has always had some appeal for theists because of its usefulness as a proselytizing device. It is sometimes tolerated only for that purpose by Christians who are otherwise opposed to it. But if faith must precede understanding, then Augustine's proof of God's existence, for example, could not possibly effect an intellectual conversion in anyone; no atheist could thereby acquire the understanding that God exists.

The Problem of "Faith seeks, understanding finds"

In some of the passages I have associated with the problem of the precedence of faith it is clear that Augustine treats faith not only as a precondition of understanding but also as a means of attaining it: "Believe *in order that* you may understand." He takes this position in the conviction that he is working out the implications of Isaiah 7:9. In his most famous interpretation of that verse he seems also to be saying *how* faith is a means to understanding:

> (A12) Faith *seeks,* understanding *finds. That's* why the Prophet says "Unless you believe, you will not understand." (*De trinitate* XV ii 2; 461.27–28)

That Augustine thinks of faith as characteristically a state of seeking what understanding finds is also suggested in several of the other passages we have already considered (especially (A8), (A9), and (A11)) and in many passages elsewhere in his writings.[29]

But, of course, to be in the state of believing a given proposition on authority is not, typically, to be seeking support or rational explanation of it. On the contrary, that sort of seeking is more generally associated not with believing but with being in doubt about (the meaning or truth of) a proposition. And so the view of propositional faith as characterized by seeking seems just wrong.

The fact that Augustine presents it as typically a state of seeking what understanding finds reinforces the ranking of understanding over faith, a feature of Augustine's account we have already noted. But at the same time that description of the working relationship between faith and understanding undercuts his claim that the combination of faith and understanding regarding the same proposition is a possible (and desirable) cognitive state. Whatever else may be said in behalf of that claim, no sense can be made of being in a state of seeking a rational explanation or an argument in support of some proposition while consciously possessing one.

"Faith seeks, understanding finds" is the heart of Augustine's charter for Christian philosophy, and I am commending the sort of Christian philosophy supported by that charter. I will, therefore, try to find solutions for these problems.

The Way of Faith and Supernatural Understanding

So far we have been looking at Augustine's account of faith and understanding from its more obviously philosophical side, but of course it also has a religious side.

The most evident observation regarding the religious side is that there is another sense of 'faith' that is essential to Augustine's account—professing Christian doctrine and trying to live in accordance with it, faith as a way of life, or what Augustine sometimes calls "the way of faith" (*iter* or *via fidei*).[30] Similarly, there is another sense of 'understanding' essential to his account, the perfect, supernatural understanding in the beatific vision: "For now we see through a glass, darkly; but then face to face: now I know in part; but then shall I know even as also I am known" (1 Cor. 13:12).

With only this much of the religious side in place, it is easy to see that the three principal problems of faith and understanding uncovered in my investigation of the philosophical side of Augustine's position simply do not arise on the religious side, regarding the way of faith and supernatural understanding. The problem of the combination of faith and understanding does not arise because no one could be both on the way of faith and enjoying the beatific vision at once. The problem of the precedence of faith does not arise, either. There are no obvious secular philosophical analogues for the way of faith and the beatific vision; and Christian doctrine, where those notions are found, stipulates that such religious faith is a necessary precondition and a means of acquiring such supernatural understanding, as Augustine emphatically recognizes.[31] Finally, there is nothing problematic in describing faith as seeking what understanding finds if the intended claim is simply that one who is on the way of faith is thereby in a state of seeking what the beatific vision confers.

This disappointingly bland outcome might suggest that Augustine's account was never meant to apply to any other sort of faith or understanding, that I have uncovered problems only because I have been misapplying his account to cases of believing some proposition on the basis of authority and achieving understanding of that proposition through a process of reasoning. Certainly Augustine often uses his two words '*fides*' and '*intellectus*' in either their religious or their philosophical senses without any terminological indication one way or the other. But we have already seen plenty of evidence that he is sometimes talking about what I have been calling propositional faith and propositional understanding. A broader and more plausible suspicion is that there is a rift in his account, that the problems that do not arise on the religious side crop up on the philosophical side because his treatment of the religious aspect of faith and understanding cannot be extended as he thought it could, that his account is religiously impeccable, perhaps, but philosophically untenable.

The Connection between the Religious and Philosophical Sides

Before trying to allay that suspicion and others, I need to clarify the connection between the religious and the philosophical sides of Augustine's account of faith and understanding. To begin with, I think Augustine takes it for granted that his account of the relationship between propositional faith and propositional understanding applies to those cognitive states only in case they have theological propositions as their objects. He sometimes writes as if he had no such restriction in mind, but I think that every context or example he provides is theological. That sort of restricted application would be perfectly compatible with the enterprise of a Christian philosophy, and without it some of what he says cannot be accepted. I will take it for granted in what follows. Against that background we can see more clearly how he connects the religious and philosophical sides of his account of faith and understanding.

Propositional faith is an essential ingredient in the way of faith. For one thing, the way of faith typically involves the profession of faith, which incorporates instances of propositional faith.[32] But even if the way of faith is considered in abstraction from such practices of a Christian community, it certainly does have an intellectual as well as a volitional component, and its intellectual component involves propositional faith. More importantly if less obviously, it seems at least psychologically impossible to live in certain ways (perform certain acts of will) without having certain beliefs. So any person living in the way of faith is, just in virtue of doing so, a person with propositional faith regarding several theological propositions.

Since faith of any sort essentially involves an imperfect cognition, faith of any sort is a condition of this life only.[33] But

Augustine views the propositional understanding attained on the basis of reasoning in this life as a foretaste of the full understanding conferred directly in the beatific vision. Of course he would not take the beatific vision to be simply a celestial version of terrestrial propositional understanding perfected in scope, depth, and accuracy, but he does think of some sort of propositional understanding as an ingredient in supernatural (celestial) understanding, as can be seen, for instance, in his remark to Evodius just before undertaking the argument for God's existence:

> (A13) What we seek at God's urging we will find by his pointing the way, to the extent to which these things can be found in this life and by people like us. For it must be believed that such things can be sorted out and apprehended very clearly and completely by better human beings even while they inhabit this earth, and certainly after this life by all those who are good and devout. (*De libero arbitrio* II ii 6;239.81–86)[34]

We now have these four elements to work with: propositional faith and the way of faith, propositional understanding and supernatural understanding. For purposes of this discussion, supernatural understanding may be set aside. Considered as a cognitive state, it is the *ideal* culmination of the enterprise of Christian philosophy, unattainable in this life.[35] Propositional understanding, on the other hand, is just what Christian philosophy promises.

The status of propositional faith is more complicated. Obviously a person who is not living the Christian life of faith may have propositional faith regarding some theological proposition: 'God exists', for example. So some propositional faith occurs outside the way of faith, and it may raise particular problems of its own. But the scope of this investigation requires me to set aside detached propositional faith of that sort and consider only the sort that concerns Augustine most—propositional faith as an ingredient in the Christian way of faith.

When we do focus our attention in that way, we find that Augustine's account of faith and understanding, his charter for Christian philosophy, is centered not on the relationship between propositional faith and propositional understanding but on the relationship between the way of faith and propositional understanding. Although we have seen some passages in which he seems to be saying that propositional faith is a necessary precondition and a means of attaining propositional understanding, the great majority of passages on the precedence of faith are clearly making that sort of claim about faith as a way of life rather than or as well as about faith as assent to some proposition on the basis of authority. For example:

(A14) Necessarily we are led to learn in two ways: by authority and by reason. Authority is temporally prior, but reason is prior in reality. . . . And so for all who desire to learn great and hidden good things it is only authority that opens the door. And whoever enters by it without any doubt, follows the precepts for the best life, and by them is made receptive to teaching will after a while learn how preeminently endowed with reason those things are which he pursued before reason. (*De ordine* II ix 26; 121.2–122.15)[36]

(A15) Hearts are purified by faith for the sake of those inner eyes whose blindness consists in not understanding, so that they may be opened and made more and more clear-sighted. For although no one can believe in God if he does not understand *anything*, nevertheless, by the very faith by which he believes he is restored in order that he may understand greater things. For there are some things we do not believe unless we understand them, and there are others we do not understand unless we believe them. (*Ennarationes in Psalmos* CXVIII, *Sermo* xviii 3; 1724.25–31)

In (A14), clearly, it is the way of faith rather than propositional faith that is being picked out as the necessary precondition. In (A15), on the other hand, the necessary precondition appears to include both the way of faith and propositional faith, presumably as an ingredient in the way of faith. The following passage presents the same sort of complex condition and also shows that the thesis regarding the precedence of faith is restricted to certain theological propositions:

(A16) There are three kinds of believable [propositions]. There are some that are always believed and never understood. Every account that ranges over temporal events and human deeds is of this kind. There are others that are believed as soon as they are understood. All human reasonings, whether about numbers or having to do with any of the disciplines, are of this kind. Thirdly, there are those that are believed first and understood afterwards. Of this kind are those that deal with divine matters which cannot be understood except by people who are pure of heart. And this is brought about by observing precepts that are accepted as rules for living rightly. (*De diversis quaestionibus LXXXIII* q. 48; 75.1–10)

How Augustinian Christian Philosophy Deals with the Problems

The aim of Christian philosophy as Augustine sees it is to combine propositional understanding with the way of faith. The most efficacious way of filling out that basic formula within the limits of this essay is to try to show how Augustinian Christian philosophy deals with the problems this investigation has uncovered. I will take them up in an order that seems helpful to the exposition.

The problem of the combination of faith and understanding points to the apparent absurdity of a person's being simultaneously in the cognitive states of propositional faith and propositional understanding with respect to the same proposition. Augustinian Christian philosophy avoids this problem. For example, the authority-based propositional faith that God exists, which is incorporated into the way of faith, would indeed be supplanted by the acquisition of understanding on the basis of a proof that God exists. What propositional understanding merely supplements or enhances is not propositional faith regarding some proposition in particular but the way of faith as a whole. I think it is very likely that passages in which Augustine speaks of understanding as supplementing faith can and must always be interpreted in that way.[37]

An epistemological transition of that sort is readily recognized in other contexts. The way of faith, which involves propositions as well as practices, is an intellectual system as well as a way of life, and in that respect it may be compared with other intellectual systems—the theory of evolution, for example. A biologist makes progress when she is finally able to put a well-founded claim in place of a conviction she had about some particular evolutionary development. Her transition from the lower- to the higher-ranking cognitive state involves supplanting her particular conviction, but it only supplements and strengthens her commitment to the theory. As a beginner in biology, she subscribed to the theory on the basis of reasonable authority alone; her commitment to it has grown as she has acquired understanding of its component claims, which earlier she had only believed.

But there may also be a way in which propositional understanding can supplement rather than supplant *propositional* faith. When the reasoning that leads to understanding is particularly hard, authoritative confirmation for the results of one's own analysis and argument is often indispensable psychologically. Even a good student of mathematics in her first calculus course will sometimes feel confident about her understanding of a word problem and her calculations only after she has checked the answer in the back of the book. She may even get some insight into the line of thought to follow by looking at the answer before beginning her work. In such a case, when she has done the reasoning, she has understanding of the answer where at first she had only faith that it was the answer; but she has *faith in her reasoning* because of her (continuing) faith in what the textbook tells her. Similarly, a Christian philosopher's reasoning about a piece of Christian doctrine obviously less accessible to unaided reason than the existence of God—the Trinity, say—is likely to be conducted within the guidelines of the doctrine in such a way that her propositional faith in the established doctrine is supplemented rather than supplanted.

The problem of characterizing faith as a state of seeking what understanding finds is likewise dispelled when the faith in question is the way of faith. I have already remarked on the doctrinally dictated recognition of the way of faith as a condition of seeking what supernatural understanding confers. But it is as a consequence of having this character that the way of faith is a state of seeking also what can be acquired in terrestrial propositional understanding, a state that gives rise to the enterprise of Christian philosophy.

(A17) So, then, as regards some things that pertain to the doctrine of salvation, things we cannot yet perceive by reason though we will be able to do so someday, let faith precede reason, and let the heart be cleansed by faith so as to receive and bear the light of great reason. This is indeed reasonable. And so the Prophet spoke with reason when he said "Unless you believe, you will not understand." In that passage he obviously distinguished those two and advised us to believe first so as to be able to understand what we believe. . . . If, then, we are faithful now, we will get to the way of faith. And, if we do not leave it, we will without doubt come not only to a great understanding of incorporeal and unchanging things, such as cannot be grasped by everyone in this life, but even to the summit of contemplation, which the Apostle calls "face to face." (*Epistula CXX* i 3–4; 706.22–29; 707.20–25)

Since the way of faith is a state of seeking theological understanding *generally*, there is no incoherence in the combination of that cognitive state with this or that particular instance of acquired propositional understanding, and so the subsidiary problem of simultaneously seeking and possessing what is sought does not arise for Augustinian Christian philosophy.

Still, this problem cannot be completely dispelled simply by interpreting 'faith' as the way of faith. I have emphasized the inclusion of propositional faith as an essential component of the way of faith, and the problem of characterizing faith as a condition of seeking seems still to be a problem where propositional faith is concerned. It surely is absurd to describe my casual, laymanly beliefs about electrons or my uninterested acceptance of what I have been told about my grandparents' birthplaces as instances of my seeking understanding. But when the propositional faith at issue is faith in the intelligibility or truth of a proposition that belongs to an intellectual system the believer is actively committed to, even that *propositional* faith seems rightly described as, at least in principle, a condition of seeking understanding of that proposition. Not every such proposition of which the actively committed believer is aware can be treated that way by every such believer: people have finite resources of time and ability. But some propositions are too prominent within the system to be covered even by that blanket excuse. Someone who has accepted but never sought understanding of 'Ontogeny recapitulates phylogeny' cannot be plausibly described as an embryologist, and a person who has accepted but never sought understanding of 'The Son of God died' cannot be plausibly described as a mature, reflective, actively committed Christian.

How does Augustinian Christian philosophy deal with the problem of the essential precedence of faith? When the faith at issue is simply propositional faith, the problem of essential precedence points to an epistemological absurdity that is so blatant as to be harmless: it is just not true that one has to believe a proposition in order to acquire philosophical understanding of it. But if the essentially precedent faith under consideration is the way of faith, "Believe in order that you may understand" (*Crede ut intelligas*) looks like "Become a Christian if you want to acquire philosophical understanding of any proposition of Christian doctrine," which is wrong in a way that is more to be censured than pitied.

When Augustine is expanding on the theme of Isaiah 7:9, as he often is, he certainly does sound as if he intends the *crede ut intelligas* injunction as broadly as he did near the beginning of his career as a Christian philosopher, when he maintained that God had "willed that none but the pure know the truth."[38] But he expressly repudiated that broad claim later, in his *Retractationes*[39] and elsewhere. As a mature Christian philosopher Augustine recognizes that some unbelievers can acquire understanding of certain theological propositions:

> (A18) If an unbeliever asks me for a reason for my faith and hope, *and* I see that he *cannot* grasp it before he believes, I give him this very reason, in which, if possible, he may see how preposterous it is for him before he has faith to ask for a reason for things he cannot grasp. (*Epistula CXX* i 4; 707.8–12)[40]

> (A19) "But," you say, "wouldn't it be better for you to give me the reason, so that I might follow wherever it should lead, without any rashness?" Perhaps it would be. Since it is so important that you must come to the knowledge of God by reason, do you think that *all* human beings are capable of apprehending the reasons by which the human mind is led to divine understanding, or many, or just a few? "A few, I think," you say. Do you believe that you belong to this number? "It is not my place," you say, "to answer that." Therefore, you think he [the person who is present-

ing Christianity to you] should believe you about this, too. And, of course, he does. (*De utilitate credendi* x 24; 29.8–16)

So Augustine's principle of the precedence of faith is not a principle of *essential* precedence: propositional faith in a proposition's intelligibility or truth is not a universally necessary precondition of acquiring understanding of that proposition. The principle therefore presents no obstacle to intellectual conversion. Augustine even acknowledges the existence of philosophers and theologians who have acquired an understanding of the intellectual system of Christianity without becoming believers:

(A20) Some people have very little [understanding], yet by walking with great perseverance in the way of faith they attain that most blessed contemplation [the beatific vision]. But there are others who, although they already know what the invisible, unchanging, incorporeal nature is, and the way that leads to the abode of such happiness, cannot attain it . . . because [the way], which is Christ crucified, seems foolish to them. (*Epistula CXX* i 4; 708.1–8)

The *crede ut intelligas* injunction, then, is not meant to apply universally but only for the most part. Augustine nevertheless thinks that it almost always does apply.

(A21) But suppose . . . that you are approaching with the right attitude to receive religion and so are one of the few people capable of understanding the reasons by which the divine power is made known with certainty. What then? . . . What about those . . . who can very easily apprehend the divine secrets with sure reasoning? Will it hinder them at all if they come by the way by which those come who believe to begin with? I do not think so. "But still," you say, "what need is there for them to delay?" Because even if by acting in that way [acquiring understanding without antecedent faith] they will in no way harm themselves, they will harm others by their example; for there is scarcely anyone who has a just estimate of his own powers. A person who thinks too little of himself should be encouraged, while one who thinks too much should be reined in, the former so that he may not be broken by despair, the latter so that he may not be carried on headlong in his brashness. This is easily done if even those who are strong enough to fly are forced to walk for a little while in the way that is also safe for others, in order not to entice anyone into danger. (*De utilitate credendi* x 24; 29.18–21; 30.6–16)

The recognition that Augustine does not intend to present either propositional faith or the way of faith as a logically or epistemologically necessary precondition of understanding dispels the formal problem of the precedence of faith I introduced earlier.[41]

But why should any Christian living the life of faith consider himself or herself to be thereby committed to seeking any terrestrial understanding of theological propositions? Augustine's answer to this question has several levels. Fundamentally and least compellingly, he recognizes understanding as a cognitive state essentially preferable to faith, as we have seen. But the situation is complicated by the fact that false reasoning is abundant, and everyone, Christian or not, is at least occasionally susceptible to it. If, for instance, certain Christians have been misled into accepting what is really an unreasonable account of the Trinity but think that they have thereby acquired understanding, then

> (A22) when true reasoning begins to break up that amalgam of carnal thought and empty fantasies, . . . we hurry to smash them and, so to speak, to shake our faith free of them, so that we do not allow even any dust of such delusions to remain there. (*Epistula* CXX ii 7; 710.27–711.5)

> (A23) The true reasoning by means of which we understand what we believe is to be preferred to false reasoning, but that very faith in things not yet understood is undoubtedly to be preferred too, since it is better to believe in what is true but not yet seen than to think that you see something true which is really false. (*Epistula* CXX ii 8; 711.11–16)

In view of such altogether sensible cautions, why should any Christian undertake the risky business of trying to attain propositional understanding?

The first thing to remember in answering this question is Augustine's repeated insistence that in acquiring propositional understanding one is always to leave one's faith intact. In the light of Augustine's view of understanding as the goal of faith, the epistemological force of his injunction to remain in the way of faith seems to be like the mathematics instructor's insistence that his students take the answers in the back of the book as definitive. The way of faith comprises a formidable intellectual system, based on authority supplemented (in our day far more than in Augustine's) by the intellectual efforts of many earnest critical minds bent on rationally attaining and elucidating the truth. This is the sort of enterprise in which human beings do make progress, as long as they do not abandon the enterprise whenever it is threatened by internal or external difficulties.

But, of course, Augustine also takes the way of faith to be the way to salvation, and it is important to see that he has no intention of inviting the Christian to risk salvation in seeking understanding.

> (A24) And if . . . the human, rational, intellectual soul, which was made in God's image, does not elude our thought and understanding, if by mind and understanding we can grasp its excellence, . . . it may not be absurd for us to try to raise our soul to understanding its creator as well, with his help. But if it fails in this and falls back on itself, let it be content with devout faith as long as it is wandering, absent from the Lord. (*Epistula CXX* ii 12; 715.6–15)

So there is a failsafe device in Augustinian Christian philosophy, and the risk is not so great as it may seem at first. But, still, why should a Christian take any risk of that sort of all?

For three reasons, the first of which is that that is the way God made us.

> (A25) Let no one think that God hates in us that in respect of which he made us superior to all other living beings. Let no one think, I say, that we should believe in such a way as not to accept or seek reason, since we could not even believe if we did not have rational souls. (*Epistula CXX* i 3; 706.18–21)[42]

The second reason for taking the risk involved in Christian philosophy is that Scripture is full of injunctions to do so, sometimes accompanied by encouragement and reassurance. Such passages are often quoted by Augustine—e.g., "be ready always to give an answer to every man that asketh you a reason of the hope that is in you" (1 Pet. 3:15); "seek, and ye shall find" (Matt. 7:7).

> (A26) But the Apostle is witness that our mind is not to shrink from it entirely [i.e., the attempt to understand the Trinity], when he says, "For the invisible things of him from the creation of the world are clearly seen, being understood by the things that are

made, even his eternal power and Godhead" [Rom. 1:20]. (*Epistula CXX* ii 12; 714.26–715.4)[43]

The third and most interesting reason why the effort after understanding (and thus at least a measure of Christian philosophy) is to be recognized as something essential to the way of faith might be described as the interdependence (if not the unity) of the theological virtues. For *faith* in God entails love for God, the primary manifestation of *charity,* and love for God entails *hope* of union with God, a union which entails understanding.

(A27) But it is better that we should use the word "faith" in connection with things that are not seen, as divine revelations have taught us. Regarding hope, too, the Apostle says, "hope that is seen is not hope: for what a man seeth, why doth he yet hope for? But if we hope for that we see not, then do we with patience wait for it" [Rom. 8:24–25]. Therefore, when we believe that good things are going to come, this is nothing other than to hope for them. Now what shall I say of love, without which faith profits nothing? But there cannot be hope without love. . . . And so the Apostle Paul approves and commends the "faith which worketh by love" [Gal. 5:6], and this certainly cannot exist without hope. Consequently, there is no love without hope, no hope without love, and neither love nor hope without faith. (*Enchiridion* ii 8; 52.49–62)

(A28) A person who already understands by true reasoning what he only believed a while ago is definitely preferable to one who still wishes to understand what he believes. But if he does not also have a desire for the things that are to be understood, he considers them as things that are only to be believed, he is ignorant of the use of faith. For a devout faith does not want to be without hope and without charity. Therefore, whatever a man of faith does not yet see he ought to believe in such a way as to hope for and love the seeing of it. (*Epistula CXX* ii 8; 711.19–25)

The union with God that is hoped for in the way of faith involves, as we have seen, the perfection of that which the propositional understanding available in this life is a sample. A person on the way of faith cannot hope for and love the ultimate perfection of vision while shrinking from the foretaste of it offered in the combination of our rational nature and the evidence of creation.

(A29) Believe me. Rather, believe him who said "Seek and ye shall find" [Matt. 7:7]. Such knowledge must not be despaired of; and it will be more manifest than those numbers [i.e., the sum $1 + 2 + 3 + 4 = 10$]. (*Contra academicos* II iii 9; 23.58–61)

How, then, does Augustinian Christian philosophy deal with the "mysteries," expressed in propositions described by Tertullian as ridiculous and impossible? I do not know of a passage in which Augustine expresses himself in general terms on that topic, but he deals with particular instances just as his program of Christian philosophy would lead us to expect. The monumental case in point is, of course, his treatise in fifteen books attempting to provide a rational understanding of the doctrine of the Trinity. But his attitude is more succinctly expressed and exhibited in his handling of a single perplexing passage, such as John 8:58: "Before Abraham was made, I am."[44] In commenting on Jesus' claim Augustine addresses the Christian reader:

(A30) Weigh the words and come to know the mystery. Understand that "was made" pertains to human formation, but "am" to the divine substance. (*In Ioannis evangelium tractatus* xliii 17; 380.4–6)[45]

Augustine does not go very far in illuminating this mystery, but he heads off in a promising direction. A sentence that may at first seem even linguistically incomprehensible is shown to be not simply a solecism but perhaps a particularly pithy way of drawing a contrast between man and God once the reader is reminded that the divine essence is expressed in 'I AM'. The divine atemporality implied in the sentence (pointed out expressly in Aquinas's comment on it) may well be implicit in Augustine's reference to the divine essence. An analysis of the sentence proceeding along the line begun here by Augustine would provide an interpretation that would cohere with already developed portions of Christian philosophy.

But what about harder cases? What about Tertullian's "ridiculous," "impossible" paradigms, 'The Son of God died, was buried, and rose again'? I think Augustinian Christian philosophy would or should treat the more recalcitrant doctrinal mysteries somewhat as physicists treat the apparent dual nature of light. Light does indeed behave both like particles and like waves, and it does indeed seem clear that nothing can be both a particle and a wave, and yet there must be a correct understanding of the nature of light. Are the Trinity, the Incarnation, the Resurrection suitable topics for investigation in Augustinian Christian philosophy? Of course they are. None of them, perhaps, would even be thought of as an appropriate object of proof, but clarification is at least as important an object of Christian philosophy as proof could ever be.[46]

Well, then, isn't it clear that Augustinian Christian philosophy is incompatible with the image of Christian doctrine as a stumbling-block to the Jews and foolishness to the Greeks? No. As Paul's language in the passage alluded to should show, Christianity should never present those appearances except from certain distorting points of view.

> (A31) Just as you ought not to give up all speech because there is false speech, so you ought not to give up all reasoning because there is false reasoning. I would say the same of wisdom. For wisdom is not to be avoided because there is also false wisdom, to which Christ crucified is foolishness, though he is himself "the power of God and the wisdom of God" [1 Cor. 1:24]. . . . Some philosophers . . . who followed not the true way but one like it, deceiving themselves and others in it, could not be persuaded of this. But other philosophers could be persuaded, and to those who could, Christ crucified is *neither* a stumbling-block *nor* foolishness. (*Epistula CXX* i 6; 709.6–11; 14–18)

Conclusion

Although I have devoted a good deal of this essay to quoting and discussing considerations that established philosophy as an integral part of Christianity 1,500 years ago, my primary aim is not historical. As I said to begin with, those considerations lead to the conclusion that normal, adult Christians who recognize no need to try to attain at least some clarification of the doctrines they profess (and in that way to move closer to Christian philosophy) are in a condition that is epistemologically unnatural and morally worrisome. And those considerations strike me as no less compelling now than they were when Augustine invoked them in providing Christian philosophy with its charter and its practitioners with a model.

(A32) In this way (*via*), that is, in the faith of Christ crucified, those who were able by the grace of God to embrace his upright righteousness, even though they were called philosophers, . . . certainly confessed with humble piety that the fishermen who went before them in the way were far superior in those matters, not only in the steadfast strength of their belief but also in the unerring truth of their understanding. (*Epistula CXX* i 6; 709.20–26)[47]

NOTES

1. By 'Christian philosophy' in the fullest sense I mean just philosophical theology carried out on Christian doctrine. A practitioner of Christian philosophy in this sense certainly need not be a Christian philosopher. On the other hand, although a Christian philosopher, medieval or contemporary, writing not on the Incarnation or the Trinity but on freedom of the will or materialism outside a doctrinal context will almost certainly approach those topics with an awareness of their bearing on certain propositions of Christian doctrine, even that sort of philosophical activity lies beyond the limits of Christian philosophy in the fullest sense as I am using the term. Gilson said, "It would be hard to imagine any expression more naturally apt to occur to the mind of the historian of medieval thought than *Christian philosophy*" (*The Spirit of Medieval Philosophy,* New York: Scribners, 1940; p. 1): One can agree with this observation without agreeing that medieval philosophy is adequately characterized as Christian philosophy in the Middle Ages.

2. As Thomas Burke pointed out to me, describing systematic Christian philosophy as the application of analysis and argument to a set of propositions with the same subject matter runs the risk of suggesting that biology, for example, might be construed as biological philosophy. What makes systematic Christian philosophy relevantly different, at least in the medieval conception of it I am recommending, is that it begins (theoretically, although not usually in its presentation) without data or, at any rate, without specifically Christian data, and develops as metaphysics (or natural theology) to the point at which the enterprise cannot proceed further without introducing doctrinal data. Christian philosophy is philosophy as biology is not, largely because it coincides with and is continuous with classical metaphysics in a way and to an extent to which biology is not. For some consideration of the

continuity between classical metaphysics and Christian philosophy, see Norman Kretzmann, "Trinity and Transcendentals," in *Trinity, Incarnation, and Atonement,* ed. Ronald. J. Feenstra and Cornelius Plantinga, Jr. (Notre Dame, Ind.: University of Notre Dame Press, forthcoming).

3. All the hundreds of medieval commentaries on Peter Lombard's *Sentences* ought to count as contributions to this project, and most of the people we recognize as medieval philosophers wrote such commentaries. The ordering of topics, the *systematic* aspect of medieval Christian philosophy, interests me in this essay less than other aspects of the application of philosophical method to Christianity, and as a feature of the presentation of Christian philosophy it is characteristic only of developments after Anselm. Since I will be considering mainly Augustine, whose contributions to philosophical theology were· thoroughgoing without being overtly systematic, I will from now on refer simply to Christian philosophy.

4. Perhaps not even one fundamental proposition of Christian doctrine has been made fully acceptable by ordinary standards of rationality; certainly none has been universally accepted by rational beings. As George Mavrodes remarked in commenting on an earlier draft of this paper, "That would seem to be precious little progress for 2000 years of work." But acceptance by rational beings is not a decisive criterion in assessing philosophy. And, in any case, philosophical theology looks no worse in this regard than ordinary metaphysics or epistemology, on which human beings have been at work for half a millenium longer. What is more, Christian philosophy has unquestionably done far better than any other brand of philosophy in the number of its practitioners and adherents. Of course progress in philosophy, Christian or not, is reckoned otherwise than by finding ourselves able to say "Thank God *that's* done!" Still, we do sometimes discover that an explanation that seemed promising will not work, or that an old, neglected concept or argument is not as bad as we had thought it was, and that is progress, too.

5. A comment of Alvin Plantinga's on an earlier draft of this essay led to these remarks about motives for Christian philosophy. For some consideration of "support" (or "proof") and "clarification" in Aquinas, see my "Trinity and Transcendentals."

6. Although I say a good deal about Augustine in this essay and quote him frequently (in my own translations), the subject of my essay is not so much Augustine as a particular conception of Christian philosophy. I have, therefore, left the literature on Augustine out of account. With some misgiving, I have also omitted any consideration of

Augustine's theory of divine illumination. It certainly plays a crucial part in his fuller account of propositional understanding, but I could not consider it along with the topics I particularly wanted to discuss in this essay. I believe that everything I have to say here is compatible with divine illumination as Augustine presents it.

7. As Tertullian puts it, "Philosophy is the core of worldly wisdom, the rash interpreter of God's nature and plan. In fact, the heresies themselves are secretly nourished by philosophy" (*De praescriptione haereticorum* vii 2–3; 192.4–7). (For the editions of Tertullian's and Augustine's works cited in this essay, see the appended list.)

8. I am adopting Kellner's conjecture of '*errorum*' instead of the edition's '*rerum*'. With '*rerum*' the passage makes the philosopher the builder of things and the Christian their destroyer—a characterization out of keeping with the rest of the paragraph.

9. *Apologeticum* xlvi 18; 162.80–83.

10. *De praescriptione haereticorum* vii 12; 193.37–39.

11. *De carne Christi* v 4; 881.27–29.

12. See, e.g., Vatican I [1870], Sess. III, "De fide et ratione," can. i: "Si quis dixerit, in revelatione divina nulla vera et proprie dìcta mysteria contineri, sed universa fidei dogmata posse per rationem rite excultam e naturalibus principiis intelligi et demonstrari: anathema sit." (If anyone should say that divine revelation contains no genuine mysteries in the strict sense, but that by means of correctly developed reason all the dogmas of the faith could be understood and demonstrated on the basis of natural principles, let him be anathema.)

13. See, e.g., *De spiritu et littera* xxxi 54; 81.4–5: "what is it to believe but to agree that what is said is true?"; *De praedestinatione sanctorum* ii 5; PL 44.963: "belief itself is nothing else than to think with assent." The dependence of this assent on authority is brought out in other passages quoted below—e.g., (A1) and (A2).

14. See also, e.g., (A4) below.

15. See, e.g., *Epistula CXXXVII* iv 15–16; *De trinitate* IV xix 25; *De vera religione* xxv 47; *De utilitate credendi* xiv 32.

16. For an example of Augustine's invoking particular rational grounds in support of accepting one authority and rejecting another, see *De utilitate credendi* xiv 31; 39.5–8: "In this matter [of Christ's existence and teachings], as I said, I believed a report which had the strength of numbers, agreement, and antiquity. And everyone knows that you [heretics], so few in number, so confused, and so new [on the scene], offer nothing that has the dignity of authority."

17. For reason in support of authority see, e.g., (A2) above and n. 30 below; also *De praedestinatione sanctorum* ii 5; PL 44.962–963; "who doesn't see that thinking is prior to believing? For no one be-

lieves anything unless he has first thought that it is to be believed"; *De ordine* II ix 26; 121.2–122.4: "Necessarily we are led to learn in two ways: by authority and by reason. Authority is temporally prior, but reason is prior in reality". (For a fuller quotation of this second passage, see (A14) below).

18. See, e.g., *Ennarationes in Psalmos* CLVIII, *Sermo* xviii 3; 1724.32–34: "how can anyone believe a person who preaches the faith if (leaving other matters aside) he does not understand the very language the preacher speaks?"; *Sermo XLIII* vii 9; PL 38.258: "unless they understand what I am saying, they cannot believe. Therefore, what he [his imagined interlocutor in this passage] says is partly true—'I want to understand in order that I may believe'. . . . Understand in order that you may believe my words." See also (A15) below.

19. Clear, correct interpretation, elucidation, or clarification, may be available for some doctrinal propositions that are not susceptible of proof. Aquinas makes this claim expressly in dividing the operations of reason into *manifestatio* and *probatio* (*ST* I q. 32, a. 1, ad 2). For further discussion, see "Trinity and Transcendentals" (n. 2 above) and "Reason in Mystery," in *The Philosophy in Christianity* ed. Godfrey Vesey (forthcoming).

20. See also (A27) below.

21. The comparison of faith and understanding in visual terms is a salient characteristic of Augustine's account in part, no doubt, because it has a scriptural background: "Now faith is the substance of things hoped for, the evidence of things not seen" (Heb. 11:1); "For the invisible things of him from the creation of the world are clearly seen, being understood by the things that are made . . . " (Rom. 1:20). For Augustine's use of the comparison see, e.g., *Sermo CXXVI* ii 3; PL 38.699: "God has given you eyes in the body, reason in the heart. Arouse the reason of the heart, wake the inner inhabitant of your inner eyes, let it take to its windows, let it examine God's creation. . . . Believe on him whom you do not see because of the things you do see"; *Ennarationes in Psalmos* CIX 8; 1607.2–4: "what reward would there be for faith, if what we believed were not hidden? But the reward of faith is to see that which we believed before we saw it"; *Epistula CXX* ii 8 (711.10–11; 16–19): "when faith acted on what pertained to it, reason, following after, found something of what faith was seeking. . . . For faith has its own eyes with which it sees, so to speak, that what it does not yet see is true, and with which it most certainly sees that it does not yet see what it believes."

22. See also, e.g., *Sermo XLIII* iii 4: "Every human being wants to understand; there is no one who does not want it. Not everyone wants to believe"; also (A25) below.

23. *De libero arbitrio* II i 5; 238.33–35; 239.59–65.

24. II xv 39; 264.19–21.

25. In at least one place Augustine sharply distinguishes between "those who have opinions, that is, those who think that they know what they do not know" and those who have propositional faith, those who recognize that they do not know what they seek to know (*De utilitate credendi* xi 25; 31.19–21). It seems to me that the ancient notion of opinion (*doxa*) is not pejorative in this way and is not for *that* reason to be distinguished from propositional faith.

26. Imagine someone's claiming to have two grounds for her present acceptance of the Pythagorean theorem: (a) remembering that her high school teacher told her it was true, and (b) being able to demonstrate it.

27. See, e.g., *De trinitate* VIII i (prooemium); 269.30–32: " . . . having observed the rule that what has not yet been made clear to our understanding must not be released from the steadfastness of faith." In invoking this rule here and elsewhere Augustine seems to ignore the possibility that a failed attempt at achieving understanding will lead to a loss of faith beyond one's control.

28. Augustine found this reading of the verse in the Ancient Latin version, translated from the Septuagint: "*Nisi credideritis, non intelligetis.*" St. Jerome's Vulgate translation from the Hebrew, which came into use during Augustine's lifetime, had the more accurate "*Si non credideritis, non permanebitis*" (KJV "If ye will not believe, surely ye shall not be established"). For Augustine's attempt to tie the two readings together, see *De doctrina christiana* II xii 17. Anselm, the thoroughgoing Augustinian, was still alluding to the old version of the verse six hundred years later: "I do not seek to understand in order that I may believe, but I believe in order that I may understand. For I believe this, too, that unless I believe, I shall not understand" (*Proslogion* 1).

29. See, e.g., *De trinitate* IX i 1; 292.21–293.25; "The person who seeks until he achieves what we are striving for and reaching toward has the most prudent plan. But the right plan is the one that starts from faith, for a sure faith somehow lays the foundation of knowledge."

30. See, e.g., (A7) above.

31. See, e.g., *Epistula CXX* i 3 (706.29–707.5, the continuation of (A17) below): "Therefore, it has been reasonably commanded that faith precede reason. For if this precept is not reasonable, it is unreasonable—which is not worth considering. And so if it is reasonable that faith precede a certain great reason which cannot yet be grasped,

there is no doubt that, however slight the reason which convinces us of this, it does precede faith."

32. The fact that the creeds tend to be statements of belief-in rather than belief-that does not mean that they do not incorporate instances of propositional faith. Believing in God the Father almighty of course entails believing that God exists, that God is almighty, and so on.

33. See, e.g., *Soliloquia* I vii 14; PL 32.876–877 (speaking of supernatural understanding): "Why would *faith* be needed when the soul already sees? . . . We must not say that the soul has *faith* that those things are true when it is not assailed by any falsehoods."

34. See also n. 36 below.

35. See, e.g., *De consensu evangelistarum* IV x 20; 416.4–10: "If anyone thinks that it could happen to a person still living that every cloud of bodily and carnal illusions was removed and dispersed so that he might possess the supremely clear light of changeless truth and keep to it steadfastly and unwaveringly with a mind entirely detached from the customary activities of this life, such a person understands neither what he is seeking nor who is seeking it."

36. The remainder of this passage provides further evidence of the closeness of the relationship between terrestrial propositional understanding and celestial supernatural understanding: " . . . and [he will learn] what reason itself is, which he now follows and comprehends, having been made steadfast and capable by the cradle of authority. [He will] also [learn] what understanding is, in which all things are or, rather, what he is who is all things, and what that is which over and above all things is the source of all things. Few people attain to that knowledge in this life, but no one can progress beyond it even after this life." To be brought into conformity with the passage quoted in n. 35 above, the final sentence of this passage should, I think, be read as "attain to *any of* that knowledge."

37. This epistemological transition figures, explicitly or implicitly, in many of the passages quoted in this paper. But see also, e.g., *Epistula* CXX i 2 (705.26–706.1; 7–17): "you [Consentius] say that you have laid down a principle for yourself that truth must be perceived on the basis of faith rather than on the basis of reason. . . . See, then, whether in accordance with those words of yours you should not follow only the authority of the saints in this matter [the doctrine of the Trinity] on which our faith is chiefly founded, rather than asking me to make it understandable to you by reason. For when I begin to lead you into the understanding of so great a mystery in any way at all (something I will be able to do only if God helps from within), the only

thing I will be doing in discussing it is giving you such reason as I can. Consequently, if you are not being unreasonable in importuning me or any other teacher in order to understand what you believe, you should correct your statement of principle—not in such a way as to repudiate faith, but in such a way that you may see by the light of reason what you now hold by faith." (This letter of Augustine's, written about 410, is an especially rich source for the topics of this essay. In this section I draw on it more than on any other source. It deserves closer study along with *Epistula CXIX*, the letter from Consentius to which Augustine is replying.)

38. *Soliloquia* I i 2; PL 32.870.

39. I iv 12; 14.12–16.

40. Augustine seems to me to be suggesting that some unbelievers seeking reasons for Augustine's faith can follow such reasons while others cannot. Here he is talking about encountering an unbeliever whom he judges to be incapable of following, say, his argument for the existence of God in *De libero arbitrio* II. Augustine's policy in such a case, I take him to be saying, is to give the unbeliever that very argument in hopes that his failure to follow it may lead him to see that he needs something else—religious instruction, presumably, and the faith it is designed to promote—before he is ready for Christian philosophy. Augustine, it seems, would also give the argument to an unbeliever he deemed capable of following it, but with different expectations of the outcome. (A19) may provide a subtler presentation of this same policy.

41. The way Augustine advocates the precedence of faith in (A21) raises epistemological problems of its own. (It suggests religious and moral problems as well, but they are less relevant to my present concerns.) *Can* "those who are strong enough" to *understand* that God exists be "forced" into merely believing it, even "for a little while"? Obviously not. But where the doctrine at issue is less accessible to un-aided reason or a mystery, strictly inaccessible to unaided reason and not fully understandable in this life, those who have acquired some understanding of it may nevertheless honestly profess faith in it as well. Augustine seems sometimes to use descriptive terms intended to pick out those doctrines (including all and perhaps only the mysteries) the understanding of which depends on faith as a precondition, at least for the most part. See, e.g., "great issues" (A3), "hidden things and secrets of the Kingdom of God" (A9), "great divine matter" (A11), "great and hidden good things" (A14), "greater things"—i.e., greater than that there is a god (A15).

42. Cf. the parallel consideration regarding the naturalness of the human desire for understanding, in (A4) above.

43. The last words of Romans 1:20, immediately following those Augustine quotes, contain a powerful indirect injunction to pursue understanding: "so that they are without excuse." And the context shows that "they" are pre-Christian thinkers who had the relevant evidence in the phenomena of creation and did not interpret it correctly.

44. The KJV "Before Abraham was, I am" is imprecise. The Greek is 'genesthai', and the Vulgate preserves it: "antequam Abraham fieret, ego sum."

45. On acquiring understanding of mysteries, see also *Epistula CXX* i 2, in n. 37 above.

46. The doctrinal inclusion of mysteries within Christian doctrine (see n. 12 above) is compatible with this Augustinian attitude. Medieval philosophers who engaged in Christian philosophy sometimes offered proofs of the unprovability of one or another doctrinal proposition (see, e.g., "Trinity and Transcendentals," n. 2 above), but of course those proofs themselves are subject to rational appraisal. And even (or especially) in the case of a doctrinal proposition thought to have been proved unprovable, those practitioners of Christian philosophy advocated and engaged in the work of clarification. (For further discussion, see my forthcoming article "Reason in Mystery" [n. 19 above].)

47. I am grateful for helpful suggestions from Thomas Burke and Alvin Plantinga, acknowledged in preceding notes, and for three further sets of detailed written comments, from Terry Irwin, George Mavrodes, and Eleonore Stump.

EDITIONS USED

CC = *Corpus Christianorum* Series Latina
CSEL = *Corpus Scriptorum Ecclesiasticorum Latinorum*
PL = *Patrologiae cursus completus Patrum Latinorum*

AUGUSTINE

Contra academicos, ed. W. M. Green, CC vol. XXIX; Turnholt: Brepols, 1970.
De consensu evangelistarum, ed. F. Weirich, CSEL vol. XXXXIII; Vienna: Tempsky, 1904.
De diversis quaestionibus LXXXIII, ed. A. Mutzenbecher, CC vol. XLIV A; Turnholt: Brepols, 1975.
De libero arbitrio, ed. W. M. Green, CC vol. XXIX; Turnholt: Brepols, 1970.

De ordine, ed. W. M. Green, CC vol. XXIX; Turnholt: Brepols, 1970.

De praedestinatione sanctorum, ed. J. -P. Migne, PL vol. 44.

De spiritu et littera, ed. W. Bright; Oxford: Clarendon Press, 1914.

De trinitate, ed. W. J. Mountain and F. Glorie, CC vols. L and L A; Turnholt: Brepols, 1968.

De utilitate credendi, ed. J. Zycha, CSEL vol. XXV, sect. VI, Pars I; Vienna: Tempsky, 1891.

De vera religione, ed. K. -D. Daur, CC vol. XXXII; Turnholt: Brepols, 1962.

Enchiridion ad Laurentium de fide et spe et caritate, ed. E. Evans, CC vol. XLVI; Turnholt: Brepols, 1969.

Ennarationes in Psalmos CI-CL, ed. D. E. Dekkers and J. Fraipont, CC vol. XL; Turnholt: Brepols, 1956.

Epistulae, ed. A. Goldbacher, CSEL vol. XXXIIII; Vienna: Tempsky, 1898.

In Ioannis evangelium tractatus, ed. D. R. Willens O.S.B., CC vol. XXXVI; Turnholt: Brepols, 1954.

Retractationes, ed. A. Mutzenbecher, CC vol. LVII; Turnholt: Brepols, 1984.

Sermones, ed. J. -P. Migne, PL vol. 38.

Soliloquia, ed. J. -P. Migne, PL vol. 32.

TERTULLIAN

Apologeticum, ed. E. Dekkers, CC vol. I; Turnholt: Brepols, 1954.

De carne Christi, ed. E. Kroymann, CC vol. II; Turnholt: Brepols, 1954.

De praescriptione haereticorum, ed. R. F. Refoulé, CC vol. I; Turnholt: Brepols, 1954.

Justice, Mercy, Supererogation, and Atonement

Richard L. Purtill

Philosophy inherits from its beginnings certain characteristic approaches. From Socrates we inherit the practice of asking hard questions about even our most cherished beliefs and practices and of not being content with easy answers. From Plato we inherit the insight that we sometimes have to answer these hard questions by producing philosophical theories which go beyond already accepted ideas. From Aristotle we inherit the method of building up a philosophical system by paying careful attention to common sense—the opinions of the many—and to previous philosophical theorizing—the opinions of our predecessors.

Each philosophical tradition has its weaknesses. Socratic questioning may degenerate into skepticism if we reject reasonable answers to our hard questions. Platonic theorizing can turn into a sort of gnosticism which rejects common sense because of a conviction that the truth can never be in the opinions of the multitude. Aristotelian systematization can turn into a rigid orthodoxy, more concerned to defend the accepted views than to be open to new truth.

When philosophers turn to philosophical theology they bring to bear all of these traditions. We sometimes affront the pious by asking searching questions about the meaning and justification of cherished beliefs. We sometimes find ourselves theorizing beyond the letter at least of revelation in order to answer these hard questions. And we sometimes find ourselves making hard choices about how to fit revelation into our philosophical systems.

37

One of the most basic and cherished Christian beliefs, surely common to any religious view which can justifiably call itself Christian, is the idea of the Atonement: that Christ suffered and died to save us from our sins. Hostile philosophical critics have often attacked this basic belief as morally monstrous. More recently Christian philosophers such as Phillip Quinn[1] have asked some hard Socratic questions about traditional understandings of the Atonement. For convenience I divide questions about the Atonement into three general categories: Is the idea of the Atonement contrary to *justice;* is it contrary to *mercy;* and finally is the idea even *intelligible?*

The objection from justice asks whether it is fair for one person to suffer for the sins of others, or fair for the others to benefit from the suffering of that one. The objection from mercy asks why the Atonement was even needed: Why could God not simply have forgiven us without the need for Christ's suffering and death? The objection from intelligibility asks if the idea of transferring merit or demerit from one person to another even makes sense.

In this essay I give an answer to these difficulties which is Aristotelian in my sense, rather than Platonic. In other words I do not think that the way out of the difficulties raised is to come up with a *new* theory about the Atonement, but rather to examine very carefully how the idea of atonement fits in with our basic moral intuitions and with the theories which earlier Christian philosophers and theologians have advanced. I try to elicit the moral intuitions by story telling, by using the method of parable as thought experiment. And with regard to our predecessors' theories I start off with the idea that very likely each of the historic theories is, as so often happens in philosophy, an exaggeration of a partial truth about the matter, and that what is needed is to put these theories together into a synthesis in which each partial truth is related to the other to get at something which approaches the whole truth.

My own view is that the "Aristotelian" method is generally the proper one in both philosophy and theology. Our predecessors were not fools; they were unlikely to be wholly wrong in their theorizing. Where they disagree it is unlikely that the truth lies wholly on one side. Similarly, our common moral intuitions may need some correction in the light of revelation or of philosophical theory, but they are unlikely to be wholly mistaken. In theology, any view which ignores or drastically revises the nearly twenty centuries of Christian belief and practice is by that very fact almost certainly mistaken. But perhaps that is only to say that I am basically Aristotelian in my philosophical outlook and orthodox in my Christianity. The questioners and the innovators must have a hearing before we can dismiss them.

The idea of the injustice of atonement is, I think, an attempt to appeal to certain moral intuitions. Is the appeal a successful one?

Consider the following parable:

A certain king had a jewel which he valued so highly that he had enlisted a band of knights, sworn to safeguard the jewel or die in the attempt. An enemy of the king, desiring the jewel, corrupted the knights one after another, some with bribes, some with threats, and some with promises. Then the enemy carried off the jewel. The king's son, who had been away with his squire while this was happening, returned to find the jewel gone. He went alone into the enemy's stronghold and after great suffering, managed to get the jewel back. On his return the king held court. The foresworn knights came before him to express their sorrow and accept their punishment. The king's son was also there, and his father praised him for his heroism, promising him whatever reward he wished. The prince said to the king, "Father, as my reward I ask that you do not punish the foresworn knights. Let my sufferings in getting back your jewel be all that anyone has to suffer in this matter." The king agreed, but the prince's squire objected, saying "This is to put these traitors on an equality with those of us who have not betrayed their king." However, the chief of the foresworn knights replied to him saying, "Sir, we are not on an equality with you, but below you in one way and above you in another. You are above us in that you have never betrayed your king, while we are forgiven traitors. But we are above you in that our prince has given us a gift which you have not received from him: his suffering has won our pardon. Therefore we have more reason to love our prince, and more motive to serve him and his father faithfully in the future."

It is tempting to elaborate this parable, but the bare bones I have just given will be enough to make my points. First it seems to me that my own moral intuitions tell me that the king's action was morally right, that the prince's action was morally admirable, and that the chief knight's reply to the squire was just. That is, to speak without parable, it is morally right to punish someone less than they deserve at the request of someone who has done a supererogatory act,[2] and this is not unfair to someone who has *not* deserved to be punished: a person who does not deserve punishment has no right to demand punishment for those who have deserved punishment if the person responsible for administering punishment has good reason to remit that punishment.

If someone's moral intuitions disagree with this, it may be for one of several reasons. First, she may be a *strict retributionist.* A retributionist is one who holds that we can *deserve* punishment and a strict retributionist is one who holds that we should never punish more *or less* than is deserved. Because deserving punishment and deserving reward are so closely linked, it would seem reasonable for a strict retributionist to also hold that we should never reward less *or more* than is deserved. Strict retribution can be contrasted with moderate retributionism, which is the view that we should never punish *more* than is deserved but may *for a good reason* punish less than is deserved. (And analogously, we may never reward *less* than is deserved, but may for a good reason reward *more* than is deserved.)[3]

Now whatever may be said in general about the merits of strict retributionism, it seems quite clear that historical Christianity has rejected strict retributionism and holds to a moderate retributionist view. The Christian God is *just* in that he never punishes more than we deserve or rewards less than we deserve, but he is *merciful* in that he sometimes punishes us less than we deserve and *generous* in that he sometimes rewards us more than we deserve. Note that for a moderate retributionist, justice and mercy are quite compatible: only a strict retributionist sees them as incompatible. (Strict retributionists also have problems about generosity: the only philosopher I know who inclines to strict retributionism is very puzzled by the parable of the vineyard and is inclined to hold that the householder acts *unjustly.*)

I want to make a few more points in terms of my parable: First, the prince was *not* punished, and *a fortiori* was not punished in place of the knights. Second, the prince, being innocent, was in a position to perform an act of supererogation: the knights, being guilty, were *not* in a position to perform such an act. Anything they did would be at best an act of *reparation*. If all of the knights had died in an effort to recover the jewel they would have been doing *less* than they were obliged to do, since they were obliged not to let it be stolen while they lived in the first place.

On the other hand the prince was in a position to perform an act of supererogation—something *more* than his position and duties required of him. This notion of supererogation is, I think, as essential to the philosophical understanding of Christianity as are the notions of justice and mercy, although *under that name* it is a less familiar idea. However, I think when Christians speak of the "generosity" or the "goodness" of God, what they often have in mind is God's *supererogatory* goodness; the good he would not be unjust in leaving undone.

This then is my answer to the accusation of injustice. It is not unjust that Christ's sufferings benefit us; it is not unjust to Christ because he was not *punished* for our sins but voluntarily did a supererogatory act in order to counteract the effects of our sins. It is not unjust that *we* benefit from Christ's sufferings, because we recognize in parallel cases the justice of allowing one person to be pardoned because of the supererogatory act of another.

Let us now turn to the difficulty involving mercy. One might feel that the king should show mercy *whether or not* the prince does any supererogatory act or makes any request. This seems to amount to the view that it is right to punish less than deserved without a good reason, or perhaps that repentance in itself is always a good reason, a view we might call "weak retributionism."

"After all," one might say, "Why shouldn't the king *simply* rescue and pardon the knights? Or if he needs a reason, why isn't the request of his son reason enough? Why should the son go through this elaborate charade to get his father to pardon the knights?"

The answer I would give is this: simple pardon or pardon at the mere request of the prince would give the knights a false idea of the seriousness of their sin, and not give them the motive for repentance which the prince's sacrifice gives them. And *unless* the knights take their sin seriously and repent of *that* sin, the sin seen as serious, the king *cannot* forgive them. For forgiving, I would maintain, has a *logical* relation to a request for forgiveness. I *cannot* forgive you, nor you me, "unilaterally." I can express my readiness to forgive you, keep bitterness and hatred against you out of my heart, and we sometimes loosely call these "forgiveness." But genuine forgiveness is "at-one-ment," and it requires action on *both* sides. God's forgiveness of us is purely supererogatory: he would not be unjust if he did not forgive us. Our forgiveness of others is *not* supererogatory, since God, who has placed us under a debt of obligation, by being prepared to forgive us for his Son's sake, has *commanded* us to forgive each other and made our forgiveness of each other a *condition* of his forgiving us. This being so, it is odd to maintain that unconditional forgiveness is *essentially* superior to conditional forgiveness, and it is not clear that we are commanded to forgive without conditions. Certainly the *logical* condition of being *asked* for forgiveness always obtains.

But consider a wife who has been repeatedly beaten by her husband. Does Christian morality require her to continue living with the husband simply because after each incident he makes a verbal profession of sorrow and asks forgiveness? Consider a teenager who has been allowed to use the family car and has repeatedly disobeyed traffic laws, driven after drinking, and overstayed curfews. Should she be given the family car again simply because she makes a verbal request for forgiveness?

The point here is that forgiveness is not a license to continue with behavior which needs forgiving. The wife may well say to the abusive husband, "I forgive you, but I will not live with you unless you begin and stick with a course of therapy." The parents may say, "We forgive you, but you may not use the car again for several months."

This is quite in line with traditional Christian beliefs and practice: for example, a criminal might be regarded as sincerely repentant, but still punished for his or her crimes. Repentance is certainly a *reason* for punishing less than deserved, but it is a reason which may be overridden; forgiveness is quite consistent with punishing exactly as much as is deserved.[4]

So my answer to the objection from mercy is that weak retribution makes an equal and opposite error to strict retributionism: by saying that we, or God, should not punish us for no good reason, or merely because we express sorrow, we are ignoring both the seriousness of deserving punishment and the tendency of human nature not to take sin seriously if it is forgiven without anyone paying the price. Suppose, for example, the prince in our parable had done nothing and the king simply said to the knights, "I will not punish you; I have another jewel to guard and will put you in charge of it." Is the second jewel likely to be guarded even as well as the first one? To simply remit punishment without anyone suffering is to encourage repeated transgression and "cheap repentance."

That, of course, is the half-truth exaggerated by strict retributionism, while the half-truth exaggerated by weak retributionism is the insight that it is just to punish less than deserved. Strict retributionism has an excess with respect to justice and a defect with respect to mercy; weak retributionism has a defect with regard to justice and an excess with regard to mercy. Either view if adopted would greatly increase the burdens of trying to live morally; strict retributionism by making it too hard on the transgressor, weak retributionism by making it easy on the transgressor (and too hard on the transgressor's victims). Both views are practical fallacies as well as intellectual fallacies.

Thus the alleged objections from justice and mercy do not, I think, call for any new approach to or theory about the Atonement, only a more careful analysis of our intuitions about justice and mercy, with some assistance from the concepts of supererogation.

Let me turn now to traditional theories about the Atonement. Are any of them satisfactory? Do even the best of them involve some idea of transferring merit from one person to another which we cannot make sense of? (Of course, an incompatibility with a specific view of morality would be a two-edged sword: if we cannot fit a theory of the Atonement into Kantian ethics, let us say, this might be a reason for abandoning Kantian ethics rather than abandoning that theory of the Atonement.)

One traditional theory of the Atonement is sometimes presented as what I will call a *strict retributionist view* of the Atonement and often, though not always, goes with a strict retributionist view in general ethics. On a strict retributionist view the idea of Atonement goes something like this: punishment has been deserved, God's justice will not allow simply ignoring the fact that punishment is deserved,[5] so Christ is punished in our place. As I said earlier, I think that strict retribution is a profoundly unChristian view and that this view of the Atonement leads to the mistaken view that Christ was *punished* for our sins, a view quite different from the view that Christ *suffered* for our sins.

Another theory of the Atonement which seems to me unsatisfactory is the "exemplary" theory: that in suffering and dying for us, Christ was *only* giving us an example of how God wants us to behave. Certainly Christ was doing *at least* this, giving us the supreme example of self-sacrificing love. But if we say that this is *all* he was doing, a problem arises. Christ could certainly have avoided suffering and dying, even by non-miraculous means. So unless his suffering and death achieved some good which could best be achieved by those means, what example is Christ giving us—the example of undergoing *useless* suffering and death? Surely that is absurd. Yet if Christ's suffering and death were not useless, what were they useful *for*?

My suggestion at the beginning of this essay was that in suffering and dying, Christ was giving God a *good reason* to punish us less and reward us more than we deserve on our own merits. His suffering and death for our sake give us a *claim* on God's mercy and generosity. God became a man; as a man he offered his suffering and death for our sake. God now has *good reason* to show us justice and mercy.

We, on our part, should realize that we *owe* our forgiveness to the self-sacrificing act of love by Christ. We see that our salvation was *costly;* that someone suffered and died to earn it. If God in his own nature had merely forgiven us without it costing anyone anything, we would not have the same motive for gratitude and repentance: we do not value what seems easy. And in one very good sense it would be easy for God to merely forgive us without anyone paying the cost.[6]

The language of "paying the cost" reminds us of a third theory of redemption, the "ransom" theory. Scorn has been heaped on this theory as being "primitive" or "naive" but it is important to remember this is the only theory which has some claim to support from Christ's own words. In Matthew 20:28, he says, "The Son of Man did not come to be served but to serve, and give his life as a ransom (λύτρον) for many." A ransom is a payment which gives a captor good reason to release a captive. If someone ransoms us from a captivity we have got into by our own fault, we have reason to be profoundly grateful to them, and to do whatever we can in return.

The puzzling part of "ransom" theories is how to answer the question "Who was our captor." To say "Satan" seems bad theology, to say "God" returns us to the picture of the strict retributionist God we rejected earlier. To say we were captives of "sin" is good New Testament language, but sin is not a personal agent who can be given a *reason* to release us.

One possible answer is that we were in a sense captives of *ourselves*, of our own self-enslavement to sin, an inability to turn ourselves around. Christ's suffering and death, then, give *God* a motive to give *us* the grace to repent and change our lives.[7] In terms of our parable, suppose that the foresworn knights had in shame and despair surrendered to the enemy and been locked into his dungeon. The prince's sacrifice would give his father a good reason to use his power to free the knights from the imprisonment, which they could no longer do themselves.

The New Testament teaching that we are somehow incorporated into Christ gives us a hint as to how we might deepen our parable: the prince locks *himself* in the dungeon with the knights, and when the king rescues him he rescues the knights as well. In this deepening of the parable, the jewel has a different importance: it is merely the symbol of and occasion for the knights' allegiance. The parable might begin:

> A certain king had a group of knights whom he loved. To give them a focus for their loyalty, he formed them into a brotherhood sworn to defend a jewel or die in the attempt. An enemy of the king, jealous of the loyalty of these knights, corrupted them . . .

Perhaps in this parable the enemy destroys the jewel, making it *impossible* for the knights to restore it. The enemy is the jailor and the shamed knights have let him imprison them. What the prince does is put himself voluntarily into the power of this jailor, then form a new brotherhood in the jail, of those whowant to return to their former allegiance. In his name the new brotherhood sends a message to the king, asking for mercy; the king defeats the enemy, releases his son and the other captives. We need not change the ending of the parable; the prince and his squire and the leader of the knights speak as before.

But the problematic idea here is the idea of our *incorporation* into Christ: of our being part of the "Body of Christ." If this is mere metaphor what is it a metaphor for? If it is not pure metaphor, how can we make sense of it? Some philosophers and theologians have found a "legal fiction" interpretation of the metaphor satisfactory: God looks at us in our sinfulness, but pretends to see Christ in his perfect obedience; our "filthy rags" are "covered with the cloak of his righteousness." But so far as I can see this interpretation (which is itself a metaphor, so we are interpreting a metaphor by a metaphor) fails because the idea of God "pretending" or "deeming" is unintelligible. The way God sees things is the way they are; the way God acts toward things is and must be based on the reality of these things.

A more attractive and innovative theory is Charles Williams's theory of "co-inherence" (eagerly adopted by C. S. Lewis).[8] In the Williams view, our incorporation in Christ is a particular application of a general "spiritual law" that there are certain things that can *only* be done for us by others and which we can only do for others, not ourselves. This theory needs a much more detailed discussion than I can give it here: it is immensely suggestive but perhaps merely restates the problem rather than solving it: *Why* are there things we can only do for others? *Why* is it a "spiritual law"? And even if it is a spiritual law in some areas, isn't deserved punishment something which is non-transferable?

It seems that there is no real substitute for a theory of our incorporation into Christ which takes our unity with Christ as a genuine metaphysical fact.[9] Just as an act done by my hand is an act done by me, so an act done by a member of Christ's mystical body is done by Christ and an act done by Christ is an act done by his mystical body.

This taking the unity of the mystical body has one seemingly embarrassing consequence and two welcome ones. The seemingly embarrassing consequence is that since members of Christ's mystical body sin, the body sins. But perhaps this makes sense of Paul's violent metaphor that Christ was "made sin for us."[10] The sins of the members become the sins of the body, just as the debts of a member of a family become family debts.

But equally if a family member's debts become family debts, the family assets become the family member's assets. This means that we have a real right to the merits which Christ has deserved: as members of his body these merits *belong* to us.

Even more crucially the sufferings of members of the body become the sufferings of the body. Christ's mystical body suffers not only in Christ's own sufferings but in the sufferings of the starving baby, the old man dying of cancer, and the woman who is raped and murdered. And *all* this suffering is redemptive; the crucifixion of Christ is going on right now in the children's wards of hospitals, in Mother Teresa's hospices for the dying, in the streets of our cities. All suffering undeserved by the sufferer and freely accepted out of love is an act of supererogation which gives God a good reason to punish members of Christ's body less than they deserve, and reward them far beyond their individual merits.

In fact, we are no longer judged as individuals, in one sense, at all: the body of Christ is judged, and judged worthy of glory. The only way of cutting ourselves off from this glory is to cut ourselves off from the body, which is what serious sin does. But unlike a cell of a natural body, we can be revivified, once cut off from the body, and be reunited to it.

In fact, the life of Christ in us as members of his body, which in some theological traditions is called sanctifying grace, is precisely what makes us share in Christ's merits. Many of us are still infected by and corrupted by sin, just as in Christ's passion many of the cells of his natural body were bruised, damaged, filled with the poisons of fatigue and trauma, yet continued to live with his life. Some of us die to Christ's life and fall away from the mystical body, just as some cells of Christ's physical body died and fell away.

This whole picture of the essential unity of individual human beings in Christ's mystical body will be profoundly unsympathetic to many moderns. But taking it as a reality and not just as a metaphor is the only way to resolve the ultimate problems of sin and suffering. The pattern should not be unfamiliar. In many philosophical problems bearing on religion, we can go quite a long way using everyday categories and judgments. For example, some suffering is obviously deserved, some obviously remedial or "soul-making." But there is always a "surd," like the sufferings of infants who die with-out any opportunity to learn or grow. This surd can *only* be dealt with by the full depths of Christian revelation. There are no *purely* philosophical answers to the deepest human problems, which is just to say that philosophy is not a substitute for religion.

What philosophy can do, however, is to show how much of revelation corresponds to our deepest human instincts, how many apparent conflicts between reason and revelation rest on confusions which can be solved by purely philosophical distinctions and arguments. But there comes a point at which philosophy can only say, "This problem is either insolvable or it is solvable by this revealed doctrine." We are always free to reject the revealed doctrine: that is why faith is a virtue. But the price we pay for rejecting the revelation is that we are left with an insoluble problem. Either the sufferings of the innocent are part of the redemptive suffering of Christ's mystical body, or there is no explanation of the sufferings of the innocent. And if there is no explanation of the sufferings of the innocent, God is not good, and we should not worship or serve God.

Thus, philosophical theology often points beyond itself.[11] It cannot give ultimate solutions to problems which can only be solved by revelation. But it can indicate the gap in our understanding which only that revelation can fill. In this sense, philosophical theology can give us reason to believe, even where it cannot give us philosophical reasons to believe. That is both the limitation and the glory of natural theology: it is a handmaiden, but it is the handmaiden of the Queen!

NOTES

1. Quinn's work is still largely unpublished: the part of it I am familiar with is a paper he read at the Society of Christian Philosophers meeting in Los Angeles in March, 1986 entitled "Christian Atonement and Kantian Justification" (published in *Faith and Philosophy* 3, no. 4 [October 1986]).

2. I was pleased to find, after working out my own views, that many of my theses agree with things said in different language by Aquinas in the *Summa theologica*. On this point, see IIIa q.49 a.4 reply obj.2, and q.38, q.48 a.2 reply.

3. I first made this distinction in print in these terms in my *Moral Dilemmas* (Belmont, Calif.: Wadsworth, 1985), p. 54. Aquinas plainly agrees with the basic point, see *ST* IIIa q.46 a.2 *ad* 3, and *ST* IIIa q.46 a.3 *ad* 3: "The man who waives satisfaction . . . acts mercifully, not unjustly."

4. See *ST* IIIa q.52 a.8 where the point is raised with regard to souls in purgatory, who are not necessarily released from due punishment by Christ's passion.

5. Aquinas clearly disagrees with this; he holds God could have forgiven us without any satisfaction for sin. See *ST* IIIa q.46 a.3 *ad* 3.

6. For Aquinas this is the major reason why God did not forgive us without satisfaction. See *ST* IIIa q.46 a.3 reply, *Primo*. Notice that this is typically Aquinas's *first* response.

7. See *ST* IIIa q.48 a.4 and q.49 a.2. It should be noted that the paradigm case of ransom for us is ransom paid a kidnapper, but the paradigm case of ransom for the ancients and the medievals was ransom for a prisoner of war, who had typically *surrendered,* thus giving a commitment to his captors. This metaphor suggests that in the war against evil we have laid down our arms and surrendered, and are thus in a sense committed to evil or to its representative, Satan.

8. On Williams's views, see Mary McDermott Shideler, *The Theology of Romantic Love* (Grand Rapids, Mich.: Eerdmans, 1962) passim and especially chap. 8. On Lewis's attitude, see, for example, the material quoted in my *C. S. Lewis's Case for the Christian Faith* (New York: Harper, 1981), 35–39.

9. Aquinas makes this his principal explanation of how and why atonement works. See *ST* IIIa q.48 a.1, reply, and q.49 a.1 *ad* 1.

10. See *ST* IIIa q.8 a.3 *ad* 2 where Aquinas deals with the sinfulness of the church as an objection to Christ's "headship" of the church.

11. Again, see Aquinas *ST* Ia q.1 a.1. Of course it is quite legiti-mate for even Christian philosophers to prefer to deal with those parts of philosophy where the "handmaiden" is "mistress in her own house," i.e., these parts of natural theology or general philosophy where purely philosophical reasons *can* be given for conclusions reached. But in my view, this unduly restricts us in philosophy of religion: see my *Thinking About Religion* (Englewood Cliffs, N.J.: Prentice Hall, 1978) *passim* 23–28. 150–151.

Providence and the Problem of Evil

Eleonore Stump

The problem of evil has often enough been presented by atheists as a problem for theists, and Christian treatments of the problem have tended to be rebuttals of an atheistic challenge.[1] But here I want to approach the problem of evil in a different way, by beginning with Christian beliefs about God and examining the problem of evil in the light of those beliefs. Furthermore, although until quite recently the divine attribute focused on in supporting or attacking proposed defenses and theodicies has been God's omnipotence, at this stage of the discussion I think we can also benefit by turning our attention from God's omnipotence to his goodness and the way it is manifested in the world. Consequently, I want first to consider what Christianity has traditionally said about God's goodness and the way in which that goodness is expressed in God's governance of creation, and then to reconsider the problem of evil in the light of those views. Roughly speaking, then, I want to focus on the elements of God's character and action comprised in the doctrine of God's providence.

I am going to take my account of God's providence from Aquinas because his view of God's goodness and governance is the one I find most appealing, philosophically and theologically. The views I attribute to Aquinas in this essay, however, can also be found in other medieval philosophers, such as Augustine or Gregory the Great[2] (though it would be harder to show that these are Augustine's or Gregory's views than that they are Aquinas's). My primary concern here, however, is not with contributing to the historical scholarship on Aquinas. My interest is

51

rather in showing a traditional view of God's providence, held in one form or another by many medievals but expounded particularly well by Aquinas. When I have presented his account of God's providence, I will show what difference it makes to the problem of evil and consider what we can say about the problem if we begin with the Christian assumption that there is a provident God.

In a previous essay on the problem of evil I proposed an approach to it that is relevant to the account I am going to give here.[3] In that essay I maintained that a Christian response to the problem of evil should be made in light of the other things Christians have traditionally believed about the world, in particular the following three beliefs:

1. At some time in the past as a result of their own choices human beings altered their nature for the worse; the alteration involved what we recognize and describe as a change in the nature of human free will; and the changed nature of the will was naturally inheritable and passed on to subsequent generations. (For the sake of brevity this belief can be referred to as the doctrine of Adam's fall.)
2. Natural evil entered the world as a result of Adam's fall (that is, no person suffered from diseases, tornadoes, droughts, etc., until Adam's fall).
3. After death, depending on their state at the time of their death, human beings go either to heaven or to hell.

Given those beliefs, I argued that on Christian doctrine the ultimate evil is not pain or even death but the unending loss of union with God which results from failure to fix the defect in the will.[4] To fix this defect in the will and still keep the will free requires the cooperation of the divine and human wills in a complicated action which includes a person's willing God's help and God's consequently altering that person's will for the better.[5] The moral and natural evil a person suffers is a means (efficacious or otherwise) for bringing him to the state in which he is willing to ask God's help because they tend to give him a humbling view of himself and his place in the world and an effective desire for a better state.[6] What justifies God's allowing any evil into his creation, then, is that the suffering occasioned by evil constitutes the most effective means for redemption, for restoring fallen persons to a state in which they can be united with God in heaven and for keeping them from the living death of hell.

It now seems to me that there are two shortcomings in that argument. In the first place, I did not do enough to illustrate the ways in which the account I was defending differs from the implausible and unpalatable view that God himself has willed the evils we suffer in order to make this the best of all possible worlds.[7] Secondly and, from my point of view, more importantly, my account is incomplete, as can be seen most readily by considering the case of martyrs. No one who has read Thomas More's Tower works, for example, can suppose that he was in need of a humbling recognition of his own sins or that his will needed stimulation in order to turn to God. On the contrary, his religious devotion and his desire for grace to overturn the evil in himself are powerfully evident. Clearly, then, the suffering he endured in his captivity and execution cannot be justified on the grounds that it converted him to God and kept him from dying in his sins. If my account is to cover cases such as that of More's suffering, it needs to be supplemented to provide a justification for God's permitting evils in cases where the sufferer has already turned to God and submitted his will to God's. In the doctrine of God's providence there is a remedy for both these shortcomings.

Aquinas's Account of Goodness

The foundation of Aquinas's ethics, as well as of his understanding of divine providence, is the claim that 'being' and 'goodness' are the same in reference but different in sense.[8] His normative ethics is constructed around a theory of virtues and vices, conceived of as habitual inclinations toward certain sorts of actions. To understand his ethical theory, then, it will be helpful to consider briefly his analysis and evaluation of actions.

On Aquinas's view every action has an object, an end, and certain circumstances in which it is done. The object of an agent's action is the state of affairs the agent intends to bring about as a direct effect of the action. We might characterize the object as the aim or purpose of the action. When More, for example, set out to write on Christ's suffering and death, his object was to produce a meditative commentary on the passion. The object of an action is to be distinguished from the action's end. We might think of an action's object as *what* the agent intends to accomplish as a direct result of his action, and the end of the action as *why* he intends to accomplish it. The end of More's action of writing about Christ's death was to strengthen himself for the painful death he anticipated. Both the object and the end of an action are taken into account in determining what the action essentially *is*. Given Aquinas's central thesis regarding being and goodness, it is not surprising to find him maintaining that the goodness or badness of any action is to be decided on the basis of an assessment of the action's object and end. If the states of affairs which the agent aims at and the desires which motivate him are good, the action is good; if either the object or the end is not good, the action is not good either.

The circumstances of an action are individuating accidents of a type of action. Consider, for example, More's refusal to take the oath of supremacy. The object of his action was to avoid perjuring himself, and the end of his action was the avoidance of what he took to be a mortal sin. The circumstances include those properties the action has in virtue of the fact that More had previously offended the king by resigning his office and by refusing to attend the coronation of the new queen, that More knew that two attempts had already been made to implicate him in some crime and that the king tended to be ruthless towards his enemies, and so on. These circumstances are accidental to the type of action More performed in refusing to take the oath, but they are not accidental to his particular action on that occasion. On the contrary, our understanding of the object and end of his action is influenced by what we know of its circumstances; they refine our understanding of what More did and contribute to our evaluation of it as an act of moral courage.

These circumstances may be thought of as intrinsic accidents of More's action, and they should be distinguished from its extrinsic accidents, such as that it was described in Roper's *Life* of More or that it was partly responsible for More's being canonized in 1935. Such extrinsic accidents contributed nothing to what More did; the connection between More's action and such extrinsic accidents was an unforeseeable and fortuitous chain of events, something More was not accountable for. On Aquinas's view, the evaluation of actions is based entirely on a consideration of what those actions *are;* and so it is based on the action's object, end, and intrinsic accidents, and not at all on the action's extrinsic accidents. Consequently, if, considered in its circumstances, the object and the end of an action are such that there is some increase in being as a result of the action, the action is morally good; and otherwise it is not.

What prevents Aquinas's view of goodness from turning into a quasi-utilitarianism based on calculations of being is his account of the virtue of justice. For Aquinas the moral virtues are dispositions of the will to choose rationally in controlling passions and directing actions. Prudence is the habit of rationally choosing means appropriate for the attaining of ends and so is concerned with directing actions; temperance and courage are concerned, in different ways, with keeping passions under the control of reason. Justice is the habitual disposition for acting rationally in actions affecting other people.

On Aquinas's view justice is generally concerned with establishing and preserving the being of a society. Distributive justice is the rational regulation of the distribution of the society's worldly goods, aiming at a rational relationship in that respect between the society as a whole and any individual member of it. Commutative justice, on the other hand, is the rational regulation of relationships among individuals or subgroups within the society. The basic notion underlying commutative justice is that persons considered just as persons are equal and that it is therefore rational for them to treat one another as equals when it is appropriate for them to consider one another just as persons. A slanderer and his victim are equals in all relevant respects; but the slanderer takes away his victim's reputation and gives nothing in return. The slanderer's action is thus a violation of commutative justice. So is murder, since in depriving the victim of life the murderer is not only providing no worldly compensation but also rendering the victim incapable of receiving such compensation.

To see how considerations of justice prevent Aquinas's account of goodness from turning into a utilitarianism of being, consider More and Cardinal Wolsey. On More's view, the cardinal was undoubtedly a dreadful priest; and, as an evil counselor to the king, through his efforts to expedite Henry's divorce and remarriage, he was also encouraging the king and clergy to follow in his own pernicious course. Using Aquinas's ethics, we might suppose that it would be acceptable for More to reason as follows. The death of one is a smaller loss of being than the death of many, and the death of the soul in hell is a greater loss of being than the death of the body. Given More's beliefs about Wolsey, then, it seems that killing Wolsey would entail a smaller loss of being than letting him live to corrupt others. Therefore, destroying Wolsey is the lesser of two evils, and it is consequently morally acceptable to murder him.

But this chain of reasoning neglects Aquinas's evaluation of actions in terms of object and end. The end of More's action in killing Wolsey would be to keep him from corrupting the secular and spiritual leaders of England. If, for the sake of argument, we simply assume the correctness of More's appraisal of Wolsey, we can say that the end of the action is good. The object of the action, however, is to kill Wolsey. But More and Wolsey are not combatants in a battle in which each is out to kill the other while defending himself from the other's attack; More is not an executioner duly appointed by the state and carrying out a judicially imposed sentence; and so on. In all the respects relevant to this case, then, More and Wolsey are equal; and if More were to kill Wolsey, More would be taking from Wolsey a great good, namely, his life, for which compensation would not (in fact, could not) be given. Therefore, in the circumstances, the object of More's action, his killing Wolsey, is an act of injustice. But no action, no matter how praiseworthy its end may be, can count as a good action unless, considered in the circumstances, both its object and its end are good. Therefore, even assuming the truth of More's appraisal of the cardinal, Aquinas's ethics would not justify More's killing Wolsey. In the same way, for the same reasons, Aquinas's ethics will not justify the sorts of cases which have seemed counterexamples to utilitarianism.

On the doctrine of divine simplicity Aquinas espouses,[9] God is identical with his nature, and God's nature is being itself. Given Aquinas's metaethical thesis that 'goodness' and 'being' are the same in reference though different in sense, God's nature is also goodness.[10] Although the doctrine of simplicity rules out predicating terms of God and of creatures univocally, it is none-theless clear, then, that Aquinas's metaethical thesis equating being and goodness is meant to hold also for God's nature and actions. We might suppose, however, that even if Aquinas is willing to apply his central metaethical thesis to God, he would be hesitant to apply his normative ethics to God and that he would in particular be unwilling to predicate justice of God. Considerations of God's sovereignty seem to militate against attributing the constraints of justice to him. If as God he owes no creature anything and can do whatever he likes[11] or if he has no obligations of any sort,[12] then it might seem that the restraints imposed by considerations of justice do not apply to him. Aquinas's view, however, is different.

God cannot enter into the sort of exchanges with his creatures on which notions of commutative justice are founded, because he is the creator of everything and therefore cannot be considered as equal to any of his creatures. Distributive justice, however, can be attributed to God. There are certain things due every creature in virtue of its condition and nature. Because God has made things as he has, there is a certain order in the created world. When God renders to each creature what is due it in the order of things, as determined by that creature's nature and current state, then God exercises distributive justice, according to Aquinas.[13] That a creature has a certain nature or is in a certain condition may itself be a result of God's mercy; but once the creature is in a particular state, considerations of justice will require that it be dealt with in certain ways. So, for example, that God made promises to the Jewish patriarchs about their descendants was an act of mercy on God's part; but once those promises had been made, justice required that God fulfill them.[14] In this sense, it is appropriate to speak of God's owing certain things to his creatures and of God's giving his creatures what is due them.[15]

Furthermore, in dealing with a creature in accordance with its nature or condition in this way, God is doing only what is objectively good for that creature.[16] Therefore, since God can do only good,[17] the constraints imposed by considerations of justice are just the constraints that operate on the divine will in any case. There is therefore no special ground for concern about the compatibility between the doctrine of divine sovereignty and the claim that God must act justly.[18] (I am not insensitive to the fact that the apparent injustice of God's dealings with his creatures is one of the guises in which the problem of evil appears to Christians, but the appropriate place for the consideration of this difficulty is in the application of the doctrine of God's providence to the problem of evil in the later sections of this essay.)

God's Providence

The notion of God's providence is derived from the concept of his goodness. Because on the doctrine of simplicity the divine nature is identical with goodness, the goodness of creatures is measured by their relationship to God. For human persons in particular, the ultimate good and the final fulfillment of their natures consists in *union* with God. And because God is good, he does what is good for his creatures. In his dealings with human beings, then, God's ultimate aim, which takes precedence over all others, is to return them to himself, to unite them to himself in heaven. The plan by which he directs the lives of human beings, influences their characters, and orders the events of their lives in order to achieve his aim is called his providence, and the actual working out of his plan is called the divine governance.[19] For the sake of brevity in what follows, I will refer to both the plan and its execution as God's providence.

Consonant with traditional Christian doctrine, it is Aquinas's claim that everything in the world is subject to divine providence. Comprised in this claim are two beliefs; (1) God in his providence directs all things in the world to their ultimate good, that is, to himself;[20] and (2) God's will is always fulfilled.[21] In other words, Aquinas believes that everything that happens happens under God's control and is chosen or allowed by him because it contributes to the ultimate good of creatures by drawing them back to him. There are obvious objections to this claim about providence, and Aquinas considers some of them from different approaches at several places in his writings. These objections fall into two groups. Those of the first group argue against the claim itself; those of the second group argue that the particular mechanism by which divine providence is said to operate is not open to God as a means of governance.[22] I will leave the objections of the second group to one side and concentrate on those of the first group.[23]

To begin with, it seems evident that God's will is not always fulfilled; in fact, there is apparently even a biblical warrant for the claim that it is not. 1 Timothy 2:4 says that God would have all men to be saved; but it is Christian doctrine that not all men are saved, and therefore it seems that the will of God is not always fulfilled. Besides, the point of God's giving human beings free will is evidently to enable them to govern themselves and make their own choices; but in that case it is possible for human persons to will something discordant with God's will. Furthermore, traditional Christianity holds that some of God's creatures, most notably Satan but also some human beings (Jonah, for example), rebelled against God; to rebel, however, is just to pit one's will against God's and deliberately act contrary to God's will. Finally, it seems that considerations of God's justice require us to say that God's will is not always fulfilled, because unless some creatures acted contrary to God's will, it seems that God would not be just in punishing them, as he is said to do.[24]

In reply Aquinas says that God always wills what is good, but sometimes what is good absolutely considered is not good in the circumstances. In such cases God may be said to have an inclination (*velleitas*) for the good absolutely considered, but what he actually wills is what is good in the circumstances. To see what Aquinas means, consider, for example, a mother who dotes on her son Aaron. If she could, she would no doubt be glad always to live in happy harmony with her child; but when he engages in deliberate mischief, she wills to scold him. What is good absolutely considered, namely, that she be pleasant to her child, is not good in the circumstances in which he misbehaves; what is good in those circumstances is that she scold him. Therefore, as a good mother who wills what is good for her son, when she is confronted with Aaron's misbehavior, she wills to scold him. Is some part of her will frustrated when she scolds him? Not if by 'will' here we mean an occurrent act of will, as distinct from a wish, desire, longing, or inclination. The mother would like to live at peace with her son, and she herself may be quite frustrated when his misbehavior keeps her from the happy relations with him which she desires; but these facts tell us only something about her emotions and aims, not about her will. In the face of Aaron's mischief her *will* is to scold him; and her will is fulfilled even if she has a longing which is unsatisfied when she and her son are at variance. Again, someone might suppose that the mother's will is contravened nonetheless just by the fact that Aaron does not will to do what he ought to do. But this objection also confuses an aim or longing with an act of will. The mother can yearn for her son to do what is right, but unless his doing what he ought to do is something she can bring about herself (as it is not so long as he has free will), *she* cannot form an act of will the content of which is what *he* does. Similarly, Aquinas says, when God considers human persons just as human, what is good for them is that they be saved, and hence a perfectly good God has an inclination (or aim or yearning) to save them all. But since some persons refuse grace and persist in sin, what God actually wills is not to save some of them.[25] The technical but familiar way to describe this situation is to say that God antecedently wills what is good absolutely, but he consequently wills the good in the circumstances. God antecedently wills all persons to be saved; but he consequently wills that some not be saved.

The distinction between antecedent and consequent will is convenient, as long as it does not mislead us into thinking that God wills first one thing and then another, or that his antecedent will is what he really wills while his consequent will is what he settles for.[26] Rather what God has ordained for his creatures insofar as it lies just in God himself to determine is what God is said to will in his antecedent will. But when a created person, because of some defect he introduces into himself, hinders himself from coming to the end God ordained for him, then God's willing nonetheless to bring that person to as much goodness as he is capable of (given the state of his will) is God's consequent will.[27] As Aquinas describes it, then, God's antecedent will is what God would will as good in the abstract, apart from the actual circumstances which obtain, as the mother in the example wills in the abstract that she might live harmoniously with her son; but what God in fact actually wills, given the circumstances that obtain, is said to be God's consequent will. For this reason Aquinas says that God's antecedent will is not strictly speaking his will at all but rather something like an inclination on God's part. What God actually wills, all the acts of will which God forms, are acts of consequent will; and understood as part of God's consequent will, all God's acts of will are fulfilled.

The objections to Aquinas's account of providence presented above can all be handled with the distinction between God's antecedent and consequent will. The biblical text that says God wills all men to be saved is referring to God's antecedent will; given that some people do not repent, it is God's consequent will that not all be saved. Furthermore, when human beings sin or rebel and so apparently will something against God's will, it is God's antecedent, not his consequent, will they contravene; his consequent will is always fulfilled.[28] In other words, when Jonah disobeys God's injunction and runs away, what are we to suppose about God's acts of will as regards Jonah's action? If God then had the *volition* that Jonah should not disobey him, he could have brought about what he willed by, for example, simply undermining Jonah's free will and causing him to will to obey. Jonah's disobeying is compatible with the existence of an omniscient and omnipotent deity only on the assumption that God's will does not dissent from Jonah's disobedience. In the circumstances, namely, Jonah's rebelliousness, the best thing for God to will (the story leads us to believe) is that Jonah be allowed to disobey, and God consequently so wills.[29] Jonah's disobedience is thus consonant with God's consequent will, which is not frustrated by what Jonah does. The initial command God gives Jonah in the story shows that Jonah's choice is not in accord with the way God would like things to be, but to say this is not to say that there is an act of God's will which is frustrated when Jonah disobeys God's command, as long as we can distinguish inclinations, desires, wishes, or longings (or their divine equivalents) from acts of will. The notion of an agent's antecedent volition is thus the notion of a desire of some sort which is nonetheless not made the agent's volition;[30] the agent's volitions are comprised in the notion of his consequent will. Consequently, we can say that Jonah's rebellion contravenes God's antecedent but not his consequent will, and that even in a case of disobedience such as Jonah's there is no unfulfilled act of God's will. Finally, that God is just in punishing a person for willing what is in accord only with God's consequent and not his antecedent will is also explainable on Aquinas's view. That a certain act is in accord with God's consequent will does not mean that the act is a good one, only that allowing the agent to perform that act is in the circumstances a good thing. Analogously, a mother might decide to allow her child to make his own mistakes and so have it as her consequent will that he be allowed to forego studying for the sake of socializing, but she might nonetheless be just in punishing him for the resulting bad grade.

This solution to the preceding objections, however, leads directly to another set of objections, because we might suppose that if evil acts are in accord with God's consequent will, then in some sense or other God himself wills moral evil and is responsible for it. In reply, Aquinas says that it is not part of God's will to exclude from his creatures entirely the power of falling away from the good or the exercise of that power.[31] It is one of Aquinas's favorite principles that God does not destroy the nature of anything he has made.[32] But it would destroy the nature of human beings if God kept them from ever doing anything evil, since the nature he has given them enables them to make significant choices for themselves. Consequently, God neither wills that moral evils occur nor wills that they do not occur. Rather he sometimes wills to permit such evils to occur when human persons have chosen to do evil, because if he always failed to give such permission, he would be acting contrary to (and to that extent destroying) the nature of human beings.[33] Therefore, in his consequent will God sometimes gives his consent to moral evil because to do otherwise would require undermining the nature he created, and the loss of being and hence of goodness entailed by doing so is a greater loss of being than whatever loss may be incurred by the evil God permits.[34]

God permits an evil on the part of his creatures, however, only in case he can direct it to some good. This claim can be understood in two senses. To do evil in order to bring about good, Aquinas says, is an evil act and can in no way be attributed to God. Why he should think so is clear from his moral theory, because the act he envisages, doing evil in order to bring about good, is an act in which the end is good but the object is not. But, as we saw above, on Aquinas's theory of morality an act is good only in case both its object and its end are good; and so what is appropriately attributed to God in permitting evil must be an action whose object and end are both good. Aquinas's formulation of the appropriate description of such an action is not entirely clear, but I think what he has in mind is something of this sort.

In George Eliot's *Silas Marner* the local Squire's dissipated son Dunstan plagues and torments his good-natured brother Godfrey, and on one occasion he bullies Godfrey into lending him his horse, contrary to Godfrey's own prudent inclination to keep his favorite animal from his reckless brother. Suppose that their father the Squire had secretly witnessed this scene and that it was entirely in his power to put a stop to Dunstan's plaguing Godfrey. Are there any circumstances we could envisage in which the Squire could be rightly said to be both just and loving towards his son Godfrey and nonetheless fail to prevent the suffering occasioned by Dunstan's mistreatment of Godfrey? Leaving aside cases which would violate agent-centered restrictions[35] and so compromise the Squire's justice, as well as cases in which Dunstan's tormenting constitutes just punishment for some moral failing of Godfrey's (as perhaps it does in Eliot's story), we can imagine circumstances of this sort. Suppose the Squire knows that Godfrey has difficulty maintaining his integrity, that he has a lamentable desire to please, and a pathetic drive to make himself popular with everyone he comes in contact with. Suppose, too, the Squire believes that allowing Dunstan to bully Godfrey into risking his horse may be exactly what it takes to wake Godfrey to the folly of his ways and to put some steel into his character. In that case the Squire can permit the evil of Dunstan's bullying of his brother, and yet both the object and the end of the Squire's action are good.

It is clear that the end of the Squire's action and the end of Dunstan's action are different; one intends to help and the other to hurt Godfrey. But the objects of their action are also different. What Dunstan intends to accomplish is not just getting the use of a horse but, more importantly, dominating and worrying Godfrey, which Dunstan enjoys. (If Dunstan got the horse without distressing Godfrey, he would feel he had been unsuccessful.) What the Squire intends to accomplish, however, is the remedying of a moral defect which would sooner or later destroy Godfrey's character. Thus, although Dunstan's will is in accord with what we can call the Squire's consequent will, Dunstan would be rightly censured for his act while the Squire would be properly praised for his.

Now the Squire in my example does not contribute much to the action. He simply decides not to stop Dunstan's evil act because he sees that allowing it to occur wards off a greater evil for Godfrey himself. Aquinas's idea, I think, is that in permitting evil God is in somewhat the same position as the Squire in the example, except that his ability to manipulate the circumstances and thus control the outcome far exceeds the Squire's, whose contribution to the final outcome consists just in not interfering when he could. God permits an evil to occur just when he knows that he can providently direct things in such a way that allowing the evil to occur will be a greater good for the sufferer than preventing that evil. In this way, although God does not do evil in order to bring about good, Aquinas says, he does permit evils from which he can draw good.

Finally, we might suppose that the doctrine of providence Aquinas espouses has the absurd consequence that there is no contingency in the world.[36] If God's will is always fulfilled, then things must go as God wills; so, apparently, nothing occurs by chance, and (even worse) whatever happens happens of necessity. This conclusion, as Aquinas says, obviously goes against common opinion.[37] To see how he replies to the objection based on the notion of chance, we should think of chance as the medievals generally did,[38] as the unforeseen and unintended convergence of causal chains. This definition plainly allows chance to be relativized to knowers. It is possible for a convergence of causal chains to be unforeseen and unintended by some persons and intended and foreseen by others. So, Aquinas says, two servants may meet by chance from their point of view, and yet the meeting may have been foreseen or even intended by their master. In the same way, events may occur by chance with respect to all human understanding and nonetheless have been intended or permitted by God as part of his providential plan.[39]

This reply to the part of the objection based on the notion of chance clearly sharpens the point of the other part of the objection, that God's providence ruled out any contingency in the world. What is certainly ruled out is that anything occur which is not part of God's providence, willed either as part of God's original plan for his creatures or as part of his consequent will warranting as good in the circumstances something he would reject considered unconditionally. But Aquinas denies that this claim rules out contingency in creation. In fact, on Aquinas's view, that God's will does not impose necessity on all things willed by God is a consequence of the efficacy of God's will, which extends both to the production of the effect willed and to the manner in which that effect occurs. Not only do those things happen that God wills to happen, but they happen necessarily or contingently according to his will. The modality of the effects of God's will are not a result of direct divine fiat. Rather, some things happen contingently because God has prepared contingent causes from which contingent effects eventuate. For example, by creating human beings with free will, God has prepared contingent causes from which contingent effects result, namely, all those effects dependent on human choice.[40] Consequently, although everything that happens happens as part of God's providential plan, it does not follow that God's governance imposes necessity on all the things governed.[41]

Providence and Evil

The doctrine of God's providence gives us the nature and purpose of God's rule, and the account of God's goodness shows us constraints on the way he can achieve his purpose. In particular, the notion of God's justice requires that undeserved suffering permitted by God be somehow compensated.[42] Undeserved suffering which is uncompensated seems clearly unjust; but so does suffering compensated only by benefits to someone other than the sufferer. Consider, for example, the notorious case in which the U.S. Army secretly administered doses of LSD to unsuspecting soldiers for the sake of understanding the drug's military potential. Perhaps the end sought in this experiment was information worth having. But the appearance of injustice in this case, which seems striking to most of us, is at least in part a consequence of the fact that the end aimed at did not directly or primarily benefit those who suffered to achieve it.

To dispel the appearance of injustice in such a case, it is not enough simply to compensate the sufferer with some greater good. Suppose a giant corporation secretly and deliberately caused a massive chemical spill in a particularly poor part of India for the sake of testing some new technology for cleaning up chemical spills. As part of their plans for this secret experiment, they might budget compensation of one thousand dollars for each seriously injured Indian. Even if we suppose that the impoverished Indians would regard the money as wealth beyond their wildest dreams and would willingly give up any further claims against the company, few of us would consider the corporation just in what it had done. In general, it seems that one is not justified in producing or permitting evil because one can compensate the evil with some greater good. Rather, other things being equal, it seems morally permissible to allow someone to suffer involuntarily only in case doing so is a necessary means or the best possible means in the circumstances to keep the sufferer from incurring even greater harm.[43]

These moral intuitions can be explained and supported on Aquinas's ethical theory, with the approach used above in the example of the Squire and Dunstan. To justify evil on the basis of the greater good which compensates it is to let the end justify the means. In such a case, although the end of the action is good, the object of the action is not. In the case of the injured Indians, the company is taking from the Indians something highly valued, namely, health (not to mention self-respect and dignity). That the Indians are so poor as to be willing to trade such a great good for the paltry sum of a thousand dollars is sign of their desperation; but that the corporation should benefit from their desperation by entering into a trade which would strike the directors of the corporation as outrageous if it were offered to *them* is a gross injustice. On the other hand, when suffering is inflicted (or allowed) just for the sake of preventing some greater harm to the unwilling sufferer, the object of the action is not causing (or concurring in) some evil but rather causing (or concurring in) the lesser of two evils for the sufferer, when the greater will occur if the lesser does not.[44] In such circumstances the object of the action is good even if the action involves inflicting (or allowing) suffering.

(It is worth noticing, however, that in certain cases, if the sufferer has previously given his assent to the suffering, then the one inflicting the suffering can be justified even when the object of the action is not the lesser of two evils but the suffering is compensated by a greater good. This is the principle which orthodontists, for example, employ. If an actor woke up one morning to find himself bandaged and in pain in consequence of orthodontia which had been done stealthily in the night, he would be justifiably outraged, even if he were subsequently to agree that the improvement in his appearance was a greater good than the pain of the treatment. On the other hand, if he had previously given his assent to the orthodontic procedures, then the suffering he underwent would be justified by his enhanced appearance. In that case, we might think of the orthodontist as an external instrument through whom the actor works his will to trade some pain and medical risk for a more attractive face. This is a trade which is perhaps not unreasonable, given his profession, and therefore it is not unreasonable for the orthodontist to assist him in accomplishing it. We would feel the same for any other medical procedure he might choose even if the drawbacks to it were greater, as long as the advantages were also commensurately greater. In such a case the object of the physician's action involves no injustice because the person undergoing the suffering is willing to do so and because that willingness is not a perverted result of dire need.)

Within these constraints set by considerations of God's goodness, the doctrine of providence tells us that God governs the world in such a way as to achieve his purpose of drawing his creatures to himself. It is important to emphasize the claim that God's overriding purpose for human persons is their union with him, just because of the standard of value which this claim establishes. Attacks on theism based on the problem of evil tend to be largely unreflective about the standard of value being employed, although consideration of the problem of evil obviously depends crucially on evaluating certain things as evil. Philosophers engaged in such attacks often seem to be presupposing what they themselves would no doubt reject vigorously if they were doing ethics rather than philosophy of religion, namely, that there is one objective standard of value which we all share regardless of our other philosophical or theological commitments. But that Christians do not hold the same standard of value as non-Christians should surprise no one. Furthermore, if Christians hold that the foundation of morality lies in God, whether in his will or in his nature, we can anticipate that their system of ethics will differ from systems which, for example, ground morality in pleasure or which relativize morality to an individual agent's beliefs and desires. Consider death, for example. If God's overriding purpose in dealing with human beings is to bring them to union with himself in heaven because that state is their greatest good, then death is not the ultimate evil. What is worthy of concern about death on this view is not whether it occurs but whether it occurs badly,[45] because death is not the end but a transition between the trials of this life and their fruition in the afterlife. The transition everyone experiences; what is to be feared and avoided as an evil is only building one's life in such a way that the transition leads away from God rather than to him. In general, then, whatever aims at a result which is discordant with God's purpose of bringing human beings to himself is evil, and what aims at furthering that purpose is good.

Aquinas's account of God's goodness and providence thus enables us to sketch the outlines of a morally sufficient reason for God's permitting evil. If we leave to one side cases in which suffering constitutes punishment for wrong-doing, then God is justified in permitting unwilling victims to suffer in case their suffering constitutes a necessary means or the best means available in the circumstances of turning them to him and keeping them from the infinitely greater evil of the loss of union with him.[46]

A number of objections to this attempted solution of the problem of evil come readily to mind.

1. This approach to the problem of evil apparently entails that nothing bad—nothing *really* bad, that is—ever happens to anybody. But this conclusion is wildly implausible.

This first objection is equivalent to insisting that the problem of evil is insoluble. *Any* attempted solution to the problem of evil must show that there is some greater good which justifies God's permitting the evil that occurs and that that good could not be achieved without allowing the evil in question. If so, however, it seems that in presenting any solution to the problem of evil we show that nothing really bad has happened to the victim of the evil, since the evil which occurred was the means to some more valued good. The objector might rejoin that the objection has force against my attempted solution in a way it does not have against others because on my account evil is not so much a regrettable means to a greater good as an apparently essential component of a greater good. But this rejoinder is based on a confusion. As I explained above, Aquinas's ethical theory rules out as not good any action whose object and end are not both good; consequently, no action which uses evil only as a means to a good end can count as good. What is justifiable on Aquinas's views is an action whose object includes suffering when that suffering is the lesser of two evils for the sufferer, because in that case the object of the action is good. The distinction here is familiar to us in its practical application. Most of us would censure a surgeon who killed one patient in order to obtain a liver for another person's needed transplant operation, but we would find nothing to blame in a surgeon who submitted his patient to the pain of surgery in order to remove gallstones. Finally, that an attempted solution to the problem of evil should have as a consequence the claim that nothing really bad happens to a person[47] is not implausible but rather just what we would expect to follow from the assumption of a provident God. If we are told that Monica has a parent who knows everything, can do anything, is perfectly good, and loves Monica unstintingly, we might understand if we heard that Monica nonetheless suffered some diseases, endured a broken heart, or failed to achieve her aspirations to be a concert pianist. But we would certainly have a hard time accounting for it if we were also told that something really, ultimately bad had happened to her.

2. If all suffering is really beneficial for the sufferer, then it seems that evildoers should be praised as the instruments of God's will, and we should never try to alleviate suffering for fear of interfering with God's work of redemption; and this conclusion is absurd.

The appropriate reply to the first part of this objection, namely, that on this account evildoers are to be praised as instruments of God's will, is inherent in the discussion of the Squire and Dunstan above. What makes a person an evildoer is that either the object or the end of his action or both are not good. When Dunstan bullies Godfrey into lending him his horse, the object of his action is not just getting the use of a horse but fretting Godfrey and forcing him to submit to his will, and the end of his action is to hurt Godfrey. That Dunstan becomes the means of turning Godfrey from pernicious moral weakness, if all goes as the Squire in my example hopes, does Dunstan no credit, because he is ignorant of the beneficial effects of his actions. In fact, there is every reason to suppose that if he knew of them, he would not engage in those actions. Similarly, evildoers can be serving God's purpose without knowing or willing it. Therefore, although they may be God's instruments, no praise accrues to them from that fact; and it will still be possible to punish them justly for the malice which prompted their actions.

The complaint that we should never alleviate suffering rests on a confusion. Norman Kretzmann and I have argued elsewhere against the claim that what counts as just is different for God and creatures,[48] but there is a claim superficially similar to that one which does seem to me correct. An agent's allowing some evil he could prevent is morally permissible only if he is justified in holding the true belief that that evil is the best means in the circumstances for drawing its victim to God; that is, the evil must have such an effect on the intellect and emotions of the sufferer as to constitute an influence on the will to turn to God in the long run if not immediately. Unless it is true that the evil in question serves this purpose, and the agent is justified in believing it does, his permitting it is not justified. But, unlike omniscient God, human beings are rarely in a position to see into the inner life of another person enough to know whether a given evil is likely to have the desired effect or how much of it is best suited to achieving the end sought. Therefore, although God might be justified in allowing an evil to occur or to continue when he could stop it, we generally would not be, not because God has rights with respect to his creatures which we as fellow creatures do not have, but rather because God in his omniscience has the information necessary for being justified in permitting evil, and we do not. Finally, it is clear that in trying to alleviate suffering we do not interfere with God's plan of redemption since whether we are successful in alleviating that suffering is up to God.

This reply to the objection has ramifications worth noting. William Rowe has argued recently that the existence of pointless suffering is apparent to us.[49] His argument depends on the presupposition that the point of any justifiably allowed suffering is the sort of thing that would be apparent to us if it were present. But Aquinas's account of God's providence undermines that presupposition. In fact, given Aquinas's views it will be very difficult ever to show that any human suffering is pointless, not because of the vacuity of the claim that no suffering is pointless but rather because of the inaccessibility of the data needed to show that claim false. To show that some suffering is pointless we would need to demonstrate that it did not serve the purpose of drawing the sufferer toward God. It would not be enough to show that the sufferer did not obviously or immediately turn to God after his suffering. In the first place, the beneficial effects of any suffering may be a hidden part of the inner life of a person and not ever apparent in behavior, or the effects may be obvious when they do occur but they may take a long time to develop. Even a person who is made more hostile to God as an immediate consequence of his suffering may subsequently find himself more drawn to God and may himself attribute the new nearness to the earlier experience of suffering. And in the second place, even if it could be shown that the suffering never eventuated in any spiritual improvement, it would not have been demonstrated that the suffering was pointless. As long as it is part of Aquinas's account that human beings have free will (where free will is understood in an incompatibilist sense), nothing God does or permits can *guarantee* that a person becomes spiritually better, because his betterment depends on his changing his will. All that is required for the suffering to count nonetheless as serving God's purpose is that it be the best available means for turning a person to God, and it is hard to see how we would ever be in a position to know that some suffering did not meet this condition.

3. It seems that some things cannot be morally used as a means to an end. Certain sorts of pain or degradation are so repugnant to us that no moral agent would choose them as a means to an end, no matter how valued the end was.[50] Therefore, this attempted solution to the problem of evil is incompatible with God's goodness and contrary to our common moral intuitions.

This objection is in fact ambiguous between two different claims, one of which seems true and the other of which is, I think, clearly false. We can understand this objection to be about actions in which the object is evil but the end is good, that is, actions in which the end sought may be good but the infliction of suffering is not the lesser of two evils for the sufferer. In this sense, I think the objection is right, and our intuition that it is so is based on the moral intuitions underlying beliefs approving agent-centered restrictions. Suppose that Henry VIII had believed More innocent of treason but had decided to condemn him to hanging and quartering anyway in order to make an example of him and thus deter others from doing anything to undermine the stability of the regime. We might for the sake of argument accept the end of the king's action as good; but the object of his action, the killing of an innocent person, is not good. And we might then side with the objection and say that the agonizing death of an innocent person must not be used as the means to an end, however good the end may be. In this sense of the third objection, however, it has no force against the account being defended here, because on Aquinas's ethical theory any action whose object is not good is itself not good and so cannot be attributed to God.

But the third objection may be taken in another sense. It can be understood as saying that intense or degrading pain may not be used as a means to an end, even when the end is preventing greater evil to the sufferer. In this sense the third objection *is* applicable to the account I am arguing for, but a visit to the cancer ward of any large hospital will show that most people do not accept the ethical intuitions on which the third objection, taken in this sense, is based. The treatments currently available for cancer and many other illnesses are often agonizing and degrading, and yet most people whose prognosis was reasonably good would undergo them readily, even if only for five or ten more years of life. On Christian doctrine, however, the loss caused by the disease of the will is infinitely greater than the loss caused by uncured terminal cancer, because the spiritual disease includes an unending loss of union with God and the perpetual torment of being left to one's sinful self; and the benefits of curing the will's disease are not a few more years of this life, with its pains and miseries, but an enduring life of fulfillment and joy. If we are willing to accept pain and degradation as a means to the benefits of physical health, we are in no position to rule out suffering as a means to the good of redemption.

4. If suffering of a certain sort is the best means of bringing a person to God, then it seems that a good God would have to will such suffering. In that case, God does not simply permit evil but wills it directly; God would thus be the instigator and initiator of all the evils that occur. But such a result is repugnant to our ordinary notion of God's goodness and love.

To understand the appropriate reply to this last objection, it will be useful to consider the biblical story of Esther.[51] It is traditionally recognized as a story demonstrating God's providence, and a thorough analysis of the story's details would no doubt give interesting insights into the mechanisms by which God's providence operates. Here I want to focus on just one part of the story to illustrate a principle about divine governance. Esther has expressed some hesitation about interceding for her people after the Jews have been put in danger of genocide as a result of Haman's insane resentment of Mordecai, Esther's cousin. In one of the most famous passages of the book, Mordecai sends Esther this message: "Think not with thyself that thou shalt escape in the king's house, more than all the Jews. For if thou altogether holdest thy peace at this time, then shall there enlargement and deliverance arise to the Jews from another place; but thou and thy father's house shall be destroyed; and who knoweth whether thou art come to the kingdom for such a time as this?"

Mordecai's speech has to do with God's providential rescue from evil, while the objection under consideration has to do with God's providential infliction of evil; but the principle behind Mordecai's speech seems to me a good one and the basis for the right reply to the objection. In Mordecai's view, God has arranged the events of Esther's life, particularly the events leading up to her becoming queen, in order to put her in a position of power from which she can help the endangered Jews. That Esther attempt to rescue the Jews is thus part of God's plan. But the fulfillment of that plan depends on Esther's free will; it is not determined by God alone. On the other hand, it does not follow that if Esther refuses to play the part open to her in God's plan, God's plan fails. The plan will still succeed, and in two respects. First, deliverance for the Jews will arise from another place. God will not let the matter of the genocide of the Jews hang solely on the free will of one post-Fall human being. The ways in which God might have rescued the Jews even without Esther's cooperation are limited only by one's imagination. Secondly, even in refusing to play her part Esther remains in God's plan, though in a different way. What God has prepared for her is drawing nearer to him in glory, through the increased reliance on him which gives her the courage to risk her life for the sake of the Jews. But if she does not draw closer to God in glory, he will draw her closer to him through the salutary pains of punishment: although there will be deliverance for the Jews in general, she will be destroyed.

In general, then, though it may be true that God does not play dice with the universe, it is perhaps possible that he plays chess with his creatures in it. A chess master achieves his aim on the board not by magically determining the will of his opponent but by being smarter and better at chess than his opponent, by anticipating what the opponent will do and having several strategies, interwoven in intricate ways, for getting what he wants no matter which of the options open to him his opponent takes at any stage. Mordecai's message to Esther suggests that God will achieve his aim if Esther cooperates but that God is perfectly prepared to achieve the same aims in a different way if Esther does not. The generalization of this claim seems to me the principle underlying God's providential permitting of evil. We can call it Mordecai's principle: God has many alternative strategies for reaching his ultimate end of uniting human beings with himself and which of these he takes is in some way a function of the choices human persons make. Those who do not fulfill his will in one way fulfill it in another, Aquinas says.[52] So, for example, God's plan is to inspire the Jews of Ahasuerus's kingdom to turn again to him with renewed fervor. Given Haman's evil will, permitting Haman to persuade the king to genocide may be the best means in the circumstances of achieving the end God wants. But it does not follow, and the last objection is mistaken in supposing, that God must either instigate Haman's evil himself or see his providential plan for the Jews fail. Even a cursory reading of the biblical account of the history of the Jews shows that there are many ways in which God draws his people closer to himself. That God allows Haman to act on his evil will accomplishes the end desired in this case and has the added advantage of perhaps also doing something for Haman, who is God's creature as much as Esther is. At any rate, the text suggests that the events attending the fall of Haman caused even Haman's wife to believe at least in the privileged position of the Jews; it may be that they also caused some rethinking in Haman.

What then is the status of the evil God permits? It is not compatible with Mordecai's principle to claim that the evil God permits is a necessary means to the good which justifies it since on Mordecai's principle God might have achieved his purpose in some way other than that brought about by a particular person's evil. What the story of Esther suggests we should say is that the evil God permits is the best means available in the circumstances for reaching God's goal, where the circumstances are taken principally to include the free choices of human beings.[53] Because Haman wills genocide, the best means to God's end involves the use of the choices Haman makes; and the reason for thinking so involves taking seriously Aquinas's dictum that God does not undermine the natures of his creatures. Since God has made human beings with free will, his governance of the world works in such a way as to allow them to will freely. But that this is so does not mean either that the amount of pain people suffer is left by God to the discretion of evildoers or that God inevitably lets the evil-hearted accomplish the evil they will. As the story of Haman illustrates, God may permit an evildoer to will an evil and yet keep him from accomplishing the evil he wills to bring about. Haman wills the slaughter of the Jews; the end result of the chain of events he initiates, however, is not genocide but a per-haps unparalleled position of power for the Jews in a foreign nation. Consequently, it is also clear that God does not let evil-doers determine the amount of suffering in the world. As Mor-decai makes clear in his message to Esther, the amount of suffering the Jews experience in Ahasuerus's kingdom is under God's control, not Haman's or Esther's.

Finally, the most rhetorically forceful objection against this attempted solution to the problem of evil consists just of pulling a particularly dreadful story from the newspapers, about some child Maggie's being beaten to death, for example, and asking whether it is plausible to suppose that the suffering of that ap-parently innocent victim is justifiable by some spiritual good for her and whether we are required by my account to suppose that Maggie is so much worse than other children that she needs such an excess of pain and terror in order to be turned to God.

The second part of this objection rests on a confusion. It assumes that because Maggie suffers intensely, she suffers more than other human beings; but that assumption is not obviously true. Her sufferings are intense but of short duration. How pains are to be compared is not clear to me, but why should we assume that the sum total of the suffering of Maggie's life is un-usually great as compared to that of other human beings just because it is compressed into a short time? (I am not here trying to defend the implausible claim that the sufferings of all human beings are precisely equal; I mean only to introduce some cau-tion into the way we make comparisons among the sufferings of different people.) But the heart of this objection is in its first part, in the rhetorical question meant to elicit disbelief in the redemptive value of Maggie's suffering. The objector wants to have explained to him how this particular suffering, which few of us could even hear described without feeling pain of our own, could possibly be thought to benefit Maggie or how anything but callous, ideological dogmatism could support the view that it does so. But what the objector wants is something which cannot be given and is not reasonable to request: a particular reason which justifies an individual instance of evil. Unless we know all that God knows about Maggie's life and character, we are in no position to give such a reason; and since we know we lack the necessary information for formulating that reason, it is unreasonable to demand it. It does not follow, however, that we cannot give an argument for a general reason justifying Maggie's suffering. Suppose that Maggie's pain was occasioned not by beating but by some particularly painful cancer treatments, the biological workings of which her mother Susan could not understand. And suppose we asked Susan the sort of question the objector is asking: how exactly does the administration of these terrible treatments benefit Maggie? She might reply that she has no notion of the biochemical intricacies of the effects of the drugs on Maggie's tumors but that she believes the doctor in charge of the case to be both competent and benevolent. Since the treatments are carried out under his authority, she reasonably concludes that they are the best hope of a cure for Maggie and therefore she has agreed to put Maggie through them.[54] Similarly, according to the arguments laid out in this essay, if we begin by assuming the providence of an omnipotent, omniscient, perfectly good God, it is reasonable to conclude that the suffering of innocents, carried out under God's authority, is turned by God into a benefit (or, a potential benefit) for the sufferer which outweighs the pain.

Providence and Martyrdom

I have been at pains to defend here the claim that God's reason for permitting suffering is to redeem human beings from their evil. Whether or not it is adequate as far as it goes, it is clearly incomplete, as can be seen by considering, for example, the suffering of martyrs, since in being willing to undergo martyrdom for their faith they are presumably already in a state of grace. To understand how to extend the account defended here to cases in which the sufferers are already committed religious believers, it will be helpful to focus on the special case of martyrs and examine what makes them willing and able to undergo martyrdom.

In Christian tradition, as in many other religious traditions, martyrs are held in high esteem as having achieved the most glorious state for believers, and that glorious state is held to endure perpetually in the afterlife. Furthermore, what is glorious about martyrs is not something extrinsic to them, conferred on them by God like a medal for valor, but something intrinsic in their nature itself, so that before a martyr whose glory was revealed an ordinary person might feel a natural awe and diffidence. What accounts for this attitude toward martyrs?

Consider More when he both believed that he would be put to death by hanging and quartering if he did not take the oath of supremacy and nonetheless was determined not to take that oath. The death he foresaw for himself is an especially painful one; and as long as we suppose More human, it seems reasonable to suppose that he had strong desires not to suffer such a death. On the other hand, given what we know of More's religious beliefs and ascetic tendencies, it is reasonable to assume that he also had desires to endure such a death rather than damn his soul through perjury. What distinguishes More from the sort of man he would have been if he had taken the oath in a reluctant spirit of fear is the presence in the real More of a second-order desire, namely, the second-order desire to make the first-order desire for martyrdom his will.[55] That this second-order desire is effective, that is, that it succeeds in governing More's first-order desires and conquering the discordant ones is a tribute to More's strength of will. If we consider the strength of will it takes to vanquish such first-order desires as the desire not to swim in an icy river or not to stand alone in adopting an unpopular position in a public meeting, we will have some idea of the strength of will required to subdue the desire not to die by torture.

That More is capable of such strength of will is a testimony to the depth of his belief in God. He could bring himself to assent to such suffering to avoid perjury only in case he were utterly convinced that there is a God to whose goodness perjury is inimical. Furthermore, his willingness to suffer must also be a function of his love of God and desire for him. If More himself were indifferent to the evil which perjury is or felt that prohibiting perjury was not required by the true goodness which characterizes God, he would somehow have temporized and escaped martyrdom, as many other Christians of his circle did. It is More's own assent to the goodness of God's prohibition against perjury and his attraction to the goodness God has that draws him to will martyrdom, against his first-order desires to avoid suffering. In forming the second-order volition to make the desire to endure suffering his will, More acts on his love of God and God's goodness and strengthens it by repressing, out of love for God, the desire to avoid torture. While More is undecided between the opposing first-order desires, to endure suffering and to escape it, he is double-minded; but in forming a second-order volition which rejects the desires discordant with what he believes, More is purifying his heart and willing one thing, the goodness of God.

That a person in such a condition sees God, as promised in the beatitudes, is asserted by More himself in a different context in one of his Tower works. How is it, he asks, that martyrs are able to endure what they do? Why don't they succumb to the pain and do what their tormentors want, for example, or at least die screaming in agony instead of praying or singing hymns, as they are often said to do? The answer, More says, can be found by considering what sometimes happens when a soldier is wounded in the heat of battle. It sometimes happens in such a case that the soldier feels no pain at all though his wound is terrible, and the reason for his insensitivity to the pain is that his mind is entirely occupied with the battle. Analogously, More claims, a person who brings himself to be willing to endure martyrdom is focused into a flame of love for God; and while he is in such a state, God draws near to him, so that while his body endures torments, his soul is rapt in the sweetness of the love of God.[56]

In consequence of his willingness to suffer, in loving God and his goodness in this way, the martyr's own goodness is completed and his being is consequently perfected. He enters the afterlife a greater person than ordinary souls, and he remains in that state perpetually. When we consider how much time, money, and trouble we are willing to sink into being healthy and attractive, although we know that physical excellence is an ephemeral thing, we may begin to understand the esteem in which martyrdom was traditionally held. The suffering the martyr endures turns him into a thing of beauty forever.

Martyrs are, of course, an extreme case, but what is true of them may also be applicable to the lesser suffering of other religious believers. So, for example, while a smaller amount of suffering may not bring a vision of God with it, the sufferer's religious beliefs may nonetheless make his experience of suffering very different from that of a person who has no religious beliefs or who does not act on his religious beliefs in his suffering. Consider the different ways in which the loss of a fortune was borne by Silas Marner and by Thomas More. Marner's grief at the thought that his gold was stolen was hysterical. He tore his hair, ran through the town, made wild accusations, and finally subsided into wretched depression, showing in every way that he was suffering an extremity of pain. When More was compelled to resign the chancellorship, he lost virtually all his income and possessions. He placed his servants with wealthier families, counselled his wife and children on their new constraints, and generally joked about his poverty and the political trouble which caused it. When the Duke of Norfolk later told More to be more careful about offending the king since the displeasure of a king is death, More is reported to have said, "Is there no more difference between your grace and me but that I shall die today and you tomorrow?" The evils that occurred to More and Marner were not exactly the same, of course, but were arguably equivalent in extent; Marner had no family to support him in his trouble, but then again the pain of the sudden poverty was not aggravated by having a family to provide for. The difference in the amount of suffering caused by the comparable evils is a function of the beliefs the two men held. And just as the martyr's willingness to undergo martyrdom for the love of God makes him into something glorious, so the acceptance of lesser suffering in a spirit of trust in God makes the sufferer a more attractive soul. If given a choice about his reactions in the face of sudden financial loss, would anyone rather be Silas Marner than Thomas More?

Someone might object that this account seems to advocate quietism, passivity in the face of social ills and religious inwardness as the appropriate responses to injustice. But such an objection would be obtuse. What More accepts is apparently inevitable suffering. What brings him into that suffering is precisely his unwillingness to endure what he takes to be an injustice, Henry's treatment of his first wife and the consequent schism in the church. Contrary to what the objection supposes, the account given here is compatible with any amount of social activism; it is, after all, Aquinas who is famous for the dictum that an unjust law is not a law[57] and who argues that a ruler's authority rests on his willingness to serve the common good.

Therefore, the reason which justifies God in permitting the evil suffered by committed believers is the greater good of the nobility of their characters. So while keeping a person from a worse evil is the reason which justifies God in allowing the suffering of those who are alienated from him, translating a person to a greater good when he is open to it is the justification for God's permitting the suffering of a committed believer. And that this is so is no violation of the ethical constraints I was at pains to argue for earlier. Then I said that for the object of an action to be good when it involved inflicting suffering, the suffering had to be the lesser of two evils for the sufferer. But there the discussion concerned those who suffered unwillingly. Those committed to Christian precepts, on the other hand, have given their assent to denying themselves, to taking up their cross daily and crucifying their old nature. In short, they have consented to let God work in their lives in order to remake them into something glorious. In their case, God is like the physician who is justified in inflicting pain to produce something beautiful because the sufferer has assented in advance to the process.

The reason for God's allowing suffering, then, is that "whom he loves he chastens," but that claim can be understood in two ways. It is Christian doctrine that all are loved, and certainly all are chastened. For those who resist the process, however, the chastening consists of weaning them away from the

things of the world and converting them to a love of the goodness that is God in order to keep them from the unending pains
of hell. For those who have accepted God's work in their lives,
on the other hand, the chastening is a means of making them
blossom into the best they can be, of turning them into something unendingly beautiful to delight themselves and others. It is
in this way, I think, through the purifying effects of suffering on
a willing soul, that all things work together for good for those
who love God.[58]

Appendix

Someone is bound to ask whether this enterprise of mine is
supposed to contribute to a defense or a theodicy. I am not sure.
A defense is typically described as providing just a *possible* morally sufficient reason why an omniscient, omnipotent, perfectly
good God might allow evil, whereas a theodicy is an attempt to
show that there is a morally sufficient reason for God's allowing
evil in the actual world. Alvin Plantinga has said that he finds
most theodicies he knows tepid, shallow, and frivolous, and
that in his view the actual reason for God's allowing evil is and
will remain mysterious.[59]

But the claim that the actual reason for God's allowing evil
is mysterious seems to me to be ambiguous. In one sense it might
mean that in any individual instance of evil, such as the case of
the woman killed by a falling wall in the recent California
earthquake, we do not know and will perhaps never know the
precise nature of the particular good which justifies God in permitting the suffering occasioned by her death. In this sense the
claim that God's allowing evil in our world is mysterious seems
to me not just true but even supported by the Apostle Paul: "Oh
the depth of the riches both of the wisdom and knowledge of
God, how unsearchable are his judgments, and his ways past
finding out" (Rom. 11:33). That evil should be mysterious in
this sense seems readily understandable. If we are told of Silas
Marner only that he loves his adopted daughter Eppie and that
he has forcibly confined her to a small, cold, lightless cellar
filled with coal, we will be in no position to understand what

morally sufficient reason justifies him in inflicting that suffering on her or how his doing so is compatible with his love for her. And in general unless we are privy to the details of an individual's life and character, details which might be hidden even from the sufferer herself, we will lack information necessary (though perhaps not sufficient) for understanding why God has dealt with her in the way he has.

But there is another sense of the claim about the mysteriousness of evil, a sense intended, I think, by neither Paul nor Plantinga. The claim could be interpreted to mean that we cannot say anything at all about God's reason for allowing evil in our world. In this sense the claim seems false, because it is clear that we can say quite a lot about God's reason for allowing evil in this world. To begin with, such a reason will have to be compatible with God's omniscience and omnipotence; it cannot be founded in any way on the supposition that God lacks knowledge or power. It will also have to be a morally appropriate reason; that is, it will have to be consonant with God's perfect goodness, and it will have to postulate some good (or goods) which outweigh all the evil in the world and for the sake of which God allows evil. Finally, we will even be able to say something about the nature of the good which justifies God's permitting evil. We know that such a good will does not consist, for example, in the experience of sensory pleasures or in the acquisition of material possessions in this life, because there is much suffering which is evidently not compensated in this world with pleasures or possessions. We could go on in this way to spell out still other features of the actual reason for God's allowing evil, some of them entailed by our account of God's nature, some specified by our theory of morality, and some required by our beliefs about the world around us. So although a Christian theodicy may not be able to give God's particular reason for allowing this or that instance of evil in the world, it can specify in some detail the range within which such a reason must fall. It can lay down the constraints operating on anything that is to count as God's reason for allowing evil, as well as some of the general characteristics it must have. And so it constitutes a theodicy (that is, it shows God's justice in the actual world) by giving a general reason for God's permitting evil, not by spelling out the details of his dealings with individual persons.

But now consider what a defense does. A defense abstracts from particular cases of actual evils and considers instead what sorts of reason could justify an omnipotent, omniscient, perfectly good being in permitting evils in circumstances much like those which do in fact obtain. That is, a defense considers possible worlds similar to the actual world, similar in the sense that they contain rational creatures, natural laws, and evils much like those in our world, and then the defense proposes a morally sufficient reason for God's allowing evil in such worlds. A defense, then, makes no claims about God's actual intentions and reasons for allowing evil, but it does in effect show us (at least some of) the constraints on candidates for God's morally sufficient reason for permitting evil, and it suggests the bounds within which such a morally sufficient reason may be found.

So although we can obviously define a theodicy and a defense in ways which show that they are not identical, the tasks of a theodicy and a defense seem to me to converge.[60] In this essay I suggest a certain approach to the problem of evil which relies on Aquinas's understanding of God's goodness and the way God governs the world. If we suppose that Aquinas is right about the nature and workings of perfect goodness, then the thrust of this essay is to specify certain characteristics anything must have to count as God's reason for permitting evil in this world, and my enterprise is the construction of a Christian theodicy. On the other hand, it seems to me that besides the usual focus on God's omnipotence and omniscience a defense must also meet certain constraints imposed by the notion of God's perfect goodness. This essay shows what those constraints are, given a certain notion of perfect goodness, and in that sense this essay can be considered part of an attempt to construct a defense.

NOTES

1. In other papers I have discussed some of these contemporary defenses and theodicies; see Eleonore Stump and Norman Kretzmann, "Being and Goodness," in *Divine and Human Action,* ed. Thomas

Morris (Ithaca, N.Y.: Cornell University Press, 1988); "The Problem of Evil," *Faith and Philosophy* 2 (1985): 392–424; and "Knowledge, Freedom, and the Problem of Evil," *International Journal for the Philosophy of Religion* 14 (1983): 49–58.

2. See, e.g., Augustine's *Commentary on the Psalms* and Gregory's *Moralia in Job,* especially xxvi.

3. "The Problem of Evil."

4. In "Dante's Hell, Aquinas's Theory of Morality, and the Love of God," *Canadian Journal of Philosophy* 16 (1986): 181–198, I argued for the compatibility of the doctrine of hell with the belief that God is perfectly good and loving.

5. How this action is related to Christ's atonement for sin is discussed in my essay "Atonement According to Aquinas" (in *Philosophy and the Christian Faith,* ed. Thomas Morris [Notre Dame, Ind.: Notre Dame University Press, 1988]); the nature of the cooperation between the divine and the human will is considered in my essay "Sanctification, Hardening of the Heart, and Frankfurt's Concept of Free Will," *Journal of Philosophy* 85 (1988): 395–420.

6. For an intriguing and detailed picture of such a process at work, see Oliver Sacks, *A Leg to Stand On* (New York: Summit Books, 1984).

7. For recent articles which find my approach implausible because they interpret it along these lines, see William Hasker, "Suffering, Soul-Making, and Salvation," forthcoming in *International Philosophical Quarterly,* and Bruce Russell, "The Persistent Problem of Evil," forthcoming in *Faith and Philosophy.*

8. For a fuller discussion of Aquinas's ethics, see "Being and Goodness"; the description of Aquinas's ethics given here is adapted from that essay.

9. For a detailed discussion and defense of the doctrine of simplicity, see Eleonore Stump and Norman Kretzmann, "Absolute Simplicity," *Faith and Philosophy* 2 (1985): 353–382.

10. *ST* Ia q.6 a.1 reply obj.2, also a.3 and a.4.

11. Cf. e.g. Marilyn Adams's helpful paper on Duns Scotus, who held such a view ("Duns Scotus on the Goodness of God," *Faith and Philosophy* 4 [1987]: 486–505.) For a related view that God as creator has rights over his creation which exceed the rights creatures have over each other and that God therefore cannot be constrained by ordinary considerations of a person's rights, see Richard Swinburne, *The Existence of God* (Oxford, Clarendon Press, 1979), 216–218. For some argument against Swinburne's view, see "Being and Goodness."

12. Cf. William Alston, "What Euthyphro Should Have Said: Some Suggestions for Divine Command Theorists," forthcoming in *Christian Theism and the Problem of Philosophy*, ed. Michael Beaty (London: Routledge and Kegan Paul).

13. *ST* Ia q.21 a.1.

14. *ST* Ia q.21 a.4 reply obj.2.

15. *ST* Ia q.21 a.4.

16. For further explanation and defense of this claim, see my essay "Dante's Hell, Aquinas's Theory of Morality, and the Love of God."

17. For arguments supporting the claim that there is no incompatibility between God's impeccability and his omnipotence, see Eleonore Stump and Norman Kretzmann, "Absolute Simplicity."

18. *ST* Ia q.21 a.1 reply obj.2.

19. *ST* Ia q.22 a.1.

20. Cf. *ST* Ia q.103 a.4.

21. Cf. *ST* Ia q.19 a.6.

22. The objections of the second group are concerned with two main points: (1) the manner of divine governance, that is, whether God's providence directly produces all human actions and events stemming from secondary causes and (2) the implications of divine governance, that is, whether divine providence can be exercised over human persons without destroying their freedom of will.

23. In comments on an earlier draft of this essay, Tom Flint raised a worry about the mechanism by which providence is exercised given the way human lives are intertwined. Since one and the same evil can have radically different effects on different people, how are we to suppose God's providence can manage to govern the world in a way that ensures maximum benefit to all people? Flint's worry, which raises important questions, is a difficulty not only for any robust account of God's providence, but even for accounts of God's benevolence. If the farmers in some area are desperately praying for rain and a commune of sculptors building a large outdoor clay sculpture are praying, with equal urgency, for dry weather, how are we to explain the way in which a benevolent God will satisfy all those who trust in him for help? I plan to address issues involving the mechanisms of God's providence in a subsequent essay.

24. See *ST* Ia q.19 a.6, q.22 a.2, q.103 a.8.

25. Cf. I *Sent.* 46.1.1.

26. In human beings it is often the case that an antecedent volition temporally precedes a consequent one, because it not infrequently happens that a person forms a volition and then learns about some

circumstance which inclines him to will differently. For the same sort of reason, a human person's consequent will is often an expression of the frustration of a previously framed antecedent will. But neither circumstance can hold for an omniscient being.

27. *De veritate* q.23 a.2.

28. Ibid. q.23 a.2.

29. That God, however, does not always will to let an evildoer accomplish what he wills is clear from the story of Haman and Mordecai, discussed below.

30. In the incarnate Christ, who as human is not impassible, the antecedent will can take the form of longing (cf. Matthew 23:37); in the impassible divine nature, the antecedent will consists in a determination that the object of the antecedent will would be the good to be pursued if the circumstances did not have to be taken into account.

31. *SCG* III ch.71.

32. See, e.g., *SCG* III ch.71.

33. *De veritate* q.5 a.4.

34. See, e.g., *ST* Ia q.19 a.9.

35. Aquinas's ethics supports agent-centered restrictions. (See "Being and Goodness.") An agent-centered restriction prohibits an agent's doing (or omitting to do) a certain type of action p, even though the agent's doing p (or omitting to do p) is the only means of preventing several other instances of p from being done (or being omitted) by other agents. (For a discussion of agent-centered restrictions, see Samuel Scheffler, "Agent-Centered Restrictions, Rationality, and the Virtues," *Mind* 94 [1985]: 409–419, and *The Rejection of Consequentialism* [Oxford: Clarendon Press, 1982].) Most of us, for example, would find it morally unthinkable to torture a child of ours even if some madman had convinced us that the penalty for our refusal would be his torturing five other children. By tying the evaluation of an action to that action's object as well as its end, Aquinas's views justify such a restriction on the agent.

36. For discussion of the relation between God and contingency in the world, see Norman Kretzmann, "Goodness, Knowledge, and Indeterminacy in the Philosophy of Thomas Aquinas," *Journal of Philosophy* 80(1983): 631–649. Kretzmann argues that Aquinas's notion of God's knowledge may not be reconcilable with the claim that there is contingency in the world.

37. See *ST* Ia q.22 a.2, q.103 a.5, q.116 a.1.

38. Cf. Norman Kretzmann, "*Nos Ipsi Principia Sumus:* Boethius and the Basis of Contingency," in *Divine Omniscience and Omnipo-*

tence in Medieval Philosophy, ed. Tamar Rudavsky, (Dordrecht: Reidel, 1985), 23–50.

39. See Peter van Inwagen, "The Place of Chance in a World Sustained by God," *Divine and Human Action: Essays in the Metaphysics of Theism*, ed. Thomas Morris (Ithaca, N.Y.: Cornell University Press, 1988). The relation of God to chance described in that paper is fundamentally reconcilable with the views being expressed here, if we add the claim that God allows chance events to occur which result in suffering only in case he can draw good out of the evil, in the way discussed just above.

40. See *ST* Ia q.19 a.8.

41. *ST* Ia q.19 a.9, q.22 a.4, q.103 a.7; Ia-IIae q.10 a.4.

42. Cases of deserved suffering I will leave to one side in what follows, since they seem not to raise the problem of evil in the way undeserved suffering does. The idea that not all suffering is punishment for sins has ample biblical warrant; see, e.g., John 9:1–3.

43. Spelling out the *ceteris paribus* clause in this principle would be complicated and controversial. Its function would be to account for the common intuition that an agent is not morally obligated to prevent the suffering of another if the cost to himself is overwhelmingly great. In the context of this essay, where the agent in question is an omnipotent and omniscient God, we can perhaps safely neglect the details of the *ceteris paribus* clause. Apart from worries about this clause, the principle is open to other objections. In an excellent essay, "The Magnitude, Duration, and Distribution of Evil: A Theodicy" (forthcoming in a special issue of *Philosophical Topics*, ed. Michael Beaty), Peter van Inwagen argues that this moral principle is false because it has the following counterexamples: the state quarantines someone with a contagious disease; the state employs the right of eminent domain to force the removal of a person's house which stands in the way of a desperately needed irrigation canal. In both these examples, he argues, we have instances which violate my principle because a person is rightly made to suffer when the benefits accrue only to someone other than the sufferer. I think that neither of these cases is a counterexample to my principle, because my principle has to do with suffering which is both nonvoluntary and undeserved. If a person knows he has a serious disease which he can easily pass on to others by moving around and if he does not voluntarily limit his movements in the way required to keep from spreading the disease, he will be guilty of an act violating commutative justice, because he will be taking something from others (namely, their health) without giving anything commensurate in return, when nothing in the case warrants his considering his victims in any

way other than as his equals. In such a case the state may with justice inflict on him the suffering of involuntary quarantine. That the sufferer endures some restriction in his movements is a consequence of the constraints entailed by having a serious and contagious disease. That he bears this suffering involuntarily may be chalked up to his fair deserts, given that he would otherwise engage in movement significantly endangering the health of others. So this apparent counterexample to my principle is not a real counterexample because the suffering in the example does not meet one of the conditions in my principle, namely, that the suffering in question be undeserved. I would analyze the second apparent counterexample in exactly the same way, except that in that case the injustice the sufferer is trying to engage in violates distributive (rather than commutative) justice. I am grateful to Professor van Inwagen for letting me see his essay in typescript as well as for many helpful discussions on the subject of this essay.

44. Where the evils in question can be prevented by some rearrangement of physical circumstances, we might suppose that an omnipotent God could never be properly justified on the grounds that he is causing or permitting the lesser of two evils; but that God might be justified this way when the evils involved are moral or spiritual I argued at length in "The Problem of Evil."

45. The physical and psychological circumstances of a death are, of course, also legitimate concerns, as are the sufferings of those connected with the person dying; my point here is just that the bare fact of death is not the ultimate evil for Christians.

46. I have argued in "Dante's Hell, Aquinas's Theory of Morality, and the Love of God," that it is possible to interpret even the pains of hell as justified in this way. That punishment does not in fact constitute an exception to the general claim I intend to argue in a forthcoming essay on retributive punishment.

47. As distinct from being chosen by him. Final impenitence, for example, is something really bad. But it does not happen to a person; it is chosen by him.

48. "Being and Goodness."

49. See William Rowe, "The Empirical Argument from Evil," in *Rationality, Religious Belief, and Moral Commitment,* ed. Robert Audi and William Wainwright (Ithaca, N.Y.: Cornell University Press, 1986), 227–247. See also Steven Wykstra, "The Humean Obstacle to Evidential Arguments from Suffering: On Avoiding the Evils of 'Appearance'," *International Journal for Philosophy of Religion* 16 (1984). Rowe's example has to do with the suffering of animals. Here, as in my earlier essay, I am omitting all consideration of the suffering of ani-

mals. Until we understand something more about the inner life of animals and the relation they have to their creator, I think we are not in a position to discuss the problem of evil with regard to animals. Is it possible for a dog to draw closer to God? How much pain does a trout suffer when it is caught and killed? Unless we can give reasoned answers to questions of this sort, we lack information crucial for considering what reasons a good God might have for permitting animals to suffer.

50. See Michael Smith, "What's So Good about Suffering?" *Faith and Philosophy* 2 (1985): 421–429; and my reply, "Suffering for Redemption," *Faith and Philosophy* 2 (1985): 430–435.

51. In what follows I am not concerned either to contribute to or to take account of contemporary biblical scholarship. I want to consider the story of Esther not as it contributes to our understanding of the history of the Jews, ancient Hebrew theology, the composition of the Old Testament, or anything else of the sort. I am interested in it as a story in the canonical Christian scriptures; I am reading it in light of Christian doctrine to see what contributions it makes to Christian theology.

52. *De veritate* q.23 a.2.

53. It is crucial to emphasize the phrase 'is the best means available' and *not* to collapse this formulation into an expression something like this: 'God permits evil which he knows will be of maximum benefit to the sufferer'. If human beings have free will in an incompatibilist sense, then suffering cannot be guaranteed to produce good effects. In that case we can know that some suffering is the best means available for bringing about some good to the sufferer without knowing that the suffering will be of maximum benefit. The short theological formulation of the point I am concerned to emphasize here is that it is possible for human beings to refuse grace.

54. Another way to put the point I want to make here is that we can give the genus of the good which constitutes God's reason for allowing evil (e.g., turning the heart to God) but not the species (e.g., turning the heart to God in virtue of helping the sufferer develop more pity for others and in consequence . . .). Similarly, Susan knows the genus of the good which justifies Maggie's suffering (i.e., employing this drug constitutes the best available chance for curing Maggie's cancer) but neither she nor the doctors may know the species of the good (e.g., employing the drug constitutes the best available chance of stimulating Maggie's body to produce interferon, which will shrink Maggie's tumors, etc.).

55. I rely on Frankfurt's notion of a hierarchical division in the will; see Harry Frankfurt, "Freedom of the Will and the Concept of a

Person," *Journal of Philosophy* 68 (1971): 5–20. For a discussion and revision of Frankfurt's view, see my paper "Sanctification, Hardening of the Heart, and Frankfurt's Concept of Free Will."

56. See Marilyn Adams's excellent paper, "Redemptive Suffering: A Christian Solution to the Problem of Evil," in *Rationality, Religious Belief, and Moral Commitment*, ed. Robert Audi and William Wainwright (Ithaca, N.Y.: Cornell University Press, 1986), 248–267.

57. Aquinas is famous for it; Augustine originates it; see Norman Kretzmann, "*Lex iniusta non est lex:* Laws on Trial in Aquinas's Court of Conscience," *American Journal of Jurisprudence,* forthcoming.

58. I am indebted to Thomas Flint, Harlan Miller, Philip Quinn, William Rowe, and Peter van Inwagen for helpful comments and questions, and I am particularly grateful to Norman Kretzmann for his many comments on earlier drafts of this paper.

59. *Alvin Plantinga,* ed. James Tomberlin and Peter van Inwagen (Dordrecht: Reidel, 1985), 35.

60. In correspondence with me Bill Rowe has suggested that it is misleading to describe a theodicy and a defense as converging, because in a case in which we know that some sufferer Maggie does *not* turn to God in consequence of her suffering, a defender but not a theodicist could claim that Maggie's turning to God is what justifies her suffering. But it seems to me that if Maggie has free will, in an incompatibilist sense of free will, then what both the defender and the theodicist should say is after all the same thing: that Maggie's suffering is justified because it is the best means available for turning Maggie to God. If the therapy cannot be guaranteed to produce a cure, then what justifies employing the therapy is not the cure (since otherwise we could never know in advance whether employing a therapy was justified, and employing the same type of therapy on the same sort of cases could be both justified and unjustified), but rather the therapy's constituting the best available means for a cure.

Can Anybody in a Post-Christian Culture Rationally Believe the Nicene Creed?

Alan Donagan

1. A Fourth-Century Creed in the Twentieth Century

The phrase, 'the Christian religion' stands for so many things that the question whether educated people in the western world today can rationally believe it is too vague to be worth answering. It is otherwise with the question whether they can rationally believe the Nicene creed. Many who call themselves Christians would reject it. Yet it is part of the liturgy of many Christian bodies, in particular of the largest of all, the Roman Catholic church, the central rite of which, the mass, requires both priest and people to profess it together. A century ago, virtually all Christians would have been willing to profess it, whether or not the liturgy of their branch of the church required it, although there is one phrase in it, 'one holy, Catholic and apostolic Church', which not all would have understood in the same sense.

Even so, what you commit yourself to when you profess the Nicene creed as part of a ritual like the mass is less than definite. Some (the present Anglican bishop of Durham, for example) act as though uttering the words, 'He [that is, Jesus] was incarnate by the Holy Spirit of the Virgin Mary,' as part of the liturgy is not logically inconsistent with addressing the words, 'Of course, as no educated person in the twentieth century can doubt, Jesus had a natural father,' to seminary students in a theology class. Yet, as far as I can tell, most educated non-Christians and most of those who say the Nicene creed as part of the liturgy of their branch of the church agree that it is logically inconsistent. They assume that 'believing the Nicene creed' means believing that its various sentences are true in the same sense as they have in non-ritual contexts. In what follows I shall also assume it.

As will appear later, I think that educated Christians in the western world share with non-Christians a scientific culture that is 'post-Christian', in a sense to be explained. This poses a number of problems for them in professing the Nicene creed understood in its everyday sense. Of those problems that seem to me acute, I propose in this paper to consider the following three.

(1) The problem of the development of Christian doctrine. The full seriousness of this problem was first made clear by Cardinal Newman, in his *Essay on Development*. There, he tried to explain to the Anglican communion he was leaving why he had come to accept the claims of the Roman communion he was entering. The Anglicans charged Rome with adding to the faith of the Apostles; but at the same time they maintained that the Nicene fathers defined part of the faith taught by the Apostles and accepted by Christians *semper, ubique, et ab omnibus*. Newman replied that, since parts of the Nicene creed would have perplexed the Apostles, the faith taught by the Apostles admits of 'development' without being added to in the sense in which adding to it would be non-apostolic. But, in that case, may not the sense in which the words in which the apostolic teaching is expressed have undergone development? Why assume that the everyday sense of the words of the Nicene creed today is the same as their sense in the fourth century, or in any time but our own?

(2) The problem of the variation of credibility with culture. Given the scientific-philosophical culture of the Mediterranean world in the first century, St. Paul reasonably held it to be incredible that the world has not a single divine creator (Rom. 1:20). However, the intellectual situation today is not what it was in the ancient world, in the Middle Ages, or even in the seventeenth and eighteenth centuries. Is the Christian faith as it was taught before the present century defensible in the ways in

which it was then defended? And if it is not, is it credible now, even if it was then?

(3) The problem of the historical claims of the Christian faith. According to the Nicene creed, not only was the second person of the divine Trinity incarnate in a named human individual, Jesus or in Aramaic, Yeshua, but that individual was sentenced to death by crucifixion by a named Roman propraetor, Pontius Pilatus, the sentence was carried out, and 'on the third day, [Jesus] rose again, according to the scriptures, [and] ascended into heaven.' This part of the creed, according to orthodox Christian belief, was attested by the Apostles from the first Pentecost after Jesus' death, and what is essential in their testimony may be found in a body of writings circulated in various parts of the early church that gradually became accepted as canonical by the church as a whole. Yet this body of testimony is now widely called into question, not only by biblical scholars outside the Christian church, but also by some within it. In view of this, is it rational to accept that body of testimony as reliable?

2. The Problem of the Development of Christian Doctrine

According to the Nicene creed, the Christian church is apostolic; and that is generally taken to imply that it teaches what the Apostles taught. The Apostles received a deposit of faith; they transmitted it to their successors, and it has remained unchanged. Part of it is formulated in the Nicene creed itself. If this were not so, the faith of Christians today would not be apostolic; they would accept as necessary to the Christian faith beliefs which the Apostles did not hold, and hence did not think necessary to it.

On the other hand, it is quite certain that the Nicene creed contains propositions that cannot be found in the canon of the New Testament, and which there is reason to believe would have baffled the Apostles: that Jesus is 'of one substance (*homoousios*) with the Father' is an example. That Jesus is in some sense 'one' with the Father was taught by the evangelist John; but the assertion that the *ousia* of Jesus and that of the Father are the same, and not merely alike, would make little sense to

Christians who were unacquainted with the terminology of Greek philosophy. Can the church's claim that all its teaching is apostolic be reconciled with the historical fact that much in its later teaching cannot be found in the canonical scriptures that are accepted as the sole authoritative source for proving what doctrines are apostolic?

The answer given to this question before the historically minded nineteenth century was that the later teachings of the church are either clarifications of what in earlier teachings had been left obscure, or deductions of what in them had been left implicit. Newman and others showed that this answer is historically false. The doctrine that the *ousia* of Jesus is that of the Father neither clarifies an obscure scriptural teaching nor is deducible from explicit scriptural teaching by recognized logical methods. Yet the church, in declaring that its teaching throughout its history neither adds to what was revealed to the Apostles nor subtracts from it, must hold that when it expressly teaches what the Apostles did not, it does not 'develop' what was revealed to them in such a way as to add to it.

Although no theory of the development of doctrine has won acceptance by Christians, the holistic conception of language worked out in contemporary analytic philosophy does enable us to elucidate it in part. According to that conception, the central function of language is to enable speakers to form complex utterances, the sense of which is that certain truth conditions are satisfied. Speakers conversing in a language would completely succeed in communicating with one another, so far as this central function goes, if and only if every utterance by each of them were to be received by his hearers as his presenting himself as believing that the same truth conditions are satisfied as he himself takes it to express. However, no uttered sentence has truth conditions in isolation from others. The simplest sentence about the simplest physical things, even those used as examples by logicians, such as that snow is white, are unintelligible apart from others about colors, the weather, and the like. Hence the simplest sentence used by a scriptural writer, for example, 'When the sabbath day was come, [Jesus] began to teach in the synagogue' (Mark 6:2) is unintelligible apart from numerous others about the institutions of rabbinic Judaism. As Donald

Davidson has shown, to the extent that a hearer does not connect the truth conditions of an uttered sentence with those of
numerous others with which the speaker connects them, and
does not largely agree with the speaker about whether or not
those truth conditions are satisfied, he will not understand what
the speaker says. For the most part, contemporaries speaking or
writing the same language do connect sentences in the same
ways and do agree about their truth.

Communication between non-contemporaries, even when
they share a common language, is another matter. For example,
in the Middle Ages, educated Jews, Christians, and Muslims
who uttered, in whatever language they spoke, a sentence that
would be correctly translated into English as 'I see a red rose'
would have taken it to be false if the surface of the petals of a
rose did not have a property which the presence of light enabled
the air to transmit to their eyes, such that the reception of that
property in their eyes was their seeing the rose's redness. Later,
from Galileo to Locke and beyond, scientifically educated west-
erners who uttered such a sentence would have taken it to be
false if the particles composing the surface of the rose's petals
did not have properties of shape, size, and motion such that they
reflected particles or waves of light emitted by an illuminating
body, thereby causing motions of the particles composing their
central nervous systems that in turn caused their minds to form
a visual representation of a red rose. Nowadays, the scientifically
educated have yet other views.

Does it follow that medieval Aristotelians and seventeenth-
century Galileans meant something different from one another
when they said that a rose they were looking at is red? No.
Neither would have said what they did unless they had meant
to express beliefs which, whether they knew it or not, the
others believed to be false. On the other hand, neither would
have retracted what they said had they become persuaded
that the others' theory of color perception was true. It does
not matter whether, in continuing to accept 'I see a red rose' as
true they changed the sense in which they used some of the
words they used, or merely changed some theoretical belief they
associated with uttering that sentence. What matters is that
each, in saying what he does, accepts a certain theory of

color perception as true, and each will continue to say what he does even if he is persuaded to change his theory of color perception.

Both philosophy and the natural sciences have made enormous advances since what Christians recognize as the revelation made by God to the Apostles. In addition, the Apostles themselves did not deny that the Greeks had a wisdom that they lacked: what they asserted was that part of that wisdom was spurious—the part that was in conflict with the revelation they had received. Hence, as the part of the wisdom of the Greeks that was not spurious was acquired by members of the Christian community, they learned new questions to ask about the deposit of faith transmitted by the church, such as the question whether the *ousia* of the only begotten Son of God the Father was identical with, or merely like, that of the Father himself. Before answering this question definitively, the church had to decide whether it is proper to speak of the *ousia* of either the Father or the Son; but, having decided that it is proper, it became part of its teaching that if philosophy were in its advance to refine the theory of *ousia*, whatever answers the church gave to questions about the *ousia* of Father or Son could be restated consistently with those refinements.

When theological questions the church recognizes as proper are framed with reference to philosophical or scientific concepts that the Apostles did not possess, the answers to them can be neither clarifications of what the Apostles left vague nor deductions of what they left implicit. They are questions which the deposit of faith enables the church—the people of God—to answer exactly, but in neither of these ways: neither by extracting something clear from a set of vague texts, each of which makes something clear that the others do not; nor by logically deriving something explicit from a set of texts, none of which by itself implies it, but which imply it as a group. They can be answered only by showing that some of the possible answers to the questions raised by the scientific or philosophical concepts the Apostles did not possess implicitly contradict something they did teach. The dogmatic teachings thus arrived at will all methodologically be of the form 'It is not true that *p*, because *p*, by itself or together with propositions that are true, implies that some part of the apostolic teaching—the deposit of faith—is false.' We can test this conclusion by considering dogmas proposed or accepted in some parts of the Church. I have no difficulty with accepting as possibly true the pious beliefs that the Blessed Virgin was immaculately conceived and at the end of her earthly life bodily assumed into heaven; but I do not accept them as dogmas because I do not find the reasoning conclusive by which their denial is held to imply that she is not, as the gospels unmistakably assert, the mother of Jesus, whom the church teaches is God.

Just as it is reasonable to conclude that the apostolic revelation comprehends much that the Apostles did not themselves conceive, so it is reasonable to assert that what Christians of the fourth or sixteenth century affirmed as dogma in terms of scientific or philosophical concepts of their day may not only have been comprehended in the apostolic revelation, but may be restated without essential addition or subtraction in the scientific or philosophical concepts of ours. Moreover, ordinary believers can honestly profess to believe dogmas they know to be part of the church's teaching, even though they have only a sketchy understanding of how orthodox theologians would expound and establish those dogmas.

Understanding the Nicene creed sufficiently to profess it in good faith does not entail being able to pass a theological examination on it. Consider some of its principal affirmations about Jesus: that he is 'begotten of his Father before all worlds, God of God, Light of Light, very God of very God; begotten not made; being of one Substance with the Father.' Confronted by some theological Socrates, few worshippers who utter those words with every sign of conviction would be able to answer a series of probing theological questions on it. Yet we should not draw a counterpart of the conclusion of the Socrates of Plato's early Socratic dialogues: that his interlocutors do not know what they profess to believe. As Plato went on to show in the *Meno*, Socrates' elenctic technique depends not only on the capacity of his interlocutors to understand and answer most of his questions, but also on the adequacy of their answers, given an intellectual midwife who can ask the right questions, to solve the theoretical problems he puts before them.

Theologically uneducated believers who make the trinitarian affirmations about Jesus I have just quoted understand very well, I submit, that they mean that Jesus stands to God the Father, maker of heaven and earth, in a relation that can figuratively be described as being begotten by him, provided that it is remembered that, since this relation is between two individuals who are not independent substances or beings, one cannot speak of one as God, or true God, or Light, and of the other as not. Of course, a hostile theologian out to show such a believer that he does not possess the theoretical knowledge he can sometimes be enticed into claiming, can often reduce him to a state of intellectual numbness about his faith. But so to employ the elenctic technique would be a malicious misuse of it, as Plato recognized by trying to show that Socrates did not so employ it.

3. A Note on the 'Demythologizing' of Dogma

While they agree that the ordinary members of the body of Christ understand their faith in a non-theoretical way, some philosophers influenced by Wittgenstein's comparison of language to a kit of tools, each with different uses, contend that in professing their faith they do not think of themselves as stating facts. Thus, when they say of Jesus, 'He will come again, with glory, to judge the living and the dead; whose kingdom will have no end,' they are expressing and embodying 'a reflection on, or vision of, the meaning of life and of death,' and not predicting 'that certain things are going to happen.'[1] The enterprise of 'demythologizing' the Christian faith, and interpreting it as teaching Heideggerian authenticity, resembles the Wittgensteinian one in obvious ways. Could the content of the belief of the ordinary Christian faithful as expressed in the Nicene creed perhaps be captured by such analyses?

The answer, while nearly obvious, is not wholly so. The Last Judgment has been depicted in painting and sculpture in numerous ways, some of which have a place in the imagination of most Christians. Most Protestant groups, while obliterating such representations in their churches, continued to allow them to be printed in books regarded as edifying. Yet no moderately educated Christian would ever have claimed that any depiction of the Last Judgment represents it as it will be. They will not say what Jesus' coming again, with glory, will be like, except that it exceeds the capacity of human imagination to express it. Does it then follow that they do not believe that it is a certain thing that is going to happen? I agree with D. Z. Phillips that, in most respects that matter, the relatively uneducated people whom their fellow-Christians recognize as leading holy lives understand the doctrine of the Last Judgment better than I do; and I also agree that most of what they have to communicate about it, when it is not practical (how it can edify and not deprave), is expressed in scriptural or liturgical formulas. Yet I deny that it follows that those formulas are nothing but figurative expressions of a vision of the meaning of life. My reasons are of two different kinds.

The expression, 'the meaning of life' is itself figurative: it likens an individual life to a spoken or written utterance that may have or lack meaning, and if it means anything, may mean something heartening or disheartening. If Christianity were true, then it would make sense figuratively to say, with reference to it, that every individual human life has a meaning: it would amount to saying that, besides being a biological event (the event that terminates in what, in one of his last speeches, Martin Luther King called 'physical death'), human life is a journey to judgment, and then to heaven or hell: and thus is not like a meaningless scribble, but like an utterance that means something edifying or unedifying. Without reference to such a specific doctrine of what human life is (I do not pretend that Christianity is the only such doctrine available to us), to affirm that human life has meaning would be almost vacuous: the equivalent of affirming that something, we know not what, is true of human life such that, if we knew it, we should be able to liken each human life to a meaningful spoken or written utterance rather than to a meaningless one. In short, we do not elucidate what is affirmed in the Nicene creed about the Last Judgment by saying that it expresses a vision of the meaning of human life and death; rather, we elucidate the figure of the meaning of life by reference to such doctrines as that of the Nicene creed.

My second difficulty is less philosophical than historical. While it is the case that most of what can usefully be said about the doctrine of the Last Judgment is practical, especially in view of the horrible evils misunderstanding of it has led to, I know of no writer whose work has been received as authoritative by any major branch of Christianity for any considerable period, who would deny that the practical teaching that can be drawn from the doctrine of the Last Judgment is drawn from it, and is not identical with it. Practical attitudes to life that can be regarded as Christian grow out of Christian beliefs about what is the case.

4. The Naturalism of Post-Christian Culture

A culture, in the sense in which I speak of 'post-Christian culture,' is a way of living, and in particular a way of thinking, that is transmitted from one generation of a human society to another. From the conversion of the Roman Empire to Christianity in the late fourth century, down to the late nineteenth century, the way of thinking about the world and humanity's place that was so transmitted in western Europe, and in its non-European colonies and former colonies, was largely Christian: and the teaching of the Nicene creed had a not unimportant place in transmitting it.

The fundamental idea of that way of thinking is expressed in the first verse of Genesis: it is that the natural universe (what is referred to in the Nicene creed as 'heaven and earth'—at least so far as each is part of 'all that is visible') was 'made' by something else, God, whose nature the creed proceeds to describe. This idea was not a superstition of the uneducated, but part of the conception of nature taken for granted by the great scientists who created the new physics (or 'natural philosophy' as Newton called it) of the seventeenth century. It was common to Galileo and to the inquisitors who condemned him, to Descartes and to Gassendi, to Newton and to Leibniz. This creationist or supernaturalist consensus was not complete: Spinoza, for one, challenged it. However, as Spinoza discovered in his correspondence with Oldenburg, his contention that what he called 'the mechanical conception of nature' entails nature's self-existence, its independence of a non-natural creator, was apt to be received not with incredulity but with incomprehension. Oldenburg's replies to Spinoza appear inept to us because Oldenburg found what Spinoza said so alien that he futilely, but I think honestly, misinterpreted it.

By the end of the nineteenth century, the culture of the educated had ceased to be creationist and supernaturalist. I do not imply that no creationist or supernaturalist groups remained within educated western society, or that none remain now. The Christian churches, like the orthodox Jewish communities, continued and still continue to believe and to teach what they always had. Yet the natural sciences are no longer taught, even in the most bibliolatrous institutions, as presupposing that nature was created from nothing by a supernatural being. Nature is presented, so far as the sciences of it go, as something whose existence needs no explanation: and it is accepted that the task of the natural sciences is not to explain why the natural universe is, but how it works—what the laws of its fundamental processes are and how those processes produced its present state from its past states.

Why is this change important? Cannot natural science be autonomous, and yet the natural universe ontologically depend on a supernatural creator? It cannot be denied that natural independence, as affirmed by the physical sciences, does not exclude ontological dependence; yet the change from a culture in which the natural universe is considered scientifically unintelligible without reference to its supernatural creator to one in which it is not is of the first importance. What exactly St. Paul meant by his remark that 'the invisible things of him from the creation of the world are clearly seen, being understood by the things that are made' (Rom. 1:20) cannot now be determined; for we do not know what principles he presumed himself to share with his correspondents in Rome. If the principles he had in mind were about how nature is to be understood, such as Descartes's principle that what the fundamental laws of physics are depends on the nature of God, or Newton's principle that the stability of the 'system of the world' must have a cause, and that it is not among the experimentally established mathematical principles of physics, then what he said would have radically different truth conditions from those it would have had if the principles he had in mind were metaphysical, like the principles of ontological dependence suggested to St. Thomas Aquinas by reflecting on Aristotle's philosophy of nature. And that difference would have an important implication: while if the former were true, natural scientists would be mistaken about natural science if they denied supernatural intervention in nature; if the latter were true, natural scientists could, consistently with truth so far as natural science can establish it, deny the existence of the supernatural, and hence of a supernatural creator.

Until the work of Darwin and Wallace gave scientists confidence that the variety of biological species could in principle be explained as the outcome of natural processes—a confidence the succeeding century of biological science has borne out—few of them believed that all reference to the supernatural could be excluded from the understanding of nature. What the full naturalization of the study of nature implies for Christian apologetics had been foreseen in the seventeenth century by Spinoza, and also, I think, by Pascal: namely, that the study of human beings might also be brought within the domain of the natural sciences, and the Christian religion itself be treated as a phenomenon to be explained. Already in the eighteenth century, although he excluded Christian origins from its scope, Gibbon had investigated what he called 'the triumph of barbarism and superstition'—that is, of Christianity—in his *Decline and Fall of the Roman Empire* and had offered an explanation of it that did not refer to supernatural causes.

The result is familiar to us as university teachers and ought to be expressly acknowledged. It is that members of the academic community as such, whatever their Christian beliefs and commitments, do their work on naturalist principles except when the content of Christianity is under discussion—and it almost never is under discussion, even in institutions committed to religious education. As a result, belief that the natural universe was created by a supernatural God, even among those who hold it, is (in sociological jargon) 'marginalized'. Perhaps that is what Nietzsche meant when he decided that God had died although most academics had not noticed it.

This situation confronts Christians with two kinds of problems, an apologetic one and a pastoral one; and neither, if I am right about them, is understood as clearly as it should be. The apologetic one, which will occupy the remainder of this essay, is to defend the traditional teachings of Christianity within a scientific culture that is post-Christian in that it is naturalist: that is, while two centuries ago its scientific ways of thinking presupposed that the natural universe depends on a supernatural creator, they no longer do. The pastoral problem is that, despite the enormous sums our society spends on education, it has not transmitted the scientific culture to the bulk of its members. Within our society, when confronted with the popular frauds of the television 'healers' and the demand for the *National Inquirer,* it is difficult not to deplore this; but when one learns that the Soviet Union is more afraid that visitors may bring in copies of the Bible in Russian than that they will bring in the AIDS virus, another side of the question emerges. It is deplorable that most of the public have little interest in scientific truth except when it directly makes their lives individually more comfortable—that they are credulous. On the other hand, it is not obviously deplorable that they have no faith that understanding the results of natural science would enable them to live better.

5. Apologetics and the Materialism of Contemporary Naturalism

Naturalism can take as many forms as there are conceptions of nature. Spinoza, for example, included mind as well as matter (substance as extended) in the one substance he identified with nature, and declined to reduce either to the other. In general, nature is what the natural sciences are about; and the conception of nature accepted within a culture reflects the sciences it recognizes as natural sciences. In the past fifty years in the western world, it has come to be generally accepted that psychology is properly a branch of biology; and that physics, chemistry, and biology all deal with different phenomena of the same fundamental subject-matter, and to the extent that the ancient term 'matter' has any scientific sense, it refers to that subject-matter. Accordingly, it has also come to be accepted that, if there is nothing but nature, then there is nothing but matter in space-time. Naturalism has become materialism.

This fact has tempted some Christian apologists to defend Christianity against naturalism by refuting the contemporary form of naturalism, materialism. That was what C. S. Lewis did, in a series of exchanges, first with H. H. Price, who had called for a religion without dogma, that is, for a liberal Christianity that renounces the traditional faith embodied in the Nicene creed, by producing a philosophical refutation of naturalism, and then with G. E. M. Anscombe, in defending his refutation. When I arrived in Oxford as a graduate student in 1951, these exchanges were still audibly, if faintly, echoing. That exchange, although out of date, has much to teach us about what apologetics today should and should not be.

Lewis confidently set out to do what few philosophers would now attempt, to show that if a familiar inference based on common beliefs about belief is sound, then naturalism in its materialist form is self-refuting. This is Lewis's own summary of this argument.

> Every particular thought . . . is always and by all men discounted the moment they believe that it can be explained, without remainder, as the result of irrational causes. Whenever you know that what the other man is saying is wholly due to his complexes or to a bit of bone pressing on his brain, you cease to attach any importance to it. But if naturalism were true, then all thoughts whatever would be wholly the result of irrational causes. Therefore, all thoughts would be equally worthless. Therefore, naturalism is worthless. If it is true, then we can know no truths. It cuts its own throat.[2]

The common belief about belief on which Lewis tacitly relies is that beliefs worth considering are held because of reasons the believer accepts; and that they are appraised according as those reasons are sound or unsound. Naturalism in its contemporary form, materialism, is then dismissed on the ground that, by asserting that all beliefs are caused without remainder by physical events, it implies that they are not held because of reasons the believer accepts.

It is true, as Lewis saw, that Christianity presupposes the common belief about beliefs on which he relies. For example, St. Paul teaches that normal human beings can form enough true opinions about themselves and their situation to understand the

moral law (Rom. 2:14–15); and that presupposes that they believe that they have certain moral obligations because of sound
reasons they accept. If that common belief is true, is Lewis's argument sound? I know of nobody who has studied Anscombe's
objection to it who believes that it is. The flaw she pointed out is
that the cause of man's believing that he is sitting before a fire
(say, that a piece of bone is pressing on his brain) is not necessarily the reason why he believes it (say, that he can see his legs
stretched out towards the fire in his study grate—this reason being an illusion caused by the pressure of the piece of bone). Admittedly, when natural events cause beliefs by way of perceptual
illusions, they are discounted. Yet when somebody who really
does see his legs stretched out towards the fire in his study grate
gives that as his reason for believing that he is sitting before a
fire, the fact that his non-illusory perception has physical (i.e.,
irrational) causes does not entitle us to discount his reason.

Yet Anscombe herself came to perceive that her objection,
although sound, is not the end of the matter. Reflecting on the
episode in introducing the second volume of her *Collected Papers*, after recording that Lewis himself agreed that her objection
was sound, she praised him for raising a problem the depth of
which she had totally failed to recognize, and which remains un-
solved: namely, 'What is the connection between the grounds
and the actual occurrence of [a] belief?'[3] And that is related to
the implicit question of Plato's Socrates in the *Phaedo*: What is
the connection between the physical causes of his limbs being in
a seated posture in prison, and his conclusion that it was better
for him to accept his lawful punishment than to escape? I myself
know of no remotely satisfying materialist answer to either of
these questions.

The most popular is that one believes something on certain
grounds when the physical event that is functionally describable
as the having of that belief is caused by another physical event
that is functionally describable as the accepting of those
grounds. This presupposes that just as the function of a physical
event (say, the firing of certain neurons in a certain brain) may
be described in physical terms (say, as the bringing about of the
firing of certain other neurons), so it may be described in inten-

tional or mental terms (say, as the having, by the person in whose brain neurons are thus firing, of a belief that he sees his legs stretched out towards his study fire). But there is an objection to this that has not to my knowledge been resolved: that, lacking an analytical reduction of the functional description in intentional terms to some description in physical terms, there is no reason to suppose that the two descriptions—the physical functional one and the intentional functional one—describe the same event. Unless the intentional description can in principle be analytically reduced to a physical one, the two descriptions would seem to be of non-identical but correlated events.

If in reality nothing happens outside nature, and whatever happens in nature is causally explicable in terms of the natural sciences, then each real event functionally describable in intentional terms must be causally explicable in terms of the natural sciences. Although it may seem to follow that every event causally explicable in terms of the natural sciences must be identical with a physical event, it does not. All that follows is that whatever happens in reality is causally explicable in terms of *ideal* natural science: natural science as it might conceivably one day be—admitting of no progress or correction because, since all possible productive research has been done, there is no room for scientific work other than mastering and teaching what has already been discovered. Nobody believes that the natural sciences as we now have them have reached this ideal state; and it is at least questionable whether human beings, given their physical and intellectual limitations, can under any natural conditions develop natural sciences that are ideal in this sense. It follows that on the one hand, understood as the doctrine that nothing happens that is not causally explicable in terms of the natural sciences as they now are, materialism is certainly false; and that on the other, understood as the doctrine that nothing happens that is not causally explicable in terms of ideal natural science, it is something we know not what.

The familiar phenomena to which Lewis drew attention, forming beliefs and persisting in them for reasons, are not causally explicable in terms of the natural sciences in their present state—indeed, the phenomena are not even intelligible in terms of them. Naturalists profess not to be put out by this: in the past half-century, enormous advances have been made in neurophysiology and in the study of artificial intelligence, they point out, and they confidently expect that the dualism of human studies and the natural sciences will not endure much longer. That, however, is a question we can dodge. What matters for Christian apologetics is that Christianity presupposes that everyday explanations of human actions (sometimes contemptuously referred to as explanations in terms of 'folk psychology') are often true. Should advances in biology and neurophysiology show that they are not, Christianity itself could not survive.

In that case, should it not be an important task of Christian apologetics to offer substitutes for Lewis's unsound argument? No. Doing so overlooks a crucial feature of the apologetic situation. Very few materialists claim that the natural sciences as they now exist furnish acceptable accounts of any of the higher mental phenomena such as beliefs. All they claim is that the progress already made gives ground for anticipating that they will, leaving it open how far the accounts they ultimately give will alter either what is commonly believed about those phenomena, or what natural scientists now believe about the subject-matter of the natural sciences. In standing by folk psychology at the present stage of the natural sciences, Christians are certainly not committed to denying either that future scientific advances may revise folk psychology, or that the natural sciences of the future may not make materialism obsolete and provide acceptable causal explanations of the higher mental phenomena.

If philosophy provides any *praeambula fidei* it is in the theory of human action, and in particular in that part of it sometimes called 'moral psychology'. In conceiving human beings as creatures of will as well as of desire, and in refusing to think of their actions as predetermined outcomes of their desires and beliefs, Christianity presents naturalism with the task either of giving a naturalist account of the will, so understood, or of showing that it is a chimaera. The poverty of existing naturalist accounts of the human psyche, and in particular of the phenomena of special interest to Christianity—those of a will that is free (in each individual case, there are options between which it can choose), and which nevertheless predictably will not in all cases make the right choice it can make—should be better recognized than they are. These phenomena point to the unique status of human beings among known animals: they alone can recognize the difference between moral good and evil, and act on it; and yet they are compelled to judge themselves evil by virtue of the ways they in fact choose to act. Even so, these phenomena do not prove naturalism to be false: that as yet there is no useful naturalist account of these phenomena does not show that there never will be.

Despite the precision of their teaching about the nature of God and about God's dealings with humankind, the Christian churches have for the most part denied that the deposit of faith confided to them includes disputable propositions about the realm of nature. They have already come to terms with three very different philosophical and scientific conceptions of nature, the neo-Platonic, the Aristotelian, and the Copernican-Galilean-Newtonian; and if they and the world have any considerable future, it seems reasonable to suppose that they will come to terms with the philosophical-scientific culture now being formed, the content of which we can no more foresee than the seventeenth-century philosophers and scientists could foresee the philosophy and science of the twentieth century.

When confronted with contemporary naturalism, Christian apologists should begin by disclaiming any view about nature other than that Christian doctrine, as embodied in traditional confessions of faith such as the Nicene creed, will prove to be compatible with any authentic advance in the natural sciences. This claim is not empty: it is not logically impossible that a future naturalist psychology could give an account of human capacities that would make nonsense of what the Christian faith presupposes about them. However, Christian apologists should deprecate as intellectually vicious the present vogue for agonizing over philosophical questions generated by fictions about scientific possibilities. They will confine themselves to the traditionally agreed content of the faith (and much more was agreed than the appalling history of Christian confessional hatred and persecution would lead one to suppose), and to well-attested results of scientific investigation. Finally, they will not be in a hurry.

These principles were well understood by Cardinal Newman, and he laid them down in explaining what was the proper response to Darwin's biological discoveries.

> It would ill become me, as if I were afraid of truth of any kind, to blame those who pursue secular facts, by means of the reason God has given them, to their logical conclusions; or to be angry with science, because religion is bound in duty to take cognizance of its teaching . . . [T]he Catholic . . . does most deeply enter into the feelings of . . . religious and sincere minds, who are simply perplexed,—frightened or rendered desperate, as the case may be,—by the utter confusion into which late discoveries or speculations have thrown their most elementary ideas of religion . . . [H]ow often has the wish risen in his heart that some one from among his own people should come forward as the champion of revealed truth against its opponents! . . . [B]ut [there are] several strong difficulties in the way. One of the greatest is this, that at the moment it is so difficult to say precisely what it is that is to be encountered and overthrown. I am far from denying that scientific knowledge is really growing, but it is by fits and starts; hypotheses rise and fall; it is difficult to imagine which of them will keep their ground, and what the state of knowledge in relation to them will turn out to be from year to year. In this condition of things, it has seemed to me to be very undignified for a Catholic to commit himself to the work of chasing what might turn out to be phantoms . . . [4]

Newman's attitude to the natural sciences seems to me to be a paradigm of Christian faith, properly understood. He implicitly acknowledges that discoveries in the natural sciences could conceivably be incompatible with the Christian faith by leaving no room for anything supernatural, and hence that philosophical refutations of naturalism must be flawed. At the same time, he asserts the rational legitimacy of accepting the Christian faith without philosophical or scientific proof. Holding the Christian faith is believing something neither philosophically or scientifically proved that could conceivably be scientifically (and hence philosophically) disproved. Why then believe it?

6. Why Do Christians Believe the Nicene Creed?

If some widespread belief, for example, that one's horoscope significantly affects what happens, is mostly harbored for bad reasons, and good reasons for it are not ready to hand, it would be silly to look for them. I therefore submit that, if there are good reasons for non-believers in a post-Christian culture to believe the Nicene creed, they should be ready to hand as the reasons why a substantial number of such persons have come to believe it. However, there is an obstacle to following this line of investigation. Conversation with such believers (of whom I am one) on what is, after all, a delicate subject, suggests that, to their embarrassment, most of them find it difficult to give any answer that seems to them more than a rationalization—and not a persuasive one. There was an intellectual process certainly, and it was complex; but what it was is hard to say.

However, in many of the intellectual processes that have culminated in many conversions, three elements can be identified.

Although all three are of philosophical interest, the only one that is strictly philosophical is not found in all conversions, but only in those of converts accustomed to think philosophically. It arises out of reflection on naturalism as a philosophy, and it is to recognize that the natural sciences as they now are cannot coherently account for human life as it is lived, and in particular for the human activity of scientific research. Perhaps the natural sciences of the future will be able to account for them, but we cannot claim to anticipate whether they will or not, as some philosophers impudently do. Once this is recognized, it must also be recognized that the explanation of part of human life as it is lived may lie outside nature.

The second element in the process by which Christianity is accepted, when it is, is ethical: it is to recognize that not only one's own life, but human life generally, whatever virtues it may exhibit, is radically tainted with evil. The gospels, in which the way for Jesus is prepared by John the Baptist preaching repentance and at the same time recognizing his own unworthiness, seem to imply that this element is to be found in all conversions.

These two elements in combination open the possibility that the remedy for human evil, if there is a remedy for it, may lie outside nature; but they establish neither that there is a remedy, nor that, if there is, it is a supernatural one. Nor, if what I have said about a possible future naturalism is true, can philosophy establish it. Our present understanding of nature is too defective for us to be able to establish either that a coherent non-theistic naturalism is possible or that it is not. We cannot take the natural science of the twentieth century along with available philosophical interpretations of it, as the medieval scholastics took the natural science of the thirteenth century and available philosophical interpretations of it, and derive from them convincing proofs of the dependence of the natural world on a supernatural God. For that a third element, a non-philosophical one, is needed.

It is found in the religious history of the human race. Of all the religions of which we have any historical knowledge, those that have spread beyond the cultures in which they emerged fall into two groups: in the first are Hinduism and its critic and descendant, Buddhism; and in the second are Judaism and the two religions that claim to continue the Jewish revelation, Christianity and Islam. With a muddle characteristic of our age, many consider it impossible, on one hand, to acknowledge that each of these great religions has characteristic virtues and must, short of idolatry, be respected both intellectually and morally, and, on the other, to deny that more than one of them can be true. They conclude that each of the world religions is a facet of the one universal religion. Such a view is the antithesis of what it claims to be: far from respecting the great religions, it refuses to take any of them seriously; for it is impossible to take seriously either Christianity or, say, Hinduism, and also to say that they might both be true. Of the affirmations each makes, one or another will be denied by each of the others, and to dismiss any of these affirmations and denials is to dismiss the religions that make them.

Nobody would accept Christianity if he also accepted certain of the cardinal ideas of Hinduism and Buddhism, for example, the law of Karma and the doctrine of reincarnation; and those ideas seem to philosophically minded Christians philosophically objectionable. Judaism and its descendants are not objectionable in this way. Anybody who studies the Jewish scriptures, and who concludes that they are the record of a special relation between the supernatural creator of the universe and one people on earth, through which all the others would one day be blessed, as it seems to me that anybody reasonably might, must inquire, in the light of what can be established historically, whether the Christian scriptures record the culmination of that relation. Of course, the Christian scriptures, or 'New Testament' as they are known as a body, are the creation of the church, and not the church of them; but all present branches of the church accept the canonical texts of the New Testament as the sole repository of evidence for proving doctrine. Can it be reasonably concluded, from an historically serious study of these texts, that the Nicene creed is true?

The obvious objection to so concluding is that many biblical scholars of standing do not. I do not think that I was unusual in absorbing, as an undergraduate, the notion that biblical scholarship (of course I did not actually read any) has shown the New Testament canon is largely a second-century work of fiction, preserving some authentic elements of the original teaching of the Apostles, and much less of that of Jesus; and that the unedifying history of it from the Tubingen school in the early nineteenth century to Bultmann has shown that it is impossible to establish what the early teaching of either was. However, what it was not could be stated with some confidence: for example, Jesus did not predict his death before he entered Jerusalem for the last time; he did not teach his uncomprehending disciples that it would be sacrificial; and he did not command them to observe the rite of the Eucharist as, *inter alia,* its perpetual memorial. Accepting the Nicene faith has been, for all I have talked to, in large part a matter of forming a critical attitude to much biblical scholarship.

The foundation of such an attitude is a distinction that leaps to the eye when the textual scholarship of non-religious Greek and Latin texts is compared with that of biblical texts. As a rough rule, one can say that, to the extent that their methods are the same, biblical scholarship is sound, valuable, and modest in its claims; and that, to the extent that biblical scholarship goes its own way, it is something else. The rule is only rough; for the garden of non-religious textual studies has its own weeds; and they are instructive for biblical studies. There is evidence that Roman historians writing just before and just after the texts of the New Testament were written used written sources that have not survived: what did they contain? Differences in our earliest texts of certain classical writers might be explained by supposing that some descend from lost third- or fourth-century editions: what did those editions contain? Given a few bold but tenuously supported hypotheses, remarkable answers to such questions can be obtained and offered as fruits of scientific scholarship—the helpless past cannot complain. Peaceable scholars who know better are apt to pass over in silence work of this sort, but fortunately not all good scholars are peaceable. I recommend those who find it difficult to credit that rubbish can be passed off as the latest thing in textual scholarship to read the passage in A. E. Housman's preface to his critical edition of Lucan's *Bellum Civile* which begins:

> I touch with reluctance, as Gibbon might say, and dispatch with impatience an idle yet pretentious game in which Lucan's less serious critics find amusement, and which they call *Ueberlieferungsgeschichte*, because that is a longer and nobler name than fudge.[5]

Yet what awaits us in biblical studies is more impudent than the fudge that now and then interrupts the studies of those who work at non-religious texts.

There is no defensible objection to attempts to determine what can be inferred from the New Testament texts about the origin of Christianity, it being expressly presupposed that nature as understood by the natural sciences of one's day is self-sufficient, and hence that whatever is narrated or reported as occurring by virtue of supernatural intervention in the natural order, whether the virgin birth of Jesus, his resurrection from the dead, or his and his Apostles' miracles of healing, is simply false. Given his naturalist assumptions, it is difficult to dispute Bultmann's conclusion that the only true history in the New Testament is the bare fact of Jesus' existence and death by crucifixion; but his scholarly caution is exceptional. For example, it has been confidently claimed that critical New Testament research establishes that Jesus was fundamentally an ethical teacher (Harnack), that he made no claim to be the Messiah (Wrede), that he was a noble but deluded fanatic who preached the imminent end of the world, and went to his death believing he could bring it about (Schweitzer), and much, much more.

Before accepting any of these results (since they contradict one another, it is impossible to accept them all), anybody who is seriously inquiring into the truth of the Nicene creed will want to know why biblical scholars should agree that nothing can happen in reality that cannot be accounted for by the natural sciences as they now are. As a day or two in a good library suffices to show, the thesis that the gospel narratives of supernatural interventions are false, although it is offered as a conclusion of textual research, is almost never a conclusion and almost always an unargued presupposition. This is sometimes concealed; for example, by working with the assumption that the authentic material from which the gospels were composed, or more accurately fabricated, were smaller pericopes that circulated as separate units in early Christian communities. Bultmann, for example, reduces these pericopes to sayings without context, with the result that he can deny that the authors of the gospels had any material implying a supernatural intervention to draw upon.

If the inquirer sets aside works of biblical criticism that simply presuppose that the naturalism of one's own day is true and traditional Christianity false, to what can he look? Devotional aids to the study of the scriptures are not what he needs either. I myself was neither directed to nor found exactly what I sought; and fell back on reading the New Testament itself, with the aid of the first (1968) edition of the *Jerome Biblical Commentary* (I chose one approved by the Roman church as least likely to confound contemporary naturalist presuppositions with results of scholarship). I devoted most attention to the earliest texts, namely, the early letters of Paul; and asked myself what can be inferred from them about the beliefs and practices of the early church and whether it is consistent with the later gospel accounts of Jesus' life and teaching. Two things I found seemed to me of special importance: first, Paul's concern, in Galatians 1 and 2, for the unity of the church and the integrity of its doctrine, his staying for fifteen days with Peter, and his recognition of James, Peter, and John as 'pillars'; and secondly, his description of the Eucharist, in 1 Corinthians 11:23–29, not only as the central rite of Christian worship, but as instituted by Jesus in terms implying that his death would be sacrificial. Both letters are reasonably believed to have been written in the 50s: less than thirty years after Jesus' death.

It seems a safe conclusion that the Apostles whom Paul recognizes as pillars were teaching soon after Jesus died that his death was sacrificial, that he was raised from the dead, and that he commanded his followers to observe the Eucharist as a memorial of his sacrifice. These teachings are the foundation of the trinitarian doctrine formulated in the Nicene creed, and they are not fabrications by unknown propagandist geniuses in the second century. The question is, are they true?

Why do converts to Christianity from pre-Christian and post-Christian cultures accept them? Part of the answer has already been suggested. When they learn what Christianity teaches, they judge it, if true, to be a remedy for their condition. In comparing it with alternatives, their verdict is, like Peter's when Jesus asked him, 'Will you also go away?' 'Lord, to whom shall we go? thou hast the words of eternal life' (John 6:67–68). Still, a fiction may be unrivalled and still a fiction. The rest of the answer is that they judge, and reasonably judge, that, from the Pentecost after they allegedly occurred, the Apostles taught the sacrificial death and resurrection of Jesus. Unless they were insanely deluded, the Apostles were in a position to know the facts, and either reported them truthfully or lied. What they reported is incredible from a contemporary naturalist point of view. Yet from a contemporary naturalist point of view much that we all reasonably believe about ourselves is unexplained, and the misery of the condition in which serious inquirers take themselves to be would have no remedy. In this situation, faith may seem to inquirers possible, and not irrational. And then, by some means they do not understand, but which the church teaches is the operation of grace, it may become actual.

NOTES

1. D. Z. Phillips, *Death and Immortality* (New York: St. Martin's Press, 1970), 67; quoted William J. Wainwright, *Philosophy of Religion* (Belmont, Calif.: Wadsworth, 1988).

2. "Religion without Dogma?" in C. S. Lewis, *The Great Miracle* (New York: Ballantine Books, 1983), 94. Originally published in *Phoenix Quarterly* 1 (1946).

3. G. E. M. Anscombe, *Collected Papers* (Minneapolis: University of Minnesota Press, 1981), vol. 2, pp. ix–x. The version of Lewis's argument which Anscombe criticized was in chap. 3 of the first edition of his book *Miracles*, which Lewis radically revised in later editions.

4. J. H. Newman, *Apologia Pro Vita Sua* (London: Oxford University Press, 1964), 272–273.

5. A. E. Housman, *M. Annaei Lucani Belli Civilis Libri Decem* (Oxford: Blackwell, 1926), xii; and cf. pp. xii–xviii.

The Remembrance of Things (Not) Past: Philosophical Reflections on Christian Liturgy

Nicholas Wolterstorff

I

A striking feature of the hymns Christian people sing, as they move through the cycle of the Church Year, is that they are cast *in the present tense*. Of course they are not all like that; some are in the past tense, as one would expect. The remarkable thing is that so many are in the present tense—and that Christians find this unremarkable. Currently many hymns are being rewritten to clean up (as it is sometimes put) the sexist language, to get rid of militaristic language, etc. No one, to the best of my knowledge, has proposed straightening out the tenses of the hymns to eliminate this strange 'hymnic present'.

Let us get some examples fresh in mind before we set out. We all know the first verse of Charles Wesley's hymn, "Hark, the Herald Angels Sing":

> Hark, the herald angels sing,
> "Glory to the new-born king.
> Peace on earth and mercy mild,
> God and sinners reconciled."
> Joyful all ye nations rise,
> Join the triumph of the skies,
> with the angelic host proclaim,

> "Christ is born in Bethlehem."
> Hark, the herald angels sing,
> "Glory to the new-born King!"

And here is the first verse of a Christmas hymn by Paul Gerhardt:

> All my heart this night rejoices
> as I hear, far and near,
> sweetest angel voices:
> "Christ is born," their choirs are singing,
> til the air everywhere
> now with joy is ringing

The first verse of another hymn by Charles Wesley, this one an Easter hymn, goes like this:

> "Christ the Lord is risen today," Alleluia!
> Sons of men and angels say: Alleluia!
> Raise your joys and triumphs high; Alleluia!
> Sing, ye heavens, and earth reply. Alleluia.

One imagines that when Wesley composed those lines, the old Latin carol, *Surrexit Christus Hodie*, was ringing in his ears. Its first verse, in English translation, goes like this:

> Jesus Christ is risen today, Alleluia!
> Our triumphant holy day, Alleluia!
> Who did once, upon the cross, Alleluia!
> Suffer to redeem our loss. Alleluia!

It may be noted that it is characteristic of hymns in the present tense to insert such indexicals as "now," "today," "this night," "this day," "this happy morn," etc., as if to make doubly sure that we do not miss the point.

What is the point? Apparently we are being invited by these hymns to imagine there being no temporal gap between the events being hymned and what is happening now—this in spite of the fact that we all know that there is by now a very large gap.

Notice that this act of imagining there being no gap has directionality to it: One can imagine Christ's birth taking place now, or one can imagine us being present at Christ's birth then. Which direction do these hymns invite us to take in our imagination? Are we being invited to imagine those events as present (actual, contemporary)? Or to imagine ourselves as participating in them then?

For the most part, they can be construed equally well either way; that seems to me true for the ones I have quoted. Sometimes, though, one of the construals would be forced; when that is so, the more natural construal is always, to the best of my knowledge, from present to past: We are invited to imagine ourselves participating in *those* events *then*, which is in any case, I think, the direction compelled by the spiritual, "Were You There When They Crucified My Lord?" and very nearly compelled by Phillips Brooks's hymn, "O Little Town of Bethlehem":

> O little town of Bethlehem,
> how still we see thee lie;
> above thy deep and dreamless sleep
> thy silent stars go by.
> Yet in thy dark streets shineth
> the everlasting light;
> the hopes and fears of all the years
> are met in thee tonight.

But consider all those Renaissance paintings in which the Nativity is unmistakably and emphatically located in some contemporary western European village, complete with ruins. Clearly the original viewers were being invited to imagine the Nativity occurring among them then. Is that evidence in favor of the opposite generalization from the one I just made—or evidence in favor of the conclusion that no such generalization can be made?

These paintings strike me, at least, as quite intentionally rubbing against the grain. We are surprised by them, set to reflecting on what could be the point. Rembrandt, by contrast, did things in the natural way: Christ and his contemporaries are dressed and housed in what a seventeenth-century Dutchman supposed to be the garb and architecture of Palestine in the first century. And is it not one of the aims of pilgrimages to "the holy land" to assist us in imagining ourselves *then*?

II

In several of his books Mircea Eliade, the great anthropologist of religion, propounds a theory as to how archaic peoples understood their rituals; along the way he suggests that the Christian liturgy and the Christian understanding thereof bear traces of this older understanding. His theory is such that if he is right, we will have in hand a fascinating and plausible answer to our question.

We must begin with Eliade's account of myth; for the core of his theory is that archaic humanity sees its rituals as enacted myth. Myth, says Eliade,

> narrates a sacred history; it relates an event that took place in primordial time, the fabled time of the "beginnings." In other words, myth tells how, through the deeds of Supernatural Beings, a reality came into existence, be it the whole of reality, the Cosmos, or only a fragment of reality—an island, a species of plant, a particular kind of human behavior, an institution. Myth, then, is always an account of a "creation"; it relates how something was produced, began to *be*. . . . The actors in myths are Supernatural Beings. They are known primarily by what they did in the transcendent times of the "beginnings." . . . In short, myths describe the various and sometimes dramatic breakthroughs of the sacred (or the "supernatural") into the World. It is this sudden breakthrough of the sacred that really *establishes* the World and makes it what it is today. Furthermore, it is as a result of the intervention of Supernatural Beings that man himself is what he is today, a mortal, sexed, and cultural being.[1]

By way of giving a narration of the origin of things, myths provide archaic humanity with paradigms, or exemplary models, for their activities. In fact, says Eliade, " . . . the foremost function of myth is to reveal the exemplary models for all human rites and all significant human activities—diet or marriage, work or education, art or wisdom" (MR 8). It is in their intentional imitation of the exemplary models that human actions have their meaning, indeed, their reality.

> Their meaning, their value, are not connected with their crude physical datum but with their property of reproducing a primordial act, of repeating a mythical example . . . . Marriage and the collective orgy echo mythical prototypes; they are repeated because they were consecrated in the beginning ("in those days," *in illo tempore, ab origine*), by gods, ancestors, or heroes. . . .
>
> This conscious repetition of given paradigmatic gestures reveals an original ontology. The crude product of nature, the object fashioned by the industry of man, acquire their reality, their

identity, only to the extent of their participation in a transcendent reality. The gesture acquires meaning, reality, solely to the extent to which it repeats a primordial act.[2]

For "archaic man, reality is a function of the imitation of a celestial archetype" (*MER* 5).

Eliade's proposal as to how archaic persons understood their rituals is an application of this general point. Indeed, archaic persons themselves made no distinction between ritual and profane activity. "Among primitives, not only do rituals have their mythical model but any human act whatsoever acquires effectiveness to the extent to which it exactly *repeats* an act performed at the beginning of time by a god, a hero, or an ancestor" (*MER* 22). Rituals are imitative repetitions of the primeval events narrated in the myths.

An implication is that a ritual cannot be performed without a knowledge of the myth which narrates its paradigm; it cannot be performed "unless its 'origin' is known, that is, the myth that tells how it was performed for the first time" (MR 17). Thus myth and ritual are linked hand in hand. Indeed, "In most cases it is not enough to *know* the origin myth, one must *recite* it; this, in a sense, is a proclamation of one's knowledge, *displays* it. But even this is not all. He who recites or performs the origin myth is thereby steeped in the sacred atmosphere in which these miraculous events took place" (*MR* 17–18). It comes then as no surprise to learn that, in general, "myths cannot be related without regard to circumstances. Among many tribes they are not recited before women or children, that is, before the uninitiated. . . . Whereas 'false stories' can be told anywhere and at any time, myths must not be recited except *during a period of sacred time*. . ." (MR 9–10).

The most striking feature of the archaic person's understanding of ritual, on Eliade's account, remains to be noted. Archaic persons do not regard their myths as mere stories; the myths relate what actually happened—once upon a time, at the beginning. Yet archaic persons do not see the times of those happenings nor the events at those times as standing in temporal relations to these historical times of ours. The thought of trying to find out *when* the mythic events took place with respect to our historical events makes no sense to them. Eliade's central thesis is that archaic persons regard themselves, when performing their rituals, and perhaps even when reciting their myths, as entering into that time of origins. They regard themselves as doing the things narrated in the myth and doing them in mythic primordial time. "The participants in the festival become contemporaries of the mythical event. In other words, they emerge from their historical time—that is, from the time constituted by the sum total of profane personal and intrapersonal events—and recover primordial time, which is always the same, which belongs to eternity. Religious man periodically finds his way into mythical and sacred time, re-enters the *time of origin*, the time that 'floweth not' because it does not participate in profane temporal duration, because it is composed of an *eternal present*, which is indefinitely recoverable."[3] The myth is lived, and it is lived in the time of the myth.[4] In ritual, the events narrated in the myths are *re-actualized*. "All rituals imitate a divine archetype and . . . their continual reactualization takes place in one and the same atemporal mythical instant. . . . The construction rites show us something beyond this: imitation, hence reactualization, of the cosmogony" (*MER* 76).

Let me halt my exposition for a moment to observe that Eliade's language suggests two quite different, and conflicting, interpretations of the archaic person's mentality. Often Eliade speaks of archaic persons as believing that they repeat, reiterate, reenact, reactualize, the events narrated in the myth; he speaks of archaic persons as trying to imitate those events, as taking them as paradigms. The suggestion carried by such language is that there are certain act-types, such as cosmos-creation, which archaic persons regard the gods as having performed in primordial time and which they now, by way of their rituals, repeatedly perform in historical time, taking the gods' performance in primordial time as paradigmatic. Admittedly it would be extraordinary if archaic persons really believed that cosmogony is an act that can be repeatedly performed, and furthermore, that they can do it. But people nowadays believe extraordinary things; presumably archaic persons could do so as well.

Another pattern of speech in Eliade suggests quite a different interpretation—one more difficult to wrap one's mind around. Eliade speaks of archaic persons as believing that, by performing their rituals, they become contemporaries of the mythical events and of the gods, they actualize the events of the myth, they enter into primordial time, they live for a while in primordial rather than historical time, etc. The interpretation these words suggest shares with the preceding one the conviction that there are two distinct time-sequences, call them historical time and primordial time, the myths narrating for us what happens in primordial time and we ordinarily living in historical time. Primordial times, and event-occurrences *at* primordial times, bear no temporal relations to our times or to the event-occurrences at our times. There is no historical time such that some event-occurrence located at a primordial time also happens at that historical time; and presumably there is also no primordial time such that some event-occurrence of historical time also happens at that primordial time. In particular, the event-occurrences in primordial time did not happen long ago with respect to what is happening now in historical time; they just happened 'once upon a time'. Though the myths speak about beginnings, the event-occurrences they narrate are not to be thought of as the *first* things that happen in our historical time.

Eliade assimilates archaic ideas to our western ideas when he speaks of primordial time as eternity, and as the time that floweth not. Perhaps speaking of it as eternity aids us in the endeavor to get some feel for what the archaic person believed. But speaking of it as the time that floweth not does not help. For it is clear that in the primordial time of the archaic person, times do flow. Things happen one after the other, some more closely after each other, others, less closely. The archaic person, if Eliade is right, works with the concept of what might be called *moving eternity*; by contrast, we in the mainline western theological tradition have worked with the concept of *stationary eternity*. In eternity, as we have thought of it, nothing succeeds anything else. The point remains true for the archaic person, however, that none of those primordial times bears either a succession or simultaneity relation to any of our historical times; and that no event-occurrence located in one time frame is also to be found in the other.

This much is shared by the two interpretations of the archaic mentality, the imitation/repetition interpretation and the actualization interpretation. Where the second differs from the first is in attributing to archaic persons the belief that by engaging in ritual—and also, perhaps, by having certain sorts of trances—they enter that primordial time. What do we mean, "enter" it? In the world of the myth only supernatural beings are to be found. One does not find there any person who is not identical with some supernatural person. So what happens upon John Doe's engaging in the ritual is that he loses his identity and takes on the identity of one of the gods in the myth, there doing whatever the god does in the myth. But of course cosmogony is not multiply performed in the myth; it is done just once. So on this interpretation it is a mistake to speak of cosmogony, or any other act of the gods narrated in the myths, as reactualized, repeated, reiterated, reenacted. So too it is a mistake to speak of any such act as the imitation of a paradigm. The gods, in primordial time, do not follow paradigms. In ritual, the events of the myth are not *re*actualized but actualized.

But surely archaic persons realize that the ritual is done repeatedly. Do they not then also perforce think of themselves as *repeating* the mythical events?

Perhaps not. We, observing the ritual, can of course see what we regard as the archaic person's body and can describe and date what the body is doing; obviously it is not actualizing the world's creation. But the archaic person thinks that he becomes a god acting in primordial time, this *becoming a god* being something that happens in historical time. If all goes well, he will at some time in our historical time recover his human identity and again do things in our historical time. But now, when the ritual is going on, he is gone. For a while, there is nothing at all that he is doing in historical time. Surely in fundamentals this is not unlike the rather common western belief that upon death, the soul of the human being enters eternity. The difference is that, on the western belief, souls do not move in and out of eternity—and that the eternity entered is a stationary eternity. Of course, the moving eternity of the archaic mentality does not include the events of archaic person John Does's taking on identity with some god and later discarding it. *These* events are to be found only in historical time. In the world of the myth, there are only gods to be found.[5]

Imagine having suffered from a delusion in which you were a god who, once upon a time, created things; and imagine further that, having come out of the delusion, you do not believe that you suffered from delusion but that you left your body and became a god acting in another time frame, doing things of which those who watched your body could tell nothing. To imagine experiencing that and believing that, is to imagine having experiences and beliefs very similar to those of the archaic person, on this second interpretation.[6]

I know of no passage in which Eliade takes note of the difference between the two interpretations which I have delineated. Yet obviously they are distinct and incompatible. It should be noted that both are what might be called *reality*-interpretations of ritual. Neither contends that ritual dramatically represents, or otherwise signifies or symbolizes, episodes from the tribe's myth. Ritual *actualizes* or *imitates*.[7] I myself am woefully lacking in the knowledge necessary to decide which, if either, is an accurate construal of the mentality of the archaic person. (Possibly the archaic person is deeply confused and holds both views.) The attribution of either one to the archaic person, but especially of the latter, strikes me as often based on a rather wooden insistence that the language of archaic persons be taken literally. Are they to be permitted no figures of speech, no tropes? But be that as it may, it is very clear that, if Eliade were faced with the need to choose, he would choose the second interpretation. Behind the myth and behind the ritual of archaic persons, he sees an ontology, coupled with a philosophy of time and history. It is in these that he is fundamentally interested, not in the details of myths and ritual. And the philosophy of time and history that he attributes to the archaic person fits the second interpretation, not the first.

"Interest in the 'irreversible' and the 'new' in history," says Eliade, "is a recent discovery in the life of humanity"—the discovery to be credited to the valorization of history as theophany by the Hebrews. By contrast, "archaic humanity . . . defended itself, to the utmost of its powers, against all the novelty and irreversibility which history entails" (*MER* 48). "For Judaism, time has a beginning and will have an end. . . . Yahweh no longer manifests himself in cosmic time (like the gods of other religions) but in a *historical time*, which is irreversible. Each new manifestation of Yahweh in history is no longer reducible to an earlier manifestation. . . . Hence the historical event acquires a new dimension; it becomes a theophany" (*SP* 110–111). By contrast, in the rituals of archaic man we see his "refusal to accept himself as a historical being, his refusal to grant value to memory and hence to the unusual events (i.e., events without an archetypal model) that in fact constitute history. In the last analysis, what we discover in all these rites and all these attitudes is the will to devalue time. . . . The life of archaic man . . . although it takes place in time, does not bear the burden of time. . . . Like the mystic, like the religious man in general, the primitive lives in a continual present" (*MER* 85–86).

When Eliade looks at Christian liturgy—and at the Christian understanding thereof—he thinks he sees some of the same phenomena to which he called attention in archaic humanity; he interprets their presence there as *remnants* from the archaic view. Narratives are recited; the participants leave behind 'profane' time and enter into the 'sacred' time of the narrated events—though with the large difference that those events are regarded as located in our historical time; and the narrated events are thereby reactualized. The "Christian liturgical year," says Eliade, "is based upon a periodic and real repetition of the Nativity, Passion, death, and Resurrection of Jesus, with all that this mystical drama implies for a Christian; that is, personal and cosmic regeneration through reactualization *in concreto* of the birth, death, and resurrection of the Savior" (*MER* 130). Thus "when a Christian of our day participates in liturgical time, he recovers the *illud tempus* in which Christ lived, suffered, and rose again—but it is no longer a mythical time, it is the time when Pontius Pilate governed Judaea" (*SP* 111).

If in celebrating the liturgy for Christmas one sees oneself as recovering "the *illud tempus* in which Christ" was born, what is more natural than to cast the hymns accompanying that celebration into the present tense? If the Eliade interpretation of the Christian liturgy and its church year setting is acceptable, the mystery surrounding the hymnic present tense is torn away. But is it acceptable?

Recall that we have divided Eliade's theory into two, an imitation/repetition theory and an actualization-theory. The questions to put to the actualization theory of Christian liturgy are such as these: Do we, by participating in the liturgy, leave behind historical time and enter another time, *sacred time*, the time of the events in the gospel narrative? Do we do that by shucking off our own identity and taking on the identity of one of the participants in the events narrated? Do we thus become participants in the narrated events of blessing and deliverance?

The answer surely is no; and for several reasons. Whether or not there is such a phenomenon as eternity distinct from the phenomenon of historical time, and whether or not God is 'in' eternity and not 'in' time, a striking feature of the Christian liturgy is that it is focused not just on God's nature but on God's actions; and more specifically, on actions which took place in historical time. Though Christians use language appropriate to temporal processes for the relations among the members of the Trinity—speaking of "begetting" and "proceeding"—they have always been careful to insist that, in this use, the words do not refer to temporal processes. The eternity of the Trinity is a stationary, not a moving eternity. And though God may be spoken of in the liturgy as eternal, immutable, impassible, etc., nonetheless the liturgy is focused on the historical events of exodus and prophecy and incarnation and crucifixion and resurrection. The Christian church has a narrative which it affirms about God's actions in history; and one thing to carry away from Eliade's discussion of the archaic mentality is the realization that the Christian liturgy is as tightly related to the Christian narrative of God's doings as is the ritual of an archaic tribe to its narrative of the doings of supernatural beings—while at the same time, let us not forget, taking account of God's present doings. Immanuel Kant, for one, saw the connection clearly; persuaded as he was that God could not act in history, he recommended, and even predicted, that Christian liturgy would disappear to be replaced by the discussions of an ethical culture society. Attacks on the conviction that God acts in history undermine the liturgy.

But the question before us is that of how, specifically, the liturgy is related to the narrative. And given that the narrative is a narrative of events from the historical past, not from some separate 'sacred' time, participating in the liturgy cannot be a way of participating in actualizing those events. The actions of blessing and redemption on which the liturgy focuses *have been* actualized; for us to participate in actualizing them is no longer an option. For us to be participants in the events narrated and liturgized would require a time-machine. To participate in the liturgy is not to climb into a time-machine.

Further, it is impossible that anyone should change his or her identity. Perhaps archaic people believed that they could change their identity; if they did, they were grievously mistaken. If it is ever the case that I am not identical with the apostle Peter, then it is always a necessary truth that I am not. Not being identical with Peter is part of my essence. For this reason, too, performing the Christian liturgy is not a way of participating in actualizing the events of the biblical narrative. It may be added that, since God is one of the prime agents in the biblical narrative, for us to actualize the biblical narrative by participating in the liturgy would require that various of us become identical with God upon entering 'sacred time.' Clearly that is untenable.[8]

The alternative theory of Christian liturgy coming out of Eliade, the repetition-theory, would go, I suppose, something like this: Incarnation (to take just one example) is an act-type capable of being repeatedly performed. Its most decisive performance occurred in Bethlehem about 2000 years ago. Christians bring about a recurrence of incarnation each year by imitating *that* occurrence in their liturgy—by imitating what might be called, given its importance, *the* Incarnation. In the liturgy we imitate the central acts of the biblical narrative; and thereby we repeat, reiterate, reactualize general act-types of which *those* were paradigmatic instances. Incarnation takes place again, atonement-by-death is repeated, resurrection from the dead occurs again, etc.

It might appear that this interpretation could be dismissed at once, on the ground of the emphatic biblical teaching concerning the uniqueness of the events of salvation. Hebrews 9 and 1 Peter 3:18 stress that the event-type, *atonement for sin by the death of a human being*, happens just once; Christ's atonement by death has been and will be the only instance thereof.[9] But what the Bible actually stresses is only the uniqueness of *certain* events of salvation. *Those* either do not enter the liturgy at all or enter in some other way than repetition. Among these will be Christ's atonement for sins by death. Perhaps, though, there are other events in the biblical narrative which can be imitated, and thereby the appropriate event-type repeated. So far, then, there seems nothing wrong with trying to interpret parts, at least, of the Christian liturgy and of its relation to *parts* of the biblical narrative in accord with the imitation/repetition theory.

The response might be that, nonetheless, only those acts from the biblical narrative which are acts of human beings can get repeated in the liturgy; the acts of God can only be recited, dramatized, etc.; and that this limitation seems to 'gut' the whole idea. But even that is not necessarily the case. It may be that God can, in one way or another, act by way of one of us doing something in the liturgy. I propose, then, to set aside for the time being this imitation/repetition theory, and return to it later when we can deal with it more adequately.

III

Remembering is as fundamental as anything in the relation of Christian people to the acts of God. Biblical scholars in recent years have emphasized that one of the fundamental injunctions in Old Testament Judaism, carried forth into New Testament Christianity, is the injunction to *remember*: to remember and not forget what God has done. Philosophers sometimes speak of memory as if the only sorts of entities which are candidates for being remembered are prior experiences of the person doing the remembering. Clearly that is mistaken. One can remember, or forget, the Pythagorean Theorem. And one can remember the Alamo without ever having been at the Alamo. Norman Malcolm's formula comes close, at least, to capturing the full range: One remembers something just in case one knows it because one knew it. The members of the people Israel, down through the generations, were to remember the Exodus, long after those who experienced it had died. The *having known* which the remembering presupposed was to be accomplished by tradition. Thus a social memory was to be maintained: The people Israel was to know because it knew, not to forget what once it knew.

A people's remembering of episodes in its experience requires a special kind of handing over, a special kind of tradition. What must be handed on is a *narrative* of the people's history. Hence, if remembering is crucial, narrative is crucial. A people's remembering is accomplished by way of the handing-on of the narrative of the events to be remembered, and by way of the narrative's being believed. If it is not believed, then what is remembered is only the narrative itself, not the events narrated.

To understand in what sense these claims just made are true, however, it is important that we take note of an ambiguity in the meaning of the word "narrative." In speaking of a narrative, we may mean either a certain kind of projected world, one that is customarily called a *story*; or we may mean a certain way of presenting a story, viz., by *narrating*, by telling, by reciting. (Or, of course, we may mean the combination of these.) When it is important to avoid the ambiguity, I shall speak either of *story* or of *narration*. A people's remembering requires the communication of its *story* and the believing acceptance thereof. It does not require that the story be narrated. Among the ancient Greeks, the stories of the people were often communicated by dramatic representation rather than by narration.

Quite obviously Christians could hand on the biblical story, and thus retain the memory of its events, without having gatherings which are recognizably liturgical. They could hand it on by narrating it in more or less private, informal situations. In fact, however, narrating the story and reading narrations of the story occupy a prominent place in the Christian gatherings. Though the canonical books of the Christian community do more than narrate the story, certainly that is a prominent element in them. And much of the liturgy consists of readings from the canonical books of the community; of speeches about, or grounded on, what is said in those books; and of expressions of praise and confession, admiration and regret, in response to what has been heard—these responses of worship themselves in good measure guided by the canonical books, and often even performed by the people taking on their lips, for their own response, *words* from the canonical books, albeit sometimes with radical alterations of meaning. Justin Martyr, in his description of the liturgy of the church of Rome around 150 A.D., remarked that

> on the day called Sunday an assembly is held in one place of all who live in town or country, and the records of the apostles or the writings of the prophets are read as time allows. Then, when the reader has finished, the president in a discourse admonishes and exhorts [us] to imitate these good things. (*First Apology*)

Yet clearly the liturgy contains more than narration and such responses to narration as indicated above. In the Eucharist, for example, we find bread and wine brought forward, the bread broken, the wine drunk. How are we to understand these additional phenomena? Do they move us outside the scope of the remembering of the story?

Not necessarily. One discovers from the Old and the New Testament that the remembering so fundamental to the life of Israel and the church was to be kept alive by strategies in addition to that of narration. It was also to be kept alive by introducing into the life of the people various objects which would function for them as what in Hebrew was called a *zikkaron*, in Greek, an *anamnesis*—translated into English as a *memorial*. Likewise the people was to *do* various things as a zikkaron, as an anamnesis, as a memorial. Its environment and its way of life were to incorporate memorials. Let us have some examples before us.

Members of Israel were to keep their fellow Hebrews as slaves for only six years, setting them free in the seventh year, so as to remember that God redeemed them from slavery in the land of Egypt (Deut. 15:12–15). Members of Israel were to render justice to the sojourners, the fatherless, and the widows, so as to remember that God redeemed them from slavery in Egypt (Deut. 24:17–18). Members of Israel were to be content with the first gleanings of their crops, leaving what remained for the sojourner, the fatherless, and the widow, so as to remember that they were slaves in the land of Egypt (Deut. 24:19–22). Members of Israel were to keep the seventh day of the week as a holy sabbath day, so as to remember that God brought them out of servanthood in Egypt; on that day, all Israel was to rest: free adults, but also children, servants, sojourners, and animals (Deut. 5:12–15). Members of Israel were to observe the Passover as a memorial, so as to remember that they were slaves in Egypt; in particular, they were to eat no leavened bread, so as to remember the day when they came out of Egypt (Deut. 16:1–12; Exodus 12:14–15; 13:3–10). And to move on to the New Testament, Jesus, at the end of the last meal which he ate with his disciples before his death, a Passover supper, and hence itself a memorial meal, instructed his disciples to "Do this as a memorial of me." Ever since, Christians have observed the Lord's Supper as a memorial of him.[10]

A striking feature of the Deuteronomic instructions to Israel, to do these various things so as to remember, is that the purpose stated is not to remember that *your forefathers* were delivered from Egypt, but to remember that *you* were delivered from Egypt. There is here an elision of intervening time similar to that which comes to expression in the hymns with which we began. The elision is even more striking in the instruction concerning Passover observance to be found in Exodus (13:8): "And you shall tell your son on that day, 'It is because of what the Lord did for me when I came out of Egypt'." The Haggadah text which to this day is recited at the Seder feast includes the words, "In every generation one ought to regard oneself as though he has personally come out of Egypt."

What is the force of the instruction, *Do this in order to remember*, or alternatively, *Do this as a memorial*? Brevard Childs, in his book, *Memory and Tradition in Israel*,[11] assumes without arguing the point that the force of the instruction is to do this to be reminded, or to do this as a reminder. This certainly seems correct. But it is difficult to resist the conclusion that it is not the whole of the matter. The old folk remedy for the forgetfulness of a husband was to tie a piece of string around his finger to remind him to buy bread, pay the butcher, or whatever. Memorials, as the Bible speaks of them, are not like that.

What is the difference? This question confronts us with a question of procedure. Some scholars have argued or assumed that the concept of memorial (zikkaron, anamnesis) is peculiar to the mentality of the Hebrews, or perhaps more generally, to that of the Semitic peoples. They have accordingly tried to grasp the concept by looking at the biblical uses—thus engaging in the project of biblical word studies so popular during the last fifty years or so. And they have argued that unless we grasp this peculiarly Hebraic concept, we will not be able to grasp the biblical understanding of the liturgy. Perhaps the best practitioner of this strategy has been Max Thurian.[12] His conclusion is that for a people to do something as a memorial of X is for them to do it so as to remind someone of X (bringing it to their attention in that way). It may be to God's attention that the people wish to bring something; then the context of the memorial action proper, often expressed in words, will be that of blessing (thanking, praising) God for his covenant fidelity, of which the memorialized event or person is an indication; and of interceding with God for his continued blessing in the future. If, on the contrary, it is the people that are to be reminded of X, then the memorial action will be done in the context of a renewed commitment to obedience, and the confidence or hope that the memorial action will effect God's blessing anew. Thurian was inclined to think that though some memorials were oriented more toward God and some, more toward the people, always there were traces of both orientations. Thus for the people to do something as a memorial of X was for them to do it so as to remind God of X in the context of praising him for his covenant fidelity and interceding for its continuation, and so as to remind themselves of X in the context of pledging fidelity to the covenant obligations and to effectuate God's blessing anew.

Fascinating and provocative though Thurian's discussion is, I do not find the underlying assumption plausible, that there is a peculiarly Hebraic (or Semitic) concept of a memorial. With the proviso, perhaps, that a sharper differentiation ought to be made between the memorials oriented toward God and those oriented toward the people, Thurian does, it seems to me, succeed in eliciting many of the features peculiar to those memorials mentioned in the Bible. But it scarcely follows from this that those features belong to the very *concept* of a memorial—that something would not be a memorial unless it showed those features. We must distinguish between the claim that there is a peculiar biblical/Hebraic concept of a memorial, and the claim that a general concept of memorial is applied in the Hebrew Scriptures to memorials which have characteristics not generally found in memorials. The linkage of memorials to remembering, and the fact that there seems little if any difference between the concept used in the Bible and called *remembering* in English translations, and the concept called *remembering* in ordinary English,[13] leads me to think that a memorial (zikkaron, anamnesis) is just a commemorative object, and that doing something as a memorial is simply doing it as a commemoration. Our modern western mentality shares with that of the ancient Hebrews the concept of *a memorial*. For we have the concept of *commemoration*: and this, I suggest, is the same concept.

All sorts of things are done in commemoration, and all sorts of things are produced as commemorations: coins are struck, stamps are issued, fireworks are shot off, speeches are given, plays are performed, dances are danced, trees are planted, academic conferences are held, portraits are painted, processions are organized, cenotaphs are raised, mausoleums are constructed, cities are founded. We are, and want to be, remembering beings. In fact, though, we find ourselves to be forgetful beings; so we fill our lives with commemorations and commemorative objects. Or if we do not actually forget what we wish to remember, often we fail to bring it to mind. Evidentally something deep about us is revealed in the fact that we surround ourselves with commemorative objects and repeatedly engage in commemorative activities; something important would be lost if we ceased to do so. Commemoration pervades our way of life and pervades the environments within which we live our lives.

Nonetheless, I know of only one substantive philosophical discussion of commemoration, that in a recent book by Edward Casey titled *Remembering*.[14] There is a good deal of insight in Casey's discussion; yet its fundamental theses seem to me not quite correct. It will be instructive to consider those theses.

Casey packs his basic theory into a few sentences: "in acts of commemoration remembering is intensified by taking place *through* the interposed agency of a text (the eulogy, the liturgy proper) and *in* the setting of a social ritual (delivering the eulogy, participating in the service). The remembering is intensified still further by the fact that both ritual and text become efficacious only in the presence of others, *with* whom we commemorate together in a public ceremony. The 'through', 'in', and 'with' that I have underlined suggest that commemoration is a highly mediated affair—that it involves a quite significant component of otherness at every turn"(218). Sometimes Casey abbreviates all this by saying that commemorating is that species of remembering which is *remembering-through*. "I commemorate, in short, by *remembering through* specific commemorative vehicles such as rituals or texts" (218).

Notice, to begin, that Casey focuses his theory entirely on commemorative *acts*. That seems to me to introduce a distortion into the theory. We must also keep in mind commemorative *objects*. As one might expect, Casey himself in the course of his discussion gives examples of commemorative objects; this does not, however, lead him to take notice of the fact that his theory speaks only of acts. If commemorative objects had been kept in mind, it would seem less plausible to treat commemoration as a species of remembering.

The central issue to consider is the relation between commemorating and remembering. Casey says two things on this point. He says that commemorating *intensifies* remembering. And he says that commemorating is a *sort of* remembering. On the former account, the essence of commemorating lies in a certain *causal effect* on remembering; on the latter, commemorating is a *species* of remembering. These accounts, on the face of it, are at war with each other. One might try to bring them into harmony by saying that Casey regards commemoratings as those cases of remembering whose intensity has been increased in a social situation by such phenomena as texts and rituals. But the attempt fails; for even on Casey's theory, *that* species of remembering is not identical with an act of commemorating, but is something *induced by* commemorative acts using texts and rituals. Commemorating, on Casey's theory, is not really a species of remembering—though that is the position it occupies in the argument of his book as a whole.

Is it true, then, that commemorating's essential function is to intensify remembering—that this causal consequence is of its essence? (One might preserve the spirit of this suggestion while yet weakening it by saying that this is its *intended* function.) Well, suppose that a group of Luther scholars decides to assemble to commemorate, say, Luther's nailing of his theses to the door of the Wittenberg church. So far as I can see, this might result in no intensification at all of their remembering of the event. Being the specialists they are, a rather intense remembering of that event is part of their daily lives. Yet they commemorate it.

The truth of the matter seems to me close by, however. An act or object is commemorative only if done or made with a certain intent; and that intent is, in one way or another, to enhance dispositional or active memory. Commemorations are meant to produce the memory of something in someone, or intensify the memory, or keep the memory alive; or to bring the remembered entity actively before the mind for a while, etc. In turn, we do this for a reason, the reason often being what is most prominent in the situation. Ordinary remembering works without a reason; it is just one of the functions of the mind. Especially prominent among our reasons for intending to induce or sustain or intensify dispositional memory, or to bring some memory actively before the mind, is the desire to praise or honor: We issue a coin to commemorate the emperor so as to honor the emperor. I am inclined to think, indeed, that if we look closely enough at commemorations we will always discern some element of honoring.[15] Honoring is not always what is most prominent, however. The Byzantines for generations commemorated the fall of Constantinople. The dominant mood was lament; but in their lament over the fall of the great city, were they not also honoring the city fallen? Nations commemorate wounds inflicted upon them so as to keep outrage alive, that justice may eventually be secured; but in doing so, do they not also honor the memory of those who fell and speak words in praise of the nation injured?

The thing commemorated must be something remembered from the past. Remembering, in some form or other, is a condition of commemoration. We must tread carefully here, however. For a group to commemorate something, there must be members of the group who remember the things being commemorated. But clearly not every member of the group need remember for the group to commemorate. Though there must be someone who can answer the question, "What mean these things?" not everyone need be able to answer this question. For some members of the group the commemoration may bring about that now they know and remember, whereas before they did not.

And what if the thing or event commemorated never existed, so that it cannot be remembered? Then that thing or event is not commemorated. The group may think it is commemorating that; but it is not.

I have been speaking about *group* commemoration. Casey defends the thesis that sociality is essential to commemoration. But that too seems to me not correct: typical, perhaps, but not essential. I see nothing at all impossible in our engaging in private commemorative acts: daily lighting a candle, perhaps, to commemorate a deceased spouse. What is true, I think, is that in commemorating there is always a *potential* for social participation. Though commemoration may be private, it cannot be purely mental. Commemorative acts are bodily acts; commemorative objects are perceptible objects. Thus privacy, though entirely possible, is accidental. You, visiting me, and noticing and understanding my hitherto private commemoration, may light a candle along with me.

What, then, about the other "mediating factors" that Casey stresses, *viz.*, text and ritual? It is the presence of text and ritual in commemorations that leads Casey to speak of commemorating as "remembering-through." So far as I can tell, what leads him to speak thus is the *representational* character of texts and rituals. The texts used in commemorative activities are *about* the commemorandum; and Casey speaks of ritual as always incorporating "an allusion, however indirect, to a pre-existing event or person" (222). I surmise that it is this representational function of commemorative acts and objects that leads Casey to speak of them as *embodying* the commemorandum. Mere reminders do not embody the commemorandum, he says; and on the other hand, when I recollect something in my mind "it presents itself to me limpidly, as if through a transparent glass" (219). Commemorations are intermediate between reminders and recollections. In commemorations "I remember the commemorated past through various commemoratively effective media in the present. It is as if this past were presenting itself to me translucently in such media—as if I were viewing the past in them, albeit darkly: as somehow set within their materiality"

(219). I suggest that what Casey has his eye on here is just the fact that texts and rituals, as he understands rituals, are non-mental phenomena that represent past objects and events.

But is it true that commemorating requires texts and rituals? Here of course we are not asking whether the meaning of a commemoration can only be transmitted by a verbal account. We are asking whether texts are required—or more generally, words—*in* the commemorative act. I think the answer is no. A commemorative act may incorporate neither words nor rituals; and a commemorative object need not be a text. A commemorative coin, for example, may have an image of the emperor and nothing more. Yet this response is an evasion of what I suspect is the point Casey really wishes to make. Though he often says that commemorations require texts and rituals, he now and then tucks in a qualifier—"or any other available *commemorabilia*" (218). Casey's real point, I think, is that to perform commemorations we must find some sort of act or object which *represents* the commemorandum. These acts or objects function as the translucent (not transparent) media which embody the commemorandum, enabling us to remember it through them.

But even this seems to me not correct; typical, perhaps, but not essential. A commemorative object may or may not, apart from its being commemorative object, itself stand for something; so too, a commemorative action. If we plant a tree to commemorate a classmate who has died, the tree, apart from being caught up in this commemoration, does not represent anything at all. It is just a tree bought from a nursery.

What is true, though, is that to do something in commemoration of a certain event is to bring it about that the action signifies, or stands in for, that event; and what is true is that to produce something as a commemoration of some entity is to bring it about that the object signifies, or stands in for, that entity. Commemorating something with something is a way of bringing it about that the one thing signifies the other. It may or may not be the case that, *apart* from this activity, the former signified the latter. Commemoration, I suggest, is *productive* of signification.

Having one thing stand for (stand in for, signify) another is as deep as anything in human life, so deep that no one, to the best of my knowledge, has succeeded in giving an illuminating explication of it. And though the concept of signifying, or standing for, or standing in for, something is far from satisfying the Cartesian demands for clarity and distinctness, we cannot do without it. Often, wanting to perform some activity on something, we find that it is impossible or undesirable to perform it on that entity directly. So we have something stand in for that thing. We want to get people to think about some entity, or remember it; so we use a word or picture or symbol or gesture to stand in for that thing. The commemorative coin, *by virtue of* being a commemorative coin, points beyond itself to the emperor—signifies him, stands for him, stands in for him; and it need contain neither an image nor name of him to do so. The names of great composers lining the balcony of the concert hall stand in for those composers, serving to remind us of them.

It is just as difficult to give an informative general account of what *brings it about* that something stands in for something else as it is to give an account of that concept itself. Always it is the consequence of the activities or intentions of persons. But no one, to the best of my knowledge, has succeeded in saying *which sort* of activities or intentions. Here we must content ourselves with stressing that one's general account must take account of the fact that one way to bring it about that one thing stands in for another is to do it or make it in commemoration of the other.

An important corollary is that that which is done in commemoration could usually also have been done without being done in commemoration, and that that which is produced as a commemorative object could usually also have been produced without being produced as that. Instead of holding the conference in commemoration of Luther's beginning of the Reformation, academics can just hold a conference on Luther; instead of planting the tree in commemoration of a classmate who died, the school children can just plant a tree in front of the school.

Up to this point, I have been using Casey's account of commemoration as a foil for developing my own account. Let me conclude with two additional points. What is commemorated is never *simply* commemorated, but is always commemorated *as so-and-so*. One way of putting this is to say that commemorative activities always have propositional content; more specifically, they always have doxastic content. If the assembly honors George Washington as so-and-so, it believes he was that. Often what the commemorandum is commemorated *as*, in a commemorative act, is made explicit in writings, testimonial speeches, etc., which are comprised within the commemoration: "We are assembled here to commemorate George Washington as. . . . " Other times, it will remain implicit in the background.

It follows that one group may commemorate a person or event as one thing, and another as quite a different thing. There may even be such distance between these that, though the commemorandum is the same, participants find it impossible, with integrity, to participate in a common commemoration. Members of the Reformed churches may commemorate the St. Bartholomew's Night Massacre as the greatest mass martyrdom of the Reformed tradition; members of the Catholic church may commemorate it as one of the greatest victories over heresy. It is not likely that they will share their commemorations. Blacks in South Africa may commemorate the Sharpesville Massacre as the epitome of innocent black suffering; Afrikaners may commemorate it as one of the glowing episodes in the attempt to stave off anarchy. They will do their commemorating separately. The division among us Christians over the Eucharist is a paradigmatic illustration of this point. Of course it is also true that some rituals done as commemorations manage to tolerate a rather wide diversity of understandings. This becomes especially clear when the *history* of the ritual is surveyed. The ritual gets established as a social practice; and it continues on its way amid many disputes over interpretation. Continuity is threatened, however, when one party succeeds in getting its interpretation expressed by words *within* the commemoration, rather than being content to let it remain in the background.

Secondly, there will always be some propriety, or purported propriety, in using that object or action to commemorate that commemorandum. What one does or makes to commemorate a certain thing is not a matter of arbitrary decision. Given the desire to commemorate some particular thing, we can rationally decide between better and worse, appropriate and inappropriate. If the aim is that Israel shall commemorate its release from the bondage of slavery in Egypt, there is an obvious propriety in that being done by freeing one's slaves every seventh year. Perhaps there are other candidates for ways of doing it which are equally appropriate. But this will do. And of course, beyond propriety of specific commemorabilia to specific commemoranda, the act or object must always genuinely *honor*. Some actions which exhibit the requisite propriety may not have the goodness and nobility required for honoring.

For none of us is the past a flat uniform array of what is over. There, in the past, are things we wish to commemorate. Commemoration is different from keeping in mind in a certain way. Commemorating requires doing something with one's body or making something with one's hands. Commemorating expands from one's way of thinking to enter one's way of living. Sometimes we find that others want to commemorate the same thing we do, and to commemorate it *as* that which we want to commemorate it *as*. So we join in a solidarity of commemorating. Typically our shared commemorating intensifies the solidarity and expands its scope. Our joint commemorating expresses, and intensifies and expands, community. And our commemorating helps to protect, against the acids of forgetfulness, what is worthy of honor and praise and lament and outrage. As we contemplate our future with each other, we see change and fickleness; to compensate, we covenant with each other. Covenants introduce a stability into the future which otherwise would not be there. So, in a similar way, commemorations introduce stability into what we carry forward from the past. Though what is commemorated recedes ever farther into the past, our commemorations keep its honored memory alive in the present. Covenants, looking ahead, introduce stability into a sea of fickleness; commemorations, looking back, introduce endurance into a sea of forgetfulness.

Given the importance, in the Jewish and Christian communities, of remembering the acts of God in history and the prophets and teachers and saints by way of whom God acted, one can expect that commemorative objects and actions will occupy an important place in the lives of these communities. Or when they do not, one can surmise that remembering has fallen away in favor of immediately experiential, or abstractly theological or ethical, approaches to God. The cross is a commemorative symbol; so too is the cock atop the Reformed churches throughout Europe: it is a memorial symbol of the Resurrection. Perhaps also many paintings of biblical episodes are to be thought of as commemorative objects. Once one begins to reflect on it, one sees that Christian lives are *filled with* commemorations of events and persons from the biblical story and the story of the church. More specifically, very much in the Christian liturgy is done in memorial; very many of the objects in the liturgical environment are commemorative objects. As we have seen, the Scriptures themselves say that Christ's followers should eat a meal as a commemoration, a memorial, of him. And down through the ages, prominent in the reasons for doing so has been thanksgiving, *eucharistia*.

In a very important way, however, that does not yet tell us much about the structure of the Eucharist. For as we have seen, the actions which can be done in memorial, and the objects which can be produced in commemoration, are tremendously diverse. Trees can be planted, coins with the image of the emperor minted, etc. What then *are* these actions of the Eucharist which are done as, or should be done as, a commemoration of Christ? By no means is the Eucharist the only important component of the liturgy; nor does understanding the Eucharist enable us automatically to understand everything else therein. But if we can understand this, we will at least have understood something central in the Christian liturgy.

At Passover, bitter herbs are placed on plates, Israel's exodus from Egypt is narrated, blessings are pronounced over unleavened bread and wine, and food is eaten. At the Eucharist, bread and wine are brought forward, praise to God is offered, episodes from Christ's last supper are recounted, words of blessing are spoken over the bread and wine, and the presider distributes the bread after breaking it and distributes the wine after pouring it, for the people to eat and drink. With an eye on such phenomena as these, the proposal has often been made that in the Passover and in the Eucharist, and perhaps in other parts of the Christian liturgy as well, we find *dramatic representations* of certain elements of the story owned by the community—that here the story is presented in the mode of dramatic representation rather than in the mode of narration (recital). One finds this theory expounded, for example, by Sigmund Mowinckel in his book, *Religion and Cult*.[16]

Mowinckel's interpretation of the cults of Judaism and Christianity is an application of his general interpretation of cult. "Cult has ... always a more or less clear dramatic stamp. It is a cultic drama. This can have a more or less realistic or symbolic form. In cult, that which happens is presented visibly through dramatic rites and symbols" (99). Thus where Eliade saw actualization of the myths, Mowinckel sees dramatic representations of the myths—an interpretation of the archaic mentality which, on the face of it, is much more plausible. Mowinckel goes on to remark that "It is not by accident that both the Greek drama and Christian mystery plays of the Middle Ages grew directly out of worship." And then he adds, strikingly, "Especially in many of the Christmas and Easter hymns, the eternal 'today' stands out clearly. '*Today* a saviour is born to us', or 'three women went *this morning* out, they came back with gladsome tide' "(105). Mowinckel does not elaborate his thought here. But presumably he has noticed that the basic tense of drama is the present tense. If the heart of the liturgy consists of dramatic representation of the Christian story, what more natural than to cast the accompanying hymns in the present tense, for good measure adding such indexicals as "today" or "this morning."

Let us get before us as clearly as we can what this theory of liturgy as dramatic representation amounts to. At the core of dramatic representation is role-playing: a world is projected by way of actors playing the role of the *dramatis personnae* and by way of objects playing the role of objects in the world of the work. Sometimes an action of one of the characters or persons in the world of the work is indicated by way of the actor *pretending* to perform that action: To represent a killing, actors typically pretend to kill; and to represent the making of an assertion, they typically pretend to make that assertion. To represent the utterance of a sentence, however, they actually utter that sentence, and to represent walking from chair to table, they actually walk from chair to table.

In appraising the dramatic-representation theory of the Christian liturgy, what strikes one at once, is that, if this is drama, it is drama of a very low grade: thin and inept. If one asked children to dramatize the story, as narrated in the gospels, of the Nativity, or the Last Supper, or the Crucifixion, or the Resurrection, they would do much better than this. Indeed, in children's programs put on by church schools they do in fact do much better than this. Better yet, Oberammergau! But of course this is not a decisive objection to the dramatic-representation theory. The theory does not claim that liturgy, *qua* dramatic representation, is very good. Indeed, someone might cite its ineptness, as compared to what children would do, as one more piece of evidence for the thesis that as children grow up, their inhibitions increase and their creativity shrinks.

So suppose we look more closely. We then discover that the language is all wrong for dramatic role-playing, even in that part of the liturgy which is the Eucharist. On the dramatic-representation theory, the celebrant at the Eucharist is presumably playing the role of Christ, or of God. Who we, the people, might be playing is not so clear. Usually there are too many of us, or too few, for us to be playing the role of the twelve disciples. And who of us wants to play Judas? But let us skip past these difficulties to scrutinize the words given to the celebrant in what, on this theory, is the script. It really does not make any difference which Eucharistic liturgy we look at, so let us pick, more or less arbitrarily, the first of the several options for the canon prayer in the post-Vatican II Catholic liturgy. It begins like this: "We come to you, Father, with praise and thanksgiving through Jesus Christ your Son." Obviously this will not do at all for someone playing the role of God the Father, nor for someone playing the role of Christ the Son. Neither will the words of the epiclesis serve: "Bless and approve our offering; make it acceptable to you, an offering in spirit and in truth. Let it become for us the body and blood of Jesus Christ, your only Son, our Lord." But may it be that, within the Institution, the minister finally glides into role-playing? The first paragraph of the Institution goes like this: "The day before he suffered he took bread in his sacred hands and looking up to heaven, to you, his almighty Father, he gave you thanks and praise. He broke the bread, gave it to his disciples, and said: "Take this, all of you, and eat it: this is my body which will be given up for you." Could it be that the celebrant, right after he says the words, "and said," starts play-ing the role of Christ? It is certainly not very plausible to think so. The obvious interpretation is that he is there, within his prayer, quoting what Christ said. To quote what someone said is not to play the role of his saying it.

I submit that there is no point at all in the Eucharistic lit-urgy where it is plausible to regard the participants as engaged in the dramatic representation of Christ's last supper, that Pass-over meal, with his disciples. Though the dramatic-representation theory is perhaps plausible as an account of archaic rituals, its considerable popularity as a theory of Christian liturgy requires not looking closely at what actually goes on in the liturgy.

Apart from its implausibility upon close scrutiny of the lit-urgy, I submit that the theory feels all wrong. The celebrant ac-tually blesses; he does not play the role of Christ blessing. We actually give thanks; we do not play the role of the disciples giv-ing thanks. What matters is that the celebrant actually gives us bread and wine, not that he plays the role of Christ long ago giving bread and wine to his disciples. What matters is that we actually eat the bread and drink the wine, not that we play the role of the disciples long ago eating the bread and drinking the wine distributed to them by Christ. The dramatic representation theory displaces the focus from the *actuality* of what is presently taking place.

The interpretation of the Eucharist which we have just been scrutinizing might be called a *signification* interpretation, in contrast to the *reality* interpretations which Eliade proposed for archaic rituals. There is another signification interpretation which, though it has never been accepted by the mainline think-ers of the church and has fallen almost entirely from view in our century, is yet of great theoretical interest, and has often enjoyed popular support. This, the so-called "allegorical interpretation," does not fall prey to the objections I have lodged against the dramatic-representation theory, except no doubt for the last.

Adumbrations of this line of interpretation are to be found in various of the church fathers; but it was first formulated with verve, imagination, and thoroughness by a student of Alcuin, Amalar, in his book *De ecclesiasticis officiis*, published in 823 or shortly before, and revised and supplemented in 831. To give a feel for this mode of interpretation, let me quote J. A. Jung-mann's summary of just a bit of the whole:

> The deacons who stand behind the celebrant are a type of the Apostles who hid themselves in fear. The subdeacons who stand opposite the celebrant on the other side of the open altar are types of the holy women who remained standing near the Cross. The prayer after the consecration signifies the Passion of our Lord on the Cross. When the priest bows down (at the *Supplices*), our Lord bows His head and dies. The slight lifting of the voice at *Nobis quoque* refers to the centurion's loud profession at the death of Jesus. The deacons at this point straighten up and begin to busy themselves with the Body of the Lord, to signify the stead-fast courage which seized the women and their work at the grave. At the concluding doxology the celebrant and the deacon elevate the Host and the Chalice and then set them down again, to signify Nicodemus' and Joseph of Arimathea's taking down our Lord's corpse from the Cross.[17]

And so forth. As it happens, Jungmann's summary concentrates on what Amalar says about the Eucharist proper. In fact Amalar had an interpretation for the entire liturgy. The introit signifies the prophets who announced the advent of Christ; the Epistle alludes to the preaching of John; the responsory, to the readiness of the Apostles when our Lord called them and they followed; and so forth.

Whether such an interpretation should be called allegorical is a good question. Certainly the liturgy on this interpretation is not a standard sort of allegory. The structure of an allegory such as *Pilgrim's Progress* is a two-world structure, the one world projected by way of the projection of the other.[18] By way of the words of the text of Bunyan's classic, a world is projected which is set in England and consists of episodes in the journey of a traveller; in turn, by way of Bunyan's projecting this world an-other world is projected which concerns the spiritual progress of the soul. The first world is projected in the fictive mode; the second, in the assertive mode. But that is not at all how the lit-urgy, on Amalar's interpretation, works. Only one world is pro-jected, a world consisting of episodes in the life of Christ.

But if the liturgy, on this interpretation, is neither an alle-gory of the two-world sort just explained nor a dramatic representation, what is it? For the most part, ritual movements and gestures are the items which function as standing for something in Amalar's interpretation; only at a few points do the words of the liturgy play a role in his account, and then their content is relevant in only a most general way. The gestures stand for things in the manner of *symbols*; and it is the *sequence of symbols* which serves to project the world of Christ's life. Thus Amalar develops what might best be called a *symbol-sequence* interpretation of the liturgy.

Let me explain briefly what I have in mind by "symbol"—examples of the sorts of things I have in mind being the cross as a symbol of the Crucifixion, the cock atop a church as a symbol of the Resurrection, the circle as a symbol of eternity, the peach blossom as a symbol of happiness, etc. I shall single out three fundamental features of symbols. Of course I assume that for X to be a symbol of Y, X must stand in for Y. My aim is to specify some of the conditions which must be satisfied if S is not only to stand in for Y, but is to be a *symbol* of Y.

(1) By way of sentences, pictures, and dramatic representations, we project *worlds*—i.e., more or less complex states of affairs. These worlds may or may not be stories. A symbol, by contrast, does not stand in for a state of affairs. The circle symbolizes eternity, not something's being so-and-so, nor something's doing so-and-so.

(2) Secondly, symbols are, to borrow a term from Goodman, relatively nonreplete. In that way they are like sentences and diagrams, and unlike pictures and dramatic representations. Let me quote Goodman on the matter:

> The difference between representations and diagrams is syntactic: The constitutive aspects of the diagrammatic as compared with the pictorial character are expressly and narrowly restricted. The only relevant features of the diagram are the ordinate and abscissa of each of the points the center of the line passes through. The thickness of the line, its color, and intensity, the absolute size of the diagram, etc., do not matter; whether a purported duplicate of the symbol belongs to the same character of the diagrammatic scheme depends not at all upon such features. For the sketch this is not true. Any thickening or thinning of the line, its

color, its contrast with the background, its size, even the qualities of the paper—none of these is ruled out, none can be ignored.[19]

Among the roosters atop churches which are used to symbolize the Resurrection there can be enormous variation. It makes no difference; they are all tokens of the same symbol, and on that account symbolize the same thing, the Resurrection. Of course what we actually have in this case is *double* signification. The things found atop churches are not flesh-and-blood roosters but three-dimensional depictions of roosters—rooster sculptures. And differences in the sculptures do signify differences in the roosters depicted. But, all of them being instances of the same symbolic character, they do not signify differences in what is symbolized. They all just symbolize the Resurrection; more specifically, they are *memorial* symbols of the Resurrection. So too, differences in the circles used to symbolize eternity are of no significance to what is symbolized, nor are differences in the swatches of purple used for advent and in the swatches of white used to symbolize purity.

One of the enormous gains for artists, in this relative non-repleteness of symbols, is that they can let their imaginations roam with respect to how they shall make the symbol, without any change occurring in what is symbolized.

(3) The assignment of symbols to symbolized is not arbitrary. Always there is some sort of fittingness or similarity between symbol and symbolized—call it the *basis* of the symbolizing relationship.[20] Of course such fittingness or similarity is not sufficient for one thing to symbolize another; it is merely necessary. It is on account of fittingness that the cock can (memorially) symbolize the Resurrection, as it is on account of fittingness that purple can be used during Lent. Shocking pink or turquoise would not do as colors for Lent; nor would a snail do as a symbol for the Resurrection.

It is, in part, because of their underlying fittingness or similarity that we often find symbols so delightful. Our imagination is stimulated by trying to discern the basis of the symbolic relation; when we do discern it, we notice connections in reality that we had not noticed before. And sometimes we are led to see either the thing symbolized or the thing which is the symbol in a new light. The names of composers marching around the interiors of concert halls is a dull business compared to the delight and instructiveness of symbols.

It may be noted that whereas many symbols stand in for abstract entities such as eternity, happiness, and purity, others stand in for concrete entities. And of the concrete entities symbolized, some are events, persons, etc., from the past. Symbols standing in for events and persons from the past will, for obvious reasons, be central in memorials (commemorations).

Let us now return to Amalar. The *introit*, says Amalar, signifies the choir of the prophets; the deacons standing behind the celebrant symbolize the apostles hiding in fear; the slight lifting of the voice at *Nobis quoque* symbolizes the centurion's loud profession at the death of Jesus, etc. Clearly on Amalar's interpretation these are all symbols, as I have explained those; and most, though not quite all, of the symbols Amalar spies symbolize events or persons from the biblical story. The individual symbols do not signify states of affairs; yet the total sequence of symbols must, I think, be seen as projecting a world, a story—a story which includes very much of the biblical story.

Jungmann is right when he says that in Amalar's writings "there is revealed a fancy that is without doubt remarkably perceptive."[21] But of course fancy does not a symbol make. The similarities and fittingnesses that Amalar notices are there to notice; but I see no reason to depart from the mainline tradition of the church, which insists that these similarities do not in fact ground symbols. (Which, of course, does not mean that the liturgy, along with its environment and instruments, contains no symbols.)

Where does that leave us? We have discarded two signification interpretations of the Eucharist, and of the liturgy in general: the dramatic-representation theory and the symbol-sequence theory. Yet are we not compelled to hold some sort of signification theory? Those actions that the celebrant performs, of taking bread and wine, giving thanks over them, breaking the bread and pouring wine, and distributing them—surely his performance of these is somehow related to Christ's acts of the same sort! These are not just acts on their own, part of an ordinary, albeit sparse, meal.

I think the correct answer is that the celebrant *imitates* the acts of Christ at that last supper, and by imitating those, *repeats* such act-types as taking bread, blessing wine, etc. Similarly we the people *imitate* the acts of the disciples at the last supper; and by imitating, *repeat* such act-types as eating bread, drinking wine, and giving thanks. The celebrant, in doing what he does, takes Christ's acts as paradigms; we, in doing what we do, take the disciples' acts as paradigms. But to imitate what someone does is not, so far forth, to play the role of that person doing that; it is, in fact, not necessary that one have signified it in any way whatsoever. Liking how you comb your hair, I may imitate it and comb mine in the same way. That does not make my combing of my hair *signify* your combing of your hair. My combing does not in any way stand in for your combing.

For the central actions of the Eucharist I propose, then, a reality interpretation rather than a signification interpretation. More specifically, it is an imitation-repetition interpretation that I propose. Thus we return to the account Eliade introduced to interpret the archaic liturgy. Earlier I pointed out that not all the acts of God to be found in the Christian story are imitated, and thereby the relevant act-types repeated, in the liturgy. Indeed with respect to most of those acts, we in the liturgy confine ourselves to reading narrations of them—and then commenting on those and responding worshipfully. But here at this central point we go beyond that to imitate and repeat what Christ and his disciples did at that last supper—imitating those specific acts in certain respects and thereby repeating certain of those act-types.

Yet this does not mean that signification, standing in for, has entirely disappeared at this central point. Remember that one can buy an ordinary tree from a nursery and plant it as a memorial of a deceased classmate. In such a case, though the thing which is the commemorative object was not itself functioning as a symbol, its being planted in commemoration has made it function like that. So too in the Eucharist. These straightforward actions of taking bread and wine, blessing them, breaking the bread and pouring the wine, distributing them, eating and drinking them, giving thanks, are caught up into a doing in memorial, into a doing in commemoration. If we take seriously what St. Paul says, however, it is not the Last Supper of Christ that we commemorate but Christ himself. "Do this as a memorial of me" he reports Christ as having said. We imitate certain of the acts of Christ's Last Supper, combine them with prayers and declarations of various sorts, and make them all together into a commemoration of Christ. Thereby it is *him* that the totality signifies, while actions within the totality imitate *Last Supper actions*. And by doing this, says Paul, we proclaim Christ's death until he comes; that is its function, or at least one of its functions. The theory I propose, then, is a blend of a reality interpretation and a signification interpretation.

It may be added that the actions of repetition at the center of the Eucharist, along with certain other actions in the liturgy, are characteristically *ritualized*—more so in the Catholic and Orthodox traditions, less so in, say, the Baptist tradition. Let me explain. To compose a work of music is to lay down a specific set of criteria for correctness and completeness in the production of musical sounds. In a wholly similar way, someone can lay down a specific set of criteria for correctness and completeness in the performance of bodily movements. Thereby a work would be composed. In some cases, the work composed would naturally be called a *dance*; in others, a *ritual*—with no sharp line between them.[22] Dance and ritual are ontological siblings. Alternatively, instead of a set of criteria for correctness and completeness of a sequence of bodily movements being laid down by an individual, they may slowly emerge in a society. Instead of being composed, they may arise—just as there is not only composed music but folk music. I think that the celebration of the Christian liturgy, and more specifically, of the Eucharist, will always be the performance of a ritual; always there will be *some* criteria of correctness and completeness of bodily movement and gesture which are in effect. The actions of the liturgy will be ritualized. But in some traditions the ritual is elaborate; in others sparse and spare. The actions are more ritualized in the former, less so in the latter.

This can still not be the whole of the matter. In every Eucharistic liturgy of which I am aware the people, shortly after the communicating has taken place, express their thanks. It is not the celebrant they thank, however, even though it is he who has given them the bread and wine; it is God they thank. In the old Reformed liturgy this was always done by reciting the opening five verses of Psalm 103, beginning like this:

> Bless the Lord, O my soul,
>   and all that is within me,
>   bless his holy name!

Not only is it obviously God who is being thanked with this recitation; God is being thanked for what he has done here and now, not for what he has done in some distant historical past. Thus the assumption is that God himself acts by way of the liturgy, that he is one of the liturgical agents, that the commemoration of Christ is efficacious of God's blessing. To participate in the liturgy is to enter the sphere of God's action—not just the sphere of God's presence but the sphere of God's action, and not just God's past action but God's present action. And God acts, in good measure, by way of *our* acting. By way of our commemorating God's prior actions, God now acts.[23] The one whom we commemorate is active by way of our commemoration.

What exactly God does by way of our liturgical actions, and then, more specifically, by way of our imitative/commemorative actions in the Eucharist, has been and remains much disputed. The topic, so it seems to me, belongs to the theologians and not to philosophers. Here let me just call attention to one view on the matter which flows directly out of some of the positions discussed earlier.

Over and over in our century it has been said that the saving events of God which are commemorated in the liturgy are *made present*, or *actualized*, by way of the performance of the liturgy. The acts of God commemorated are not just acknowledged as having present significance; in some way the commemoration makes them actually present. One finds this position espoused, for example, in the comments of Mowinckel and Childs on the liturgy of biblical Israel. Here is what Childs says in one place: "When Israel observes the Sabbath in order to remember the events of her redemption, she is participating again in the Exodus event. Memory functions as an actualization (Vergegenwärtigung) of the decisive event in her tradition" (53).

Perhaps the most famous exponent of the position, however, was the Roman Catholic liturgical theologian, Dom Odo

Casel, who argued for what he called a "mystery" conception of the liturgy. In espousing this conception, Casel very consciously saw himself as applying to Christian liturgy a model derived from the study of pagan rituals—especially pagan mystery rituals. He says that "for the ancients. . . . the play is a sacred thing. Men carry out its actions in a way all can see; but the real actors are the gods who dwell at the feast. They are the ones through whom men fulfill the action which they do. For this reason what the play represents is made real in the deepest fashion."[24]

Casel then applies the mystery model to the Christian liturgy in the following way:

> When the church on Septuagesima Sunday begins her reading of the book of Genesis, she brings the primaeval fact to life: creation, the Fall and all the rest. . . . With the reading of the Scripture we return to the first age; we place ourselves into the primaeval act which is made present.(124)
>
> Still more strongly do we perceive the power of the primaeval saving act made present, in the Eucharist; by the transformation and the consumption of the bread and wine man is filled with the power of Christ. He returns to that primaeval force with which God gave life to the world in the death and resurrection of Christ. Man's action in the rite is made one with God's action.(125)
>
> In the view of some theologians Christ placed the grace which he had earned by his sacrifice in the sacraments; when the sacrament is performed those who perform it receive the grace it contains. The sacrament is the cause of grace. In the mystery conception it is the primaeval saving act which is made present. . . . The myth is lived out in worship; the rite is living myth.(124–125)
>
> All these examples show that the myth is no mere tale; rather it is a reality which is lived.(125)
>
> Worship is the means which brings back the Origin; in it the new Beginning is made present for the Christian. What he experiences in his worship is not only an after-effect of the saving act; the saving act itself takes on presence.(128)
>
> The mystery is no mere recalling of Christ and his saving deed; it is a memorial in worship. The church does what the Lord did, and thereby makes his act present.(141)

I think it is clear that these words, if taken literally, are not true. Whatever God does by way of the liturgy, God does not bring it about that the resurrection of Christ occurs when the liturgy is performed. There is clear evidence that those who espouse the 'commemorated-acts-made-present' view realize this; every now and then they offer paraphrases of what they have been saying. Unfortunately the paraphrases are so bewilderingly diverse, even within a single writer, that it would not be profitable to carry the matter further. Childs indicates in one passage (84–85) that what he means is that God now speaks to us the same imperative which he spoke to the contemporaries of the event which we commemorate. That strikes me, at least, as an unwarrantedly narrow view of what God does in the liturgy; God does much more than speak imperatively. But in any case, others who speak along these lines offer quite different paraphrases.

As to *how* God acts by way of our participation in the liturgy, that is a rich field waiting for exploration by philosophers. I am myself inclined toward a combination of a proxy view and an occasionalist view. In the liturgy God *speaks* by way of someone serving as his proxy—speaking on his behalf. And in the liturgy God *acts causally* by way of making something happen on the occasion of someone in the liturgy doing a certain thing. But here is not the place to explore further this beckoning terrain. To do so would be to open up for philosophical discussion the sacramental dimension of liturgy. The Christian liturgy has many dimensions, not just one: the sacramental, the commemorative, the dedicatory, etc. In this essay I have set as my project to do no more than open up the commemorative dimension.

IV

Why do Christians find it so important to remember and commemorate? Why not just live out one's life alert to the contemporary and open to the future? In his fascinating book, *Pagans and Christians*, Robin Lane Fox has a long discussion about the multitude of theophanies claimed by people of the Roman empire in late antiquity. Much of the evidence for these theophanies is taken from inscriptions on commemorative stones. Yet the memory of those theophanies has not been kept alive—nor did anyone at the time think it important to keep them alive for long. With Christianity and Judaism—and Islam as well—things are obviously different. Why is that?

The answer, surely, is that the theophanies and other acts of God held in memory by Christians not only *were* relevant to those to whom God spoke or appeared, but *are* relevant to us and to all humanity. Though their direct recipients then were few, their import abides and is universal. When Apollo spoke to those visiting his shrine in Claros, he usually rendered advice relevant to only a few persons, and that for a limited time. It is the Christian confession that the death and resurrection of the man from Nazareth are relevant to all at all times. They changed the standing of humanity down through the ages before God. That which we commemorate inaugurated the reality in which we now live.

What more natural, then, than to cast our hymns into the present tense? What happened then and there is as relevant to us as it was to them. We are all contemporaries. The Haggadah declares, "Not only our forefathers did the Holy One, Blessed be He, redeem, but also ourselves did He redeem with them." If one believes that, then naturally one will talk as if one walked through the Red Sea in flight from Pharaoh. For the same reason, Christians will talk as if they were present when our Lord was born in Bethlehem, as if they were there on Golgotha when our Lord was crucified, as if they were there at the tomb when the stone was rolled away. When we celebrate birthdays, we count off the years; "How old are you today?" we ask. One who turns forty does not naturally speak of himself then as born "to-day." But when we commemorate Easter, we do not count off the years. It might as well have happened this morning. "Becoming a Christian," said Kierkegaard, means "to become contemporary with Christ. . . . For in relation to the absolute there is only one tense: the present. For him who is not contemporary with the absolute—for him it has no existence. And as Christ is the absolute, it is easy to see that with respect to Him there is only one situation: that of contemporaneousness."[25]

V

Christian existence incorporates Christian belief and Christian ethical action, Christian experience and Christian ritual. In our century we who are Christian philosophers have thought especially about Christian belief and Christian ethics, somewhat about Christian experience. We have thought scarcely at all about Christian liturgy. To my mind that shows remnants of the mentality of the Enlightenment, remnants which we should try to eliminate. Someone might reply that it shows nothing of the sort; it shows simply that there is little of interest for philosophers in liturgy. If I have done nothing else in this essay, I hope I have made you suspect, if not actually believe, that that is false. It would be a pity if philosophers had nothing to say about this fundamental dimension of Christian existence. On the other hand, before some things, philosophers had best be silent.

NOTES

1. Mircea Eliade, *Myth and Reality* (New York: Harper and Row, 1963), 5–6. Subsequent references will be incorporated into the text as *MR*.

2. Mircea Eliade, *The Myth of the Eternal Return* (Princeton, N.J.: Princeton University Press, 1974), 4–5. Subsequent references will be incorporated into the text as *MER*.

3. Mircea Eliade, *The Sacred and the Profane* (New York: Harcourt Brace Jovanovich, 1959), 88. Subsequent references will be incorporated into the text as *SP*. Cf. *SP*, 105–106:

> The religious festival is the reactualization of a primordial event, of a sacred history in which the actors are the gods or semidivine beings. But sacred history is recounted in the myths. Hence, the participants in the festival become contemporaries of the gods and the semidivine beings. They live in the primordial time that is sanctified by the presence and activities of the gods. The sacred calendar periodically regenerates time, because it makes it coincide with the *time of origin*, the strong, pure time. The religious experience of the festival—that is, participation in the sacred—

enables man periodically to live in the presence of the gods . . . In so far as he imitates his gods, religious man lives in the *time of origin*, the time of the myths. In other words, he emerges from profane duration to recover an unmoving time, eternity.

4. And living the myth

implies a genuinely 'religious' experience, since it differs from the ordinary experience of everyday life. The 'religiousness' of this experience is due to the fact that one re-enacts fabulous, exalting, significant events, one again witnesses the creative deeds of the Supernaturals; one ceases to exist in the everyday world and enters a transfigured, auroral world impregnated with the Supernaturals' presence. What is involved is not a commemoration of mythical events but a reiteration of them. The protagonists of the myth are made present, one becomes their contemporary. This also implies that one is no longer living in chronological time, but in the primordial Time, the Time when the event *first took place*. This is why we can use the term the "strong time" of myth; it is the prodigious, "sacred" time when something *new, strong* and *significant* was manifested. To re-experience that time, to re-enact it as often as possible, to witness again the spectacle of the divine works, to meet with the Supernaturals and relearn their creative lesson is the desire that runs like a pattern through all the ritual reiterations of myths. (*MR* 19)

5. I think that a determined attempt to unravel the states of affairs true in historical time from those true in primordial time would reveal that in fact this view is not coherent; but I shall have to skip past those difficulties. I think that essentially the same incoherence turns up in the attempt to unravel time from eternity, in the western sense of "eternity." So the archaic person is not alone in his difficulties.

6. Cf. the passage from the ancient philosopher Synesius, cited by Robin Lane Fox in his *Pagans and Christians* (New York: Alfred A. Knopf, 1987), 149–150: "None of the laws of Necessity stops me being more successful than Icarus while I am asleep, from passing from earth to soar higher than an eagle, to reach the highest spheres . . . and thence, from afar, to look down on the earth, to discourse with the stars, to keep company with the gods, an impossibility in our world. For what is said to be 'hard', is then easy. 'The gods appear clearly'. They are not in the least jealous."

7. Eliade does, infrequently, use the language of symbolism. In one passage he speaks of "a symbolic return to the atemporal instant of

primordial plentitude" (*MER* 82). But infrequency of such language reflects the fact that it plays no role in Eliade's theory.

8. It would be relevant here, though space forbids it, to explore Levy-Bruhl's notion of participation: the archaic person does not see himself as becoming *identical* with some god or ancestor, but as *participating in* that being.

9. This is recognized by Eliade; see *MER*, 143.

10. It would be a mistake not to note that the Old Testament writers also speak of *God* as remembering, that they offer pleas to *God* to remember, and that they even say that various items in the world and various phenomena in the life of Israel function for God as memorials. Fundamentally these are all pleas and memorials that God remember his *covenant* with Israel. In Exodus it is said that the two stones of the ephod of the high priest, inscribed with the names of the twelve sons of Israel, are for remembrance before the Lord (Exodus 28:12), as are the twelve stones inscribed with the names of the sons of Israel on his breastpiece. In Numbers it is said that two silver trumpets shall be blown on feast days, over sacrifices, and before going to war, "for a memorial before your God," "that you may be remembered before the Lord your God:" (Numbers 10:1–10). Isaiah, in the context of the prospect of a renewed covenant, says that

> Instead of the thorn shall come up the cypress;
>> instead of the briar shall come up the myrtle;
> and it shall be to the Lord for a memorial,
>> for an everlasting sign which shall not be cut off.
>>>> (Isaiah 55:12)

And, to break off the list, in Genesis (9:12–17) it is said that after the Flood the rainbow is a reminder to God of his covenant.

Compare the following Jewish prayer for Passover: "Our God and God of our fathers, may there arise in your sight, and come, and be present, and be regarded, and be pleasing, and be heard, and be visited, and be remembered, our remembrance and our visitation, and the remembrance of our fathers, and the remembrance of the Messiah, the son of your servant David, and the remembrance of Jerusalem, the city of your holiness, and the remembrance of all your people, the house of Israel ... " (Quoted from Jasper and Cummings, *Prayers of the Eucharist* [New York: Pueblo, 1987], 11).

11. Brevard S. Childs, *Memory and Tradition in Israel* (London: SCM Press, 1962).

12. Max Thurian, *The Eucharistic Memorial*, 2 vols. (Richmond, Va.: John Knox Press, 1960).

13. Here I follow Childs, *Memory and Tradition*.

14. Edward S. Casey, *Remembering: A Phenomenological Study* (Bloomington, Ind.: Indiana University Press, 1987). References will be incorporated into the text.

15. Cf. Casey in an earlier essay, "Commemoration in the Eucharist" in *God: Experience or Origin*, ed. A. T. de Nicolas and E. Moutsopoulos (New York: Paragon House, 1985), 217: "Paying tribute is an important part of any memorialization."

16. Sigmund Mowinckel, *Religion and Cult*, trans. John F. X. Sheehan (Milwaukee, Wisc.: Marquette University Press, 1981). The theory is also accepted, without hesitation, by Israel Scheffler in "Ritual and Reference," *Synthese* 46 (March 1981): 421–431. It is also accepted by Gareth B. Matthews in "Comments on Israel Scheffler" in the same issue, pp. 439–444.

17. Joseph A. Jungmann, *The Mass of the Roman Rite*, 2 vols. (Westminster, Md.: Christian Classics, 1986), vol. 1, p. 90.

18. For a general theory of world-projection, see my *Works and Worlds of Art* (Oxford: Clarendon Press, 1980).

19. Nelson Goodman, *Languages of Art* (Indianapolis, Ind.: Bobbs-Merrill, 1968), 229.

20. As to what I mean by "fittingness," see part 3, chapter 2, section 2 of my *Art in Action* (Grand Rapids, Mich.: Eerdmans, 1980).

21. Jungmann, *The Mass of the Roman Rite*, 91.

22. Thus I do not agree with Casey that ritual must be representational. It may be purely abstract—just as dance may be purely abstract.

23. Cf. Mowinckel:

The essential thing about the cultic drama is that it does not merely portray for consideration or memory but rather that it is a *creative* drama. It is not a play for the education of the people, but something really happens in it. The drama which takes place is that God comes and meets mankind in its situation and with the display of his wondrous power in battle and victory creates a new situation for mankind. That which is created through this meeting is nothing less than all of the reality which the community or assembly needs in order to live. This includes the natural, historical and the spiritual realities among which, of course, the ancients did not distinguish. It is "life" in its fullest. Moreover, the spiritual "benefits of salvation" which more and more in the higher religions become the focal point, are present in it. It is all of existence in its fluctuating rhythms which is newly created in the cultic drama; it is the world. It is, therefore, the cultic drama which is an actual reliving and reexperiencing of whatever happened in the beginning. (*Religion and Cult*, 109)

In the cultic festival, it is the past which is reenacted and the future which is created. (*Religion and Cult*, 109)

Cf. Sigmund Mowinckel, *The Psalms in Israel's Worship* (Oxford: Basil Blackwell, 1962), 15–22.

24. Odo Casel, *The Mystery of Christian Worship* (Westminster, Md.: Newman Press, 1962), 159. Subsequent references will be incorporated into the text.

25. S. Kierkegaard, *Training in Christianity* (Princeton, N. J.: Princeton University Press, 1964), 67.

Love and Absolutes in Christian Ethics

J. L. A. Garcia

Christian Scripture enjoins us to love God and neighbors, offering as models numerous real and fictional exemplars of love. Oftentimes these figures are not merely *described* as loving, they *manifest* their love in action, especially in costly or self-sacrificial action. These actions are impressive in a variety of ways but especially important for my purpose here is that they are *morally* impressive. Indeed, in the eyes of a Christian, the connection between morality and love must be tight, for we are told that it is on love that the whole of the law depends, and "the law" here appears to include what people sometimes call 'the Moral Law'.

This indicates that morality, for a Christian, must be derivative from, and thus centered on, love. A philosophical conception of moral assessment should be acceptable to a Christian,[1] it would thus seem, only if it holds that any favorable (approbative) moral judgment on an action or type of action, or on a character trait or some instantiation of it, or on some type or particular instance of some psychological state or activity, or on some person, must be based on a judgment that the action or trait, etc., is rightly connected to love. We can go a bit further and say that in any approach to moral judgment properly acceptable to Christians—what I shall hereafter call 'a Christian ethics'—one of the central and most basic questions must be 'Is this action, trait, etc., *loving* in the appropriate and relevant way?' Doubtless an excessively simple approach to this question can lead to theoretical disaster in Christian ethics, as the example of Joseph Fletcher attests. Still, no view of morals that does not take as central being loving, and thus responding and acting lovingly, can be adequate for a Christian.

In this essay I attempt in the first two sections to sketch the broad outlines of a moral approach that, I think, meets this test and to show some of its advantages, and, in the third, fourth, and fifth sections, I try to show how it could be used to lend support to the claim, traditional within Christian ethics, that some familiar prohibitions on certain classes of actions admit of no exceptions. I conclude with some observations about the admissibility of moral dilemmas into a Christian ethics and its relevance for exceptionless norms.

I. Introduction

As I shall see it, a person's moral life comprises certain salient relationships or roles she stands in. To be morally good or bad is to be good or bad in such roles as friend, parent, offspring, spouse, neighbor (in the scriptural sense), confidante, informant, promiser, etc. Some of these roles are quite institution-bound, some are not; some are entered voluntarily, into others we are born; some are permanent, some temporary. One's moral duty, at least in the first instance, is one's duty in some such role; any moral right one has is a right one has as an R (where R is replaced by a term for one who fills a role); moral virtues will be some of the features that make one a good R; and what one morally ought to be or do in the first instance is what one ought as an R to be or do.[2]

What makes these roles and not some others to be morally determinative in this respect? That is a difficult question to which I have no good answer. My hypothesis is that it is the fact that these and similar roles are such that both (a) it is natural for one to want someone to fill them in one's life, and (b) it is not a part of one's nature to be averse to filling them. We want to have (or to have had) friends, informants, confidantes, parents, etc. This is just part of human nature; there would be something wrong in an important way about a person who did not want these roles filled in her life, though, of course, there need be nothing wrong with her if she *chooses* to go without one or more of them. In contrast, it is not part of human nature to be averse to filling such a role, being someone's friend, spouse, confidante, etc. (whether or not such an aversion would itself be unnatural).

This, however, is just a hypothesis. I surely do not know enough about human nature to argue for it and I am doubtful whether any experts in the scientific study of psychology can, at the present state of knowledge, prove it either true or false. In any case, my thesis that the moral life is all about acquitting oneself adequately in the roles I have mentioned has a certain commonsense appeal and here I shall try neither to argue for it nor to propose and defend some principle that selects all and only these roles as being morally determinative.

It will be important for my purposes to go into a bit of detail on two parts of my own version of this moral conception. The first concerns the theory of value and the second concerns the assessment of behavior, especially ascriptions of wrongdoing to agents.

II. A Conception of Moral Life

The approach I take in value theory is a simple one. I think that when we say of some state of affairs, say, Smythe's dying, that it is bad or undesirable, meaning not just that it is bad for Smythe (but not, perhaps, for me, who run a funeral home), but bad in itself or impersonally, what we are getting at is that it is a bad thing to desire, or, better, that the desire for it is a bad one. The sort of badness involved I take to be moral badness and it applies not merely to desire but also to other relevant forms of favoring or endorsing or embracing states of affairs. Thus, the immorality of wanting Smythe to die extends to hoping she will die, wishing she would, intending her to, and also to taking pleasure in the prospect that she will. In general, we can understand talk of objectively or intrinsically good states of affairs in terms of what it would be morally good to desire, hope for, be pleased with, intend, etc.

Various details of this account are spelled out elsewhere. Here let me say only that it is derived from the axiological approach taken by Brentano, Meinong, and Ewing and has several advantages to moral theory.[3] First, it leads *directly* from value judgments to claims about how people should respond by analyzing the former in terms of the latter. This can save us some steps since in ethics our interest is in value response more than it is in value itself. Second, it makes it a logical truth that desiring (and otherwise favoring) what is bad is itself bad, since on this account, this thesis comes only to the trivial truth that desiring what it is bad to desire is bad. Third, in its talk of good and bad desires, it makes theoretical progress by reducing the sometimes mystifying predicative use of 'good' and 'bad' to the more manageable adjunctive use.[4]

We think that desiring, wishing, and intending Smythe to die are immoral because we think such attitudes malevolent, i.e., we think them morally vicious. In contrast, we think that desiring, wishing, and intending Smythe to stay alive are morally good because we think such attitudes kindly and benevolent, i.e., we think them morally virtuous. If Aristotle is right in telling us that a virtue is what makes a thing and its work good,[5] then the question arises 'In what way does desiring the states of affairs we call objectively good make us and our 'work' good?'

My answer is that such an attitude, if characteristic of a person, tends to make her good in filling some morally significant role in the life of a person; that is, they tend to make her a good R to somebody. One's moral life, as I see it, is entirely a matter of being the sort of person who fills such roles in a satisfactory way.[6] It is a matter of having the virtues and lacking the vices of a friend, spouse, etc. However, not every virtue in a friend or spouse is a moral virtue. For purposes of moral evaluation it is of no import that one is a witty friend or a comely spouse. Moral assessment looks to the *character* of the one evaluated, not her appearance or personality. A conception that is thus role-centered has a pleasing richness, for not only does the vocabulary of virtues and vices seem most sensible in the context of roles, the same is true of duties and rights, goodness and badness, and of 'ought'-evaluations. A common way of defending and clarifying our claim that S has a duty or ought to V is to specify that we meant she ought or has a duty *as an* R to V.

Such an account has several theoretical advantages. First, like other accounts propounded by members of what Frankena has called "the Movement" against modernist moral philosophy, it tends to demystify moral 'ought'-judgments by assimilating them to what he calls "Ordinary Oughts," on a par with familiar functional 'ought'-judgments.[7]

Second, such an account allows for a victim-oriented account of wrongdoing. In utilitarian and equalitarian (and divine command) moral theories the person who suffers at the agent's hands tends to figure merely as a *locus* of wrongdoing—the point at which attainable utility is lost, or the person whose holdings make for a less equitable distribution (or the one with respect to whom one's behavior violates God's command). What is needed is an account, like the one sketched here, in which harming S is morally wrong (when it is wrong) because it *wrongs S*, constitutes a breach of the agent's relationship with S.[8] Of course, the world may be so arranged that whatever wrongs one of our neighbors *also* and thereby wrongs God insofar as it constitutes disobedience to him.[9] Christians will believe that whatever is wrong violates God's legislative will, but this no more requires them to think it wrong *only* because it does this (making violating God's will to be the only ultimate wrong-making feature) than does their conviction that whatever is true is also believed by God compel them to hold that whatever is true is true because God believes it and only because of that.

Third, such an account promises to do a much better job of explaining the moral importance of such special personal relationships as friendship than do the more familiar modernist approaches. Indeed, my fourth point builds on this. The analysis of value judgments sketched above, in conjunction with the role-centered conception of morality we have been discussing, yields a simple defense of what Sen has dubbed the "position-relativity" of objective values, the fact that what is, for example, bad in itself may be *more* bad with respect to one person than it is with respect to another. Consider Smythe's death. On my account, to say it is an objectively bad thing is to say that wanting her death is morally bad. However, if to be morally bad is to be (or tend to be) bad in some such morally significant role as spouse or sibling, then it is easy to see that it will be worse for you as S's spouse or sibling to desire her death than it is for someone to desire it who is not so closely connected to her.[10]

My concern here is not to extol this conception of morality but rather to focus on and draw out some implications of one aspect of it. We observed above that morality is concerned with character and also noted that what makes it immoral to want someone to suffer or die is that such desire, when characteristic, tends to make one bad in some morally significant role. Bad, because malevolent. What is striking and, I think, important is that malevolence is a vice in *any* of the morally significant roles and that benevolence, either in general or in the form of willing some specific form of good, is good in any of them. It is whether one has goodwill, i.e., wills me the variety of things that make for good human living, that determines whether she is a good sibling, friend, or neighbor (in the broad scriptural sense) to me. It is whether she wills me some more specific type of good that determines whether she is good in certain other morally significant roles—whether she wills me some relevant knowledge that determines whether she is a good informant to me, for example. On my view, developed elsewhere,[11] one's treatment of another is morally good or bad, right or wrong, according to how it stands in relation to the sort of goodwill that determines what counts as virtue in the relationships or roles one fills in the other's life.

'Will' is a term that can be used in a variety of ways, but in its most focused and most relevant use it picks out a certain practical orientation or endorsement. What one wills in this sense is what one aims at, makes her objective, adopts as a goal (even if only a goal instrumental to the attainment of some further goal). In short, to will something in this narrower sense of 'will' is to intend it. Intentions are commonly linked to decisions—to decide to V is to adopt the intention to V and to decide not to V, usually, at least, consists in rejecting (after giving practical consideration to) any intention to V. Actions acquire moral status according to the orientation of the agent's will, that is, according to whether they are properly related to the agent's having or rejecting good or bad intentions. Some illustrations may be helpful at this point. If A kills B out of hatred, then A's action, in my view, is immoral because it reflects A's evil intention, her making it her objective that *B* die. If *A* lets *B* die out of hatred, her omission is immoral for the same reason. If *A* wrongfully kills *B* as a foreseen or forseeable side effect of something else *A* does intentionally, e.g., kills *B* by polluting the drinking water through *A*'s careless waste disposal, then her action is immoral because it reflects *A*'s evil failure to adopt a good intention, her failure to try to make sure she does not cause harm to *B*. If she unintentionally but wrongfully lets *B* die, her behavior is immoral because it too reflects her wicked failure to see to it that *B* stays alive, and this also is wrong because it is a failure of goodwill, literally a failure to will *B* some relevant good.

Several points need to be stressed here. First, not all failures of goodwill are immoral. One obviously is not able to secure each good for each person; one cannot rationally intend to do what she knows she cannot,[12] and moral principles normally do not require one to do what one cannot.[13] Moreover, it does not require one even to will others all the good one could will them. Many philosophers have talked of the ways "integrity," "autonomy," or "the personal point of view" work to provide moral justification for us on at least some of the occasions when we pursue our own personal projects and interests at cost to others who would have profited from our acting otherwise.

Second, while such failures of goodwill are often justified, they do stand in need of justification; for benevolence is not merely a virtue, it is a duty. We have a responsibility to each person, defeasible though it is, not only to wish her well but, more practically, to will her good.

Third, such an account helps us to see why greater deviations from goodwill are morally permitted with respect to evildoers, for such persons have already violated their relationships by their wicked adoption or rejection of certain intentions and have thus weakened the bonds of goodwill that tie them to us in their role relations. Hence, a deviation from the minimal standards of goodwill which would never be justified on the grounds of integrity (e.g., an intentionally lethal attack) may be justifiable in defense of self or others. At least, this is open to argue, given the foundation of a role-centered conception of moral life.

Fourth, when goodwill, or some special form of it, is seen as the ultimate duty in any morally significant role, then it is apparent that there are two basic ways of violating duty—one can deviate from goodwill either by dereliction, i.e., by failure to will what is good or, more seriously, by transgression, i.e., by willing what is evil (e.g., the loss of some good).[14] Taking our duties to be linked to our roles or 'offices', I shall call the first sort of violation of duty 'inofficious' behavior, and call the second type 'counter-officious'. The first type is privative in that one does not will in accord with the demands of one's 'office'; in the second type, the will has as its object the opposite of what it should have as object in keeping with the agent's office. It is one thing not to care enough for someone to trouble myself by trying to save or spare his life. That is a deviation from goodwill and one it will be difficult to justify. But it is another thing altogether, a difference not merely of degree, to go beyond such *inattention* to his good to the extreme of actually making the destruction of his life one of my goals. This distinction between two forms of wrongdoing is a crucial one and one to which I shall return.

Sixth, such an account serves to remind Christian ethicists of a point to which our immersion in modern secular moral philosophies may blind us: that every instance of wrongdoing, every sin, is a sin *against* some virtue.

In the course of trying to lay out various features of this intentionalist[15] and role-centered conception of morality I have already tried to highlight some of its appealing features. Let me turn, then, to a brief consideration of some salient objections that might be raised against it.

The first objection is the least philosophical. It holds simply that intentions and decisions cannot capture the heart of morality in the way I have claimed, on the grounds that it is common knowledge that good intentions are not enough in life. As the saying has it, they pave the road to hell. I can think of three kinds of cases that might lead one to think this way about the road to hell. In the first, an agent has good *general* intentions, say, to contribute to charities, phone home more often, etc., but never gets around actually to *acting* on them. In the second, an agent with good *ultimate* intentions adopts immoral *means* in pursuit of them. In the third, an agent with good ultimate intentions employs foolish and harmful means in pursuit of them. In all three cases one might feel some temptation to think that we need to look beyond these agents' good intentions and to consider the agent's external behavior—what she does or leaves undone.

I think this is, at best, only half-right. We do need to look beyond these agents' good general and ultimate intentions; but we do not need to look beyond the intentions she adopts or rejects. In the first case, the agent is wrong for never having adopted the right kind of what Brand calls "immediate intention," an intention to contribute or phone "here and now."[16] If she does form such an intention but fails to get her contribution through to the needy or fails to complete her call, whether because of some breakdown or bad luck in the external situation or (rather less likely) because of some malfunction in her neurological or muscular system which prevents her will from moving her body, the agent is not to blame and, as far as this incident goes, is headed for heaven rather than for hell.

In the second case, it should be obvious that using an immoral means involves acting with an immoral instrumental intention and thus the case does not require us to look beyond the agent's intention in making our moral judgment.

In the third case, we need to know whether the choice of foolish and harmful means reflected the agent's recklessness in failing to attend to manifest dangers or showed her negligence in failing to take adequate precautions against possible ill effects. In either case she is to blame for this past failure of goodwill which now infects this action, though neither her current instrumental nor ultimate intention is immoral. So, again, we need not look beyond intentions and decisions. Of course, her choice of means may be foolish and harmful without being in any way connected to some past immoral failure of goodwill. However, in that instance, I see no reason to think the agent bound for hell. She has not acted immorally, though she has acted harmfully, indeed, disastrously.

The second objection is captured in Jonathan Bennett's complaint that appeal to intentions has no place in what he calls "first-order" morality.[17] He seems to mean that whereas it is appropriate to consider the agent's intentions in evaluating her and in determining her blameworthiness, such consideration is inappropriate in trying to figure out simply whether she acted wrongly.

I can see no good reason to think this true. Suppose that I have promised a hostess to be kind or nice or loving towards a certain guest with whom I have had strained dealings. Then, to find out whether in making a certain remark at her party I acted wrongly by breaking this promise, we need to know with what intentions I acted. For if my goal was to hurt the guest's feelings, then I surely did break the promise.

Moreover, there are plainly many situations in which one has an obligation to treat another kindly or lovingly even absent such a promise. Everyone should admit that; and that is sufficient to prove it wrong to think that appeal to intentions never has a place in determining wrongdoing. Indeed, I think this shows that the distinction between act-evaluations and agent-evaluations has been overemphasized.[18] Most of our moral discourse involves both kinds of evaluation simultaneously, as when we say, 'It was cruel (or kind, or dishonest, or malevolent, or clever, or unwise) of S to V.' In fact, in using most of our substantive negative moral vocabulary for the appraisal and classification of actions, we evaluate the actions while at the same time ascribing certain immoral intentions to the agent—consider 'theft', 'lie', 'murder', 'adultery', 'blasphemy'. In any case, Bennett's view does not fit well with Christianity, since Christians will think that all of us are always under a moral requirement, rooted in our relationship with God, to love, and therefore to act lovingly. Indeed, they will think all other moral requirements hang on, are derived from, this demand for love—a love in the heart that naturally finds expression in behavior.

The third objection stems from an argument sometimes used against Abelard.[19] Its thrust is that it cannot be bad intentions that make bad actions bad, for the direction of explanation must be the reverse—we know whether an intention is bad by knowing whether what it is an intention to do is a bad thing to do.

To this I reply that there is no reason to think it true. Plainly it is not its bad effects that make a malevolent act vicious, for it may have no bad effect. Nor is it the fact that ma-

levolent actions *usually* have such effects, for we should
condemn malevolence as vicious even in an imaginary world
where malevolent actions were usually ineffectual (perhaps because the agents have no communication or other interaction
with one another). Where Abelard's opponents go astray is in
fallaciously reasoning from the fact it is its content that determines whether an intention is morally good or bad to the conclusion that it is the moral goodness or badness of its content
that determines whether the intention is morally good or bad.
That conclusion does not follow and, in my opinion, it is not
true.

This is important for Christians seeking to understand
moral life. They must think that ultimately an action is morally
right or wrong depending on how it comports with the Law of
Love and plainly they should find attractive an intentionalist account of moral right and wrong, one focused on the agent's motivational structure.[20] Of course, there will be certain kinds of
action which no sane agent can conceive of as loving, but that
does not show there must be kinds of action which are immoral
independently of the decisions and intentions from which they
flow. 'Love' in its most generic sense means benevolence or
goodwill, and these concepts take us directly to will and thus to
intention and decision. An ethics of love is most plausibly understood as an intentionalist ethics.

III. On Intention and Its Counterfeits

Let us try to get a bit clearer about intentions.[21] Intentions
are goals, aims, objectives. What we intend to do is what we
mean to do. Intentions are what is adopted or rejected when we
make decisions to do things. Intentions are what get linked together in the practical networks we call plans. We are in the
realm of intentions when we speak of what we act in order to
achieve or of that for whose sake we act. Intentions are not actions but psychological states and they are neither cognitive nor
affective nor desiderative states but are rather *practical* ones,
states of will. We need not intend only our actions but we can
intend only what we think it possible relevantly to affect

through our actions. We need not think it probable we will do what we intend to do, but we must think it possible we will. We can intend that something happen only if and because we prefer its happening (to its not happening), and thus we always want what we intend, want it, at least, in preference to its not being the case. This last point is sometimes obscured by the fact that some of what we intend we also want *not* to happen.[22] However, since one can reasonably want something to happen while also reasonably wanting it not to happen, this does not show that I am wrong in thinking we always want whatever we intend. Though each of these claims is denied by some philosopher, it would take me too far afield to try to argue for them here[23] and I shall instead simply assert them without supporting considerations. Each has strong intuitive warrant.

It is sometimes said that what one foresees or expects she will do in the course of doing something she intends to do, she therefore intends to do.[24] I will briefly speak against this claim. Suppose that while I present a lecture I foresee that as I continue to speak some of the audience will be bored by me; and yet I fully intend to continue to speak. Why think that I intend to make them bored?

Note, first, that there is nothing I do *in order to* bore them. Second, note that, plainly, I do not bore them for the sake of boring and, just as plainly, I do not bore them in order to accomplish some further end. I talk in order to accomplish some further end, it is true, but I intend to bore people by my talking only if I intend that my talking bore them and I have no reason to adopt such an intention. After all, their being bored does me no good, advances no purpose of mine. So why think I have adopted such an intention? Third, imagine that my expectation is incorrect and, because of some intense interest in their hearts, none of the audience is bored by my talk. Whenever one intends her talk to bore someone and it does not, then she and the talk are failures, in part at least. But note that we should not want to say in our imaginary case that I or the talk are even partial failures. Fourth, keeping this imaginary case in mind, notice we should not say I *tried* to bore the audience. However, when one intends her efforts to have a certain effect and they do not, then it is correct to say she tried (but failed) to achieve that effect.

I think all this shows that one need not intend to do all that one expects to do in pursuit of her intentions. Indeed, it would be helpful to think of my four points as demonstrations that my practical attitude fails four tests for intent. These tests are perfectly generalizable ones, though I will not here devise general schematizations of them. Instead, let me offer one final proof that I do not intend to bore (and thus need not intend all that I expect to do), for this proof introduces some points that will shortly prove helpful for my larger project.

Consider the fact that as I speak I might start using a funny accent, or tossing in wisecracks, or making silly faces. I *could* do these things in an attempt, perhaps futile, to avoid boring the audience. That I could rationally make such an attempt and *do so without abandoning any of the reasons for which I give the talk* shows that I cannot in talking *intend* to bore. For one cannot rationally try to avoid what one intends to do. Any such attempt must introduce such inconsistency into one's practical aims (for notice that whatever I attempt to do I make it my aim to do) as to demand their revision.[25] Of course, if I go ahead and talk while expecting it to bore, I must be *willing* to bore. But that does not mean I will to, where 'will' is to be understood as intent. For I may (rationally) be willing to do something (stay home to read, for example) while I am also willing not to do it (e.g., to go out to visit friends), but, again, I cannot (rationally) *intend* to do what I at the same time *intend* not to do.[26] So being willing to V neither entails nor is identical with willing (intending) to V.

It is not true that one need intend to do all that one foresees she will do in the course of doing what she intends to do. Still, I think we can understand what has led some to think it is true. That I foresee I will do A and go ahead and do it shows something interesting, and sometimes morally significant, about my practical or volitional orientation towards doing A. It shows what we might call a limitation to my volitional distance from doing it. We can get a little clearer about this, I hope, if we compare two schematic situations and flesh each out in a concrete illustration.

Consider first this possible conjuction: (a) S intends and expects that p. (b) S intends that if p then q. (c) S intends that q.

And yet, (d) S does not expect that q.[27] To flesh this out we can imagine that S is trapped at the bottom of a deep shaft and that her only hope of salvation is to throw a rope to the top in such fashion that it will catch on a branch and enable her to climb out. We can let 'p' stand for 'S throws up her rope' and let 'q' stand for 'S is in position to climb to safety.' She intends to be in a position to climb out, since this is her aim in, her reason for, throwing the rope. Nonetheless, she does not *expect* to be so positioned; she realizes it is a very long shot. Still, while she does not expect to be in a position to climb out, the fact that she intends to does indicate a limit to what we might call her epistemic distance from q. One can only intend what one apprehends as possible, so the information that she intends that q tells us that, while S need not believe that q, she must believe in its *possibility*. We can say that she must at least allow that it *may* be that q, where 'may' is used epistemically.

Now construct from this a different conjunction, replacing every appearance of 'intend' with 'expect' and *vice versa*. This yields: (e) S expects and intends that p. (f) S expects that if p then q. (g) S expects that q. And yet (h) S does not intend that q. To flesh this out we can imagine that S is trapped in a tunnel with no way out. Her only hope is to call for help, though she thinks the probability of being heard is low while the likelihood of her setting off vibrations that cause the tunnel's collapse is high. We can let 'p' stand for 'S calls out' and let 'q' stand for 'S destroys the tunnel.' Any suggestion that S intends to destroy the tunnel is grotesque. Nonetheless, the fact that she expects to destroy it indicates a limit to what we might call her practical or volitional distance from q. If she were determined to avoid q at all costs, then she would not intentionally do something which is such that she expects that if she does it then q. Hence, the information that she expects that q in this circumstance tells us that, while S need not intend (will) that q, she must be willing that q. We can say that she must at least allow that it *may* be that q, where 'may' is used to indicate a sort of permission or toleration.

Obviously, this can have moral significance. What is objectively undesirable (bad) is not only bad to desire and intend, it is also a good thing to oppose; that is, it is good to want and intend its nonexistence. When q is something objectively bad, then there is a strong moral presumption against being willing or permitting that q. Thus, the information that the agent expects that q gives us grounds to question the morality of her behavior and, moreover, to question it on the basis of the volitional relationship we can ascribe to q and the agent in virtue of the information about her expectation. It is this last fact that seems to lead people into thinking S must intend that q; they simply misidentify and overestimate the volitional connection that must hold between the agent and q.

This explanation of the psychological mistake also lends support to my backward-looking (intentionalist) account of moral justification.[28] It is a commonplace that it matters for morality whether an agent expects to do the harmful things she does. *Why* does this matter? The simple answer, that expectation implies intention, is false. One might be tempted to think that we must account for the moral importance of expectation by tying it to probabilities and thus moving toward a forward-looking account of moral justification. The explanation I have just offered indicates a better alternative. The fact that she expected to do harm shows that she was not as volitionally opposed to doing harm as she might have been, she was not trying as hard as she might have tried to avoid it. It indicates she may be to blame, not for having a bad intention, but rather for failing to have a good one—the intention to avoid doing harm. Thus, information about the agent's epistemic state matters morally because of what it says about her volitional states. This still leaves the will center stage in matters of moral justification.

Incidentally, the triple—(i) believing that r, (ii) failing to believe that r, and (iii) believing that not-r—seems to exhibit the same interrelationship in the epistemic realm that I will try to show holds in the volitional realm among the triple: (iv) intending that r, (v) failing to intend that r, (vi) intending that not-r. Intuitively we think (iii) is more opposed to or more distant from (i) than is (ii), though we may be unsure just how to analyze this notion of 'opposition'. Indeed, this interrelationship also seems to hold for the desiderative triple: (vii) desiring that r, (viii) failing to desire that r, and (ix) desiring that not-r. This pattern, in fact, is so widespread throughout our epistemic, desiderative, and affective attitudes that it would be quite surprising if it did *not* occur in the volitional realm.

IV. Towards Moral Absolutes

These last observations can help us defend a claim made earlier about the comparative immorality of inofficious and counter-officious behavior. Let us recall and try to clarify those notions. According to the conception of moral life I have been employing, one's moral life is a matter of discharging well the various morally significant roles she fills in the lives of various persons. For each such role, being good in it, being a good R, depends crucially on being benevolent in some relevant way. For some roles, such as informant, this consists in willing some relatively particular type of human good, e.g., knowledge. For others, such as neighbor or friend, the relevant notion of benevolence is a less specific one. I think that the basic idea of such less specific benevolence, what constitutes virtue and the standard of duty for these roles, is that of willing for someone the most basic components of a flourishing human life. This is what the virtue and the duty of goodwill is all about. Unless it is justified by some other consideration, any action manifesting a failure in such benevolence is a violation of one's moral duty to someone, a violation of the sort I have called 'inofficious.' Likewise, absent such justification, an action manifesting a decision in which one has made it one's aim that a person not have some basic component of a flourishing human life is a violation of one's moral duty to her, a violation of the sort I have called 'counter-officious.'

While resembling the traditional distinction between positive and negative duties, this distinction is not the same as that one. That distinction is usually drawn on the basis of a distinction between actions and omissions, or between acts of commission and acts of omission, or between helping and not-harming.[29] However, one's behavior may be inofficious whether it is an omission or a commission, whether it harms or just does not help. The same holds for counter-officious behavior.

My claim is that when we are dealing with basic components of human flourishing and with their privation, what I shall hereafter call basic goods and evils, then presumptively counter-officious behavior is both harder to justify and (presumptively) morally worse than is presumptively inofficious behavior. It is harder to justify trying to harm me in a basic way than it is to justify not trying to help me, or even not trying not to harm me. It is harder to justify because counter-officious behavior is morally worse than is inofficious behavior.

Let me try to show this. Things are more bad or less bad, Aquinas tells us, according to their distance from the good.[30] Less metaphorically, we can say that what is worse is worse in that it is somehow more opposed to the good. Taking benevolence, goodwill, to be the relevant sort of good, we can show that counter-officious behavior (willing what is bad) is worse than inofficious behavior (failing to will what is good) if we can show that (1) willing what is bad is, in a relevant way, more opposed to (2) willing what is good than is (3) a failure to will what is good. (This is true even when the failure is accompanied by the belief that, because of this failure, what is good will be lost.)

We can show this if we can show both that (a) acting from one decision[31] which consists in one's deciding against pursuing a certain intention (in light of a certain cost) is rationally consistent with *at the same time* acting from a second decision which consists in adopting that intention, and (b) acting from a decision which consists in adopting an intention to do something is not rationally consistent with at the same time acting from a decision which consists in adopting an intention not to do it. This is rather complicated but returning to the simple example above of my talk's boring the audience can help to illustrate the point.

In that case I could have been so concerned to avoid boring the audience that I decided against giving the talk. But I was not. Given the choice between giving the talk on the one hand and, on the other, of aborting the speech in pursuit of the goal of not boring, I decided against pursuing the latter intention. My speech stems from that first decision. However, I may then face a second choice—a choice between behaving in a professional and sober manner on the one hand and, on the other, pursuing my goal of not boring (by making wisecracks, silly faces, etc.). Nothing in the first decision precludes now, in this second decision, my pursuing the very goal I rejected in the first. In now pursuing a goal (through my wisecracking) which I had earlier decided against pursuing (I could have pursued it by aborting the talk) I *do not repudiate* the earlier decision. So much for (a). As for (b) we need only note what was said before about the irrationality of intending not to do something one at the same time intends to do. The point here can be illustrated in many ways. A mother who goes into the baby's room in order to retrieve something, and expects thereby to wake her, may nonetheless take measures, e.g., tiptoeing, in order to avoid waking her. In deciding to go into the room she is deciding against taking *certain* measures (abandoning the trip) in order to avoid waking her but in tiptoeing she decides to take other measures with just that aim.

What I take this to show is that a decision against pursuing a certain goal need not be so opposed to that goal that it precludes rationally making a second decision (without repudiating the first) in which one does decide to pursue that goal. In contrast, to decide to *oppose* that goal *does* preclude rationally making a second decision (without repudiating the first) in which one decides to pursue the goal. Contrast the mother's situation just mentioned with that of a father who reluctantly decides to enter the baby's room to wake her to give her some medicine. Whereas the mother could consistently take steps to avoid waking the baby, the father cannot.

Now consider two more controversial cases, those of Terror Bomber and Tactical Bomber.[32] Terror Bomber is, without justification, resolved to drop her bombs on an enemy infant-orphanage in order to kill the orphans, demoralizing the population and thereby advancing her cause. Tactical Bomber, without justification, aims to drop her bombs on a supply depot in order to impede the movement of *materiel* and thereby advance her cause. She sees that the bombs dropped will also kill orphans in a nearby orphanage. Both decide against sparing the orphans by withholding their bombs. Notice that Tactical Bomber, however, who expects but does not intend to kill the orphans, may take measures in order to spare the orphans. She may, for example, wait an extra split-second before she pushes her button, in order to get the bombs to drop on the side of the supply depot farthest from the orphanage, thereby trying to avoid killing the orphans. She may do this with such an intention even if she recognizes that the chances of any orphan's being better off for this delay are small indeed.

In contrast, Terror Bomber cannot rationally do anything in order to avoid killing the orphans. Killing them is one of her objectives. Whereas, in deciding to drop her bombs, Tactical Bomber fails to will the orphans the good of continued life, she may consistently will them this good in a *further* decision, her decision to delay on the button. Terror Bomber cannot consistently will the orphans the good of continued life, for in deciding to drop her bombs she wills them the loss of this good.[33]

This gives us what we have needed, for it shows us a way in which failure to will a good is less opposed to willing that good than is willing its non-existence. It is less opposed because it can be embodied in a decision which itself is rationally consistent with a further decision which consists in willing that good. Any decision embodying an intention that the good not exist is *not*, in contrast, rationally consistent with a further decision which consists in willing that good. Thus, Tactical Bomber's inofficious bombing is less wrong than is Terror Bomber's counter-officious bombing, even when justifying considerations are equally lacking. It is less wrong because its motivational background is less opposed to goodwill. Since this is true for purely structural reasons, the same will hold for all other comparable pairs of inofficious and counter-officious pieces of behavior.

The same conclusion can, I think, be reached along a different route. (a) Willing the non-existence of a good *as a means* is more opposed to (b) willing that good than is (c) failure to will the good, because (a) is less opposed to (d) willing the non-existence of a good *as one's ultimate goal* than is (c). Since (b) and (d) are maximally opposed, it follows that what is *less* opposed to (d) is *eo ipso more* opposed to (b). This can be made more vivid if we follow Aquinas in taking being more or less opposed to be expressible in terms of being more or less distant.[34] Failure to will a good is less distant from willing a good than is instrumentally willing that good's destruction because this last is closer to willing the good's destruction for its own sake. Since willing the destruction of the good is more distant from virtue (goodwill) than is failure to will the good, willing the destruction of a good and the acts that come from it are worse.

Nozick is getting at roughly the same point when he says that one with intentions like Terror Bomber's is more "closely aligned" with disvalue than one with intentions like Tactical Bomber's need be.[35] Nagel makes a similar point, going on to observe that Terror Bomber must let herself be *guided* by disvalue (that is, evil) in a way that Tactical Bomber need not.[36] Such subservience to evil is diametrically opposed to the active opposition which evil should call forth.

This insight is especially forceful if we utilize here the axiological analysis offered at the beginning of this essay. According to that analysis, to say something, e.g., the death of the orphans, is bad not just for them but *impersonally* is to say that desiring, hoping for, and intending it is immoral. While it is easy to see why what is only instrumentally or conditionally undesirable may not be an immoral thing to want or intend in special circumstances, I do not see how what is undesirable impersonally or unconditionally can be such that wanting or intending it can be other than immoral under *any* circumstances. The death of an innocent is unconditionally bad as such, for the innocent cannot *de dicto* have done anything to deserve death. It can only be immoral to will such a death, for willing it is willing what is, in itself and unconditionally, bad (where that is to say it is unconditionally immoral to make it the object of one's desires, hopes, or intentions).

Is death, even the death of an innocent, an unconditional evil? Death itself is bad only insofar as life is good. However, some think life only instrumentally and, hence, conditionally, good.[37] I doubt that is true. For most of us, our lives have value despite, not because of, the lives we lead. In this respect being alive is, I think, like being human and like making choices. For most of us, being human is valuable despite, not because of, the (usually wretched and loathsome) humans we turn out to be, and making choices is valuable despite, not because of, the disastrous or pathetic choices we usually make. My point is simply the negative one that the value of such things as being alive, being human, and making choices is not simply derivative from the value of what comes from them. Hence, they are not simply instrumentally valuable.

I have no positive account of their value to offer, but I will hazard a conjecture. Perhaps life, humanity, and choice are basic goods for humans simply in that each is a realization, a fulfillment, of some fundamental capacity that helps define us and what constitutes flourishing for our kind. If true, this may be enough to explain why death is always an evil *for the deceased*. The larger task of showing that the death of innocents is always impersonally and unconditionally evil should, I think, be developed in the context of the axiological analysis and the role-centered moral conceptions sketched earlier.

At last, with our talk of what it can only be immoral to will, we have reached the notion of moral absolutes, exceptionless moral norms. How can such norms be justified? In light of the conception of moral life with which we have been dealing one sort of answer seems immediately appealing. Such norms may constitute a reasonable response to the fact, mentioned earlier, that we are neither able to will to secure every good for each person nor willing to will anybody all the good we could will her. In view of this limit on our goodwill, it seems reasonable to establish a floor beneath which we will not go in our departures from goodwill.[38] In morality we need a line drawn between the kinds of deviations from goodwill which are sometimes justifiable on the grounds simply of our own projects and interests and those which are not. The idea of absolutism is that this line falls roughly along the line already drawn between the two kinds of presumptive duty-violation. (Because of questions of ill-desert and other consequences of wrongdoing, the line between the justifiable and the unjustifiable does not *exactly* follow that between the inofficious and the counter-officious.) But *can* this be reasonable? To see whether any sort of traditional moral absolutism is philosophically defensible we need to respond to Samuel Scheffler's recent challenge. It is to this we now turn.

V. Moral Absolutes

Scheffler's challenge is a simple one to show how it can be rationally acceptable for one to refuse to act so as to minimize violations of a norm when the only way to minimize such violations is to violate it oneself.[39] Consider the traditional absolute norm against intentionally killing the innocent. Scheffler's claim is that no matter where we locate whatever it is that is so objectionable about doing this, whether in some features of the agent or of the action itself, there will be *more* of this objectionable feature if the agent refuses intentionally to kill the innocent when by doing so she could reduce the number of such killings that occur. Take, for example, the Kantians' claims that such a killing breaches the respect due to the victim. Scheffler's point is that unless this innocent is killed by me now there will be even more breaches of respect in the world. If their disvalue is what makes killing innocents so bad, why is it not more rational to *minimize* the breaches of respect by minimizing the killings?

I will try to respond by offering my own account of how one should undertake the moral evaluation of such a case. Let us present the case in schematized form: Victims V_2 and V_3, innocent people, are not intentionally killed by agent A_2 if and only if agent A_1 intentionally kills V_1, another innocent. The first thing to note is that what A_1 ought to do is whatever is less presumptively bad in the circumstances. She should choose the less evil of the alternative courses of action. The second thing we need to note is that A_1's choice is between killing V_1 in order to save V_2 and V_3 and, alternatively, letting V_2 and V_3 die by refusing to do what is needed to save them. Thus, so far we do not need to ask whether A_1's killing V_1 would be worse than A_2's killing V_2 and V_3. We need to consider the immorality of A_2's action only if we assume that the value/disvalue of A_1's refusing to kill V_1 is determined by the value of its results. But why make the assumption that moral justification is in this way forward-looking? The intentionalist account of moral justification I sketched above takes the justification of an action to be backward-looking, dependent on the decisions from which it flows.

It is not difficult to classify and assess the alternative courses of action open to A_1. If she kills V_1 to save the others she kills him intentionally and thus intends to kill him. It is not hard to establish this. First, she does something (e.g., shoots him) *in order to* kill him, she kills him *in order to* achieve some further goal, the release of V_2 and V_3. Second, his death does her some *good*, since it sets the stage (she hopes) for the others' release. Third, her situation is such that if her shot misses or he survives her stab wounds, it would be true that she *tried* to kill him. Fourth, if he survives her attack, then she and her plan are at least partial *failures*. (Note, by the way, that this last is true even if, unexpectedly, A_2 releases V_2 and V_3 unharmed after A_1's attempt to kill fails. For though she tried to get V_2 and V_3 released unharmed and she did get them thus released, she failed to get them released *in the way she planned (intended) to*.)

On the other hand, if A_1 refuses to kill V_1 and thereby lets V_2 and V_3 die, she does not *intend* to let them die. She does not do anything in order to let them die. Their dying does her no good, since it is irrelevant to her goal of sparing V_1's life. If they get miraculously spared this would not make her even a partial failure, nor would it be correct to say that she had tried (but failed) to let them die. Since A_1's mental state clearly fails all these tests for intent, she plainly does not intend to let V_2 and V_3 die. One might feel some inclination to think her mental state passes one test for intent, for one might feel some inclination to say she let them die *in order to* achieve some further goal. I think this inclination is to be resisted; she refuses to kill in order to secure her goal but she does not *let them die* in order to secure any goal. However, even if one is inclined to call this hard test differently, the clear negative judgment from the other tests must take precedence.

So if A_1 kills V_1 she intends to kill him but if she instead lets V_2 and V_3 die she does not intend them to die. This means that the case against killing V_1 is that it involves willing him the destruction of a basic form of good, whereas the case against letting V_2 and V_3 die (by refusing to kill V_1) is that it involves failing to will them the good of continued life. Killing V_1 is, therefore, presumptively counter-officious, while letting V_2 and V_3 die is presumptively inofficious. Since, as I tried to show in the previous section, the former is worse than the latter, what A_1 ought to do is avoid the more evil act—she ought not to kill V_1 even in this case. She would wrong V_1 more by killing him than she would wrong either V_2 or V_3 by letting them die. Hence, killing V_1 is the worse of her alternative actions.

At this point, a Benthamite objection will be raised, of course. It will be said that even if I have shown that killing V_1 here would be worse than letting V_2 die and have shown that killing V_1 would be worse than letting V_3 die, I have not shown that it is worse than letting *both* die. 'Every man is to count for one,' the Benthamite will cry. Of course, I have no complaint with one person's counting for one. The question is 'How is each to be counted?'

My answer is that a moral method that takes seriously the fact that one's moral duties are duties owed to this person or that person on account of the role(s) one fills in that person's life will require that the cases for and against acting to prolong the life of each interested party must be made serially. What I have in mind can be made clear if we imagine moral reasoning to be like an adversary proceeding in a kind of courtroom. My claim is that the correct way to organize the moral hearings, the way most consistent with the sort of role-centered conception of moral life we have been discussing, is to demand that V_2 comes before the bar *alone* to make the case for saving his life (by taking V_1's). Only after that case is adjudicated does V_3 get to come before the bar to make the case for saving his life. Each of these litigants will meet V_1 as adversary, trying to show that the moral case against killing him is stronger than the moral case against letting the other die. Only such a procedure as this will remain faithful to the fact that to act wrongly is *to wrong someone* by violating one's relationship with her and that, for this reason, acting more wrongly must consist in wronging someone more gravely (i.e., more gravely than one wrongs anyone by acting in an alternative way). Of course, my contention is that V_1 will win each such contest, since intentionally killing him wrongs him more gravely than does refusing to kill him wrong any other individual.

This will not be cheerfully accepted. I will treat four objections to my view. The first directly addresses the last point I made. The objection is that even if killing V_1 wrongs him more gravely than letting V_2 and V_3 die wrongs any individual, nonetheless they are *jointly* more gravely wronged than V_1 is.

To this I reply that to act wrongly is to fail in a role. However, A_1 stands in no morally significant role to V_2 and V_3. So

A_1 cannot wrong them jointly. She can only wrong each, and she does that only if in letting each die she does no good to another comparable to the loss *each* undergoes.

The second objection picks up the argument at this point. This objector reasons that talk of wronging V_2 and V_3 together, i.e., jointly, is no more objectionable than is talk of my total debt of ten dollars owed to X and Y jointly, when I owe each five dollars.[40] The point is that moral wrongness may be aggregated; the wrongness of letting V_2 die may be summed with that of letting V_3 die in such a way that, as victims are added, eventually the aggregate wrongness of letting others die in refusing to kill V_1 will outweigh that of killing him.

I wish to make three points against this objection. First, this conception vulgarizes the concept of immorality, treating it as if it were reducible to some system of demerits, so that even if A_1 gets, say, six demerits for intentionally killing V_1 but only, say, four for unintentionally (but foreseeably) letting V_2 die, the additional four demerits she gets for letting V_3 die, will combine to outweigh the six and tip the scales in favor of killing V_1. Such an account of immorality has no place in the conception of moral life I sketched and, indeed, is inferior to the one contained in that conception. I say it is inferior because it does not take seriously the fact that there is no wrongdoing which is not the wronging *of* somebody, no immorality which is not a matter of falling short in some morally significant relationship.

Second, this objection misunderstands the debt-analogy from which it seeks to draw suppport. In the case imagined where I owe five dollars to X and five dollars to Y, talk of 'the total debt owed X and Y jointly' or of my 'joint debt to X and Y' is useful but *fictive*. There is, of course, a real sum of the amounts owed each, but there is no real total debt, just as there is a mathematical average of the numbers giving the weight in pounds of each American, but there is no real 'average American' who weighs it. Suppose I promised six dollars to A on Monday and then promised four dollars to B on Tuesday. We can then usefully talk of my total joint promissory obligation of ten dollars. Nevertheless, there is no joint promise since there is no joint act of promising; there are only the two acts, one on Monday, and one on Tuesday. To think otherwise would be to make a mistake similar to that made by one who assumes that because my average indebtedness is five dollars, there must be a real average debt I owe. But to whom is it owed? On which day did I incur it? As there is no average and no joint promise I make spread out over Monday and Tuesday, so there is no average and no joint promise I have made to A and B jointly.

Third, whereas in the debt and weight cases (and perhaps, in the promising case) there is a use for the arithmetical procedures, this is not always the case, and it may well be true that the moral situation is more similar to the cases where the arithmetic makes no sense than it is to the debt case. Suppose I dive to a depth of six feet on my first high-dive and to a depth of four feet on each of two subsequent dives. Have I dived on the later dives to a joint, total depth of eight feet? What would one mean in saying this? The moral case is interestingly like this diving case. In failing to save V_2, it is as if one sinks below (to use a relevant metaphor) the normal mark of benevolence with respect to him and so too in letting V_3 die. However, A_1 sinks to a far greater depth, as we might say, if she intentionally kills V_1. What sense are we to make of demands that we 'add the depths' to which the agent sinks in two of the presumptive violations of duty and then compare this total with that of the third? I can assign none.

The third objection appeals to rights. With Anscombe, I think no one is wronged by A_1 when she lets V_2 and V_3 die rather than kill V_1. And like her I concluded from this that no wrong is done by A_1. One might claim instead that everyone has a right that agents act so as to save the larger number and thus that everyone is wronged. However, this has the absurd result that V_1 is wronged, his rights are violated, by A_1 when she decides against killing him.

More plausibly, one might insist that when the choice must be made between acting so as to save from death either a larger group or a smaller group, then everyone in *the larger group* has a right that the larger group be saved, while those in the smaller group do not. Thus, there will be people wronged if the agent acts to spare the smaller number from being killed and thus the act will be wrong.

However, the problem for this line of argument is that it is not clear what reason there is to think that each member of the *larger* group has a right that it be spared which reason does not also allow that each member of the *smaller* group has a right that *it* be spared. After all, either way such a right protects the interests of those who have it. The only reason that seems to work in the needed way giving rights to be saved to those in the larger group but not to those in the smaller group is one that *presupposes* it is morally important to save more rather than fewer. However, this begs the question of whether it is worse of the agent to spare the one and let the two be killed than it is to spare the two and let the one be killed. (Ignoring what obviously is not to be ignored—that the one is, and the two are not, killed *by the agent.*)

The fourth objection is the simplest. Its claim is merely that the deaths of two people (V_2 and V_3) are a worse thing than is the death of just one (V_1), the deaths of three worse than two, and so on, and that these facts must figure in our moral reasoning in such a way as to favor killing one rather than letting the multitude die.

To reply to this we must first understand what is meant by the claim that the deaths of V_2 and V_3 are a worse thing than is the death of V_1.[41] Using the axiological analysis we have been employing, this must come to the claim that desiring the deaths of V_2 and V_3 is worse than is desiring V_1's death. But using the account of moral badness I have sketched, this claim is ambiguous, open to interpretation *inter alia* as (a) the thesis that desiring V_2's and V_3's deaths tends to make one *more bad in some role* one plays in another's life, (b) the thesis that desiring V_2's and V_3's deaths tends to make one *bad in more roles,* and (c) the thesis that desiring V_2's and V_3's deaths tends to make one *bad in one's roles (relationships) to more people.*

The last interpretation is the one that seems most natural and the one on which the claim most plainly turns out true. However, now we require an argument showing that A_1 has a duty owed to someone that she minimize the number of people in her relationships to whom she falls short of the minimal relevant standard of goodwill. To whom is this duty owed?[42] Everyone? But why think it is owed to anyone? In our moral life, as we have conceived it, we are tied to *each* person, to some more tightly than to others. Nothing in this points to a duty to minimize the *extent* of breaches of relationship. However, this conception does indicate that we should minimize the *intensity* of any breaches which we occasion for that way we avoid distancing ourselves too greatly from anyone.

This suggests it is rational to see in our morality a sort of minimax rule requiring an agent in relevant conflict situations to minimize the maximum degree to which she deviates from her responsibility to will the good to each affected party.[43] Fidelity to such a rule can be seen as part of the goodwill owed each person in virtue of our relationship to her. This is captured by the decision procedure outlined above, which, we saw, systematically found in favor of the case for sparing V_1's life. Even if the world does not permit us to act lovingly to everyone, we can and should eschew all ill will. 'With malice toward none' must remain our guide as a minimal gesture towards the ideal of charity to all.

The line of argument developed with respect to the case of A_1 and A_2 can, with further philosophical work, be extended to cover other kinds of actions. Consider A_3 who knows that, unless she kills some innocent person now, she will wind up killing even more in the future. Though these future killings would be just as evilly intended as her killing this victim now, her choice now is between an action performed with an intent to kill and a course of action (refusing to kill now) with no such intention and against which one can say only that it involves a failure to try to avoid the future killings. This choice pits the (presumptively) counter-officious against the inofficious and can thus be resolved in the same way. Morally, she must choose against killing now. The same holds even if the victim of the contemplated present killing would be among the victims of those possible future ones. If I intend to kill him now my intention is evil even if this intention is instrumental to sparing him later and perhaps worse death. For to intend death is to intend the loss of a basic form of good and this is so opposed to the goodwill that constitutes virtue and duty in one's moral role that its wrongness will always be greater than that of any failure to secure the other a good.

With this, of course, we are on the way to an explanation of the impermissibility of mercy-killing and, when we consider the virtues and duties internal to our role as steward of oneself, we may be positioned to explain the impermissibility of suicide, sterilization, and other forms of self-mutilation, and perhaps of other assaults on our bodies and our dignity. With an adequate account of the goods devotion to which is constitutive of the virtues and duties of a spouse, we should be able to apply the same line of argument to derive the impermissibility of abandonment, adultery, and so on. Of course, all this is going much too fast. I mean only to gesture toward the work that lies before those interested in continuing, along the lines I have indicated, the project of explaining the place of some of the traditional exceptionless norms in a Christian ethics.

The approach taken here in clearing the way for a philosophical defense of certain traditional moral absolutes may well have advantages over its principal rivals. Foot relies on a distinction between positive and negative duties, holding that the latter are more stringent because they are duties of justice while positive duties are duties of charity.[44] This leaves it quite unclear why duties of justice are more stringent, especially given her claim that violations of duties of justice need not be morally worse acts than violations of duties of charity. Donagan relies on a Kantian principle of respect but his approach has been criticized by Kagan for leaving it unexplained just how the absolutist is to make the crucial move from the uncontroversial premise that the respect principle prohibits killing people "at will" to the needed conclusion that it prohibits killing one person to avert more such killings.[45] Finnis and Grisez rely on a supposedly self-evident requirement of practical reason that we never "choose directly against" any basic form of human good.[46] However, this appeal to self-evidence is notoriously unevident to many philosophers. Nor is it clear just how they respond to the charge that it is implausible to maintain that reason really does require something that is, if Scheffler is right, so strongly irrational on its face. Nozick relies on natural rights, but leaves it unclear how we acquire them, why we have them, just which ones we have, and why they are so stringent.[47] Nagel roots his "deontological restrictions" in the independence of what he calls "the subjective

point of view." However, his discussion of this is full of perplexing sayings, "Perhaps reality should not be identified with objective reality," " . . . there is no way things are in themselves,"
"the problem is not that something has been left out [of the objective account of the world]," but " . . . an objective account,
whatever it shows, will omit something." One concerned to justify certain exceptionless norms in the tradition is well advised
to be wary of conceding that her opponent is on the side of objectivity while conceding that her own position is, as Nagel calls
it, "a form of romanticism."[48]

VI. Moral Dilemmas

Permit me to close with some observations about moral
dilemmas.[49] One might think these have nothing to do with
moral absolutism, but that would be wrong. Allowing dilemmas
into the moral framework can make some of the traditional exceptionless norms more palatable to some.[50] Suppose one thinks,
like Kant, Augustine, Aquinas, and others, that lying is always
immoral. This seems severely to restrict one's acceptable options.
However, if one also accepts that there are situations where one
cannot but do wrong and that some wrongdoing is therefore
somehow eligible, then the exceptionless norm about the wrong-
fulness of lying does not by itself serve to exclude lying from the
range of one's legitimate options. To me, making absolutes eligible in this way amounts to denaturing them, robbing them of
their proper status as conclusive reasons, factors that close off
options as unfit for practical consideration. Hence, I wish to
speak against dilemmas.

The philosophical waters are now muddied on this issue,
making it difficult to see just what the alternative positions are
and what is to be said for them. However, there are, I think,
strong reasons for thinking Christians to be well advised in seeking to exclude moral dilemmas from Christian ethics, whatever
their status in secular ethics may be.[51]

First, Christians will think that part of what makes wrong
acts wrong is that they are contrary to God's will. His will,
moreover, is paradigmatically rational, and his knowledge com-

plete. Now a rational agent never wills each of two things she knows to be mutually exclusive. However, if there are situations in which one acts wrongly no matter how one acts and therefore situations in which one acts against God's will no matter how one acts, then it would seem God must will things which are, and which he therefore knows to be, mutually exclusive. Since God cannot act in such an irrational way, it appears we need to give up either some traditional Christian beliefs about God's will and knowledge or the thesis that there are situations in which one cannot but act wrongly.

Second, it is a commonplace of both secular and Christian morality that it is immoral to will another to do evil. However, if God wills one to do something which she cannot do without doing evil, then God, it would seem, wills her to do evil. Since this would be immoral, we are again faced with a choice between traditional Christian belief and the thesis of moral dilemmas.

It might be thought one could evade these arguments by insisting that Christian morality requires only fidelity to divine *commands,* not to divine *will.*[52] I doubt such a strategy can work. First, it is not clear that one can command a person to do something without intending her to do it. Some philosophers have thought such an intention to be internal to commands. But, second and more important, Christian morality cannot sensibly consider people bound to obey God's commands unless there is some presumption that his commands reflect his will. Without such a presumption why pay attention to his commands? The difficulty is precisely analogous to that which would afflict any claim that we ought to believe what God tells us irrespective of whether it can be thought accurately to reflect his knowledge.

Having had my say against admitting moral dilemmas into Christian ethics, I should point out that such admission poses less of a threat of undermining the practical significance of my defense of traditional absolute norms than of other possible defenses. On my view, the reason such types of action as intentionally killing the innocent, lying, blaspheming, etc., are always wrong (I mean wrong *simpliciter,* not merely *prima facie* wrong) is that an action of such a type is always morally *worse* than its alternatives, worse because it involves wickedly intending the destruction of some basic form of human good, i.e., a good the willing of which constitutes the standard of virtue and duty in some morally significant role.

That being so, even if one allows that there are cases where all the alternative actions open to an agent are immoral, there could still be no good reason to lie, to kill the innocent, etc. For there can be no justification for selecting, even in a situation where all alternatives are immoral, an action which is *more* immoral than some alternative. I think the partisans of moral dilemmas should not be permitted to bring their Trojan Horse inside the gates of Christian ethics. But even if they do, we may not be lacking in the resources needed to overcome the enemy lurking in its bowels.[53]

NOTES

I am grateful to Stephen Evans for his comments delivered when this paper was first read in February 1988, at a conference sponsored by the Center for the Philosophy of Religion at the University of Notre Dame. I also benefited from questions posed at that session, from written comments sent me by John Whelan and Philip Devine, and from discussions with Laura Garcia and Robert Audi.

1. Because I do from time to time argue that a certain position is more or less acceptable to Christians, the question arises whether I have crossed the traditional line between philosophical and theological discourse. I think I have not. To argue that *p* is false because it ill fits with Christian belief is, perhaps, to argue theologically. However, one need not rely on one's own Christian convictions (indeed, one need not have any) to argue, as I sometimes do in this essay, that *p* complements or clashes with what Christians believe and for that reason is or is not an epistemically attractive or acceptable position for a Christian. This essay was written, of course, for an audience predominantly Christian but surely that does not make it into theology.

2. I offer some considerations in favor of such a conception of moral life in Garcia (1985; 1986a).

3. See Brentano (1889; 1952); Meinong (1917); Ewing (1939). Some important secondary works include Chisholm (1986), McAlister (1976), and Findlay (1963).

4. For more on this approach to value theory, see Garcia (1987).

5. *Nicomachean Ethics* 1106a15–20.

6. For a different defense and understanding of the claim that moral assessment centers on what one is to be rather than on what one is to do, see Kekes (1984). Recently, some feminist critics of contemporary moral philosophy have urged the centrality of one's relationships and, particularly, the significance of personal responsibility and caring in contrast to the usual overemphasis on rights, reasoning, principles, and impartiality. For an introduction, see Held (1988) and Gilligan (1982). There are also interesting similarities between my view and the 'relationship-responsibility' model of moral life offered as an alternative to the old deontological/teleological division in Curran (1985), chaps. 1, 6.

7. Frankena (1980, 4–6).

8. Gass (1957) drew attention to this constraint on an adequate account of morality. For a more recent view, see the methodological remarks in Thomson (1986, 258ff).

9. We can say, consistent with the conception of moral life sketched above, that one fulfills her moral roles *vis-à-vis* God when she responds to him as it is his nature to want her to respond. Christians presumably will take their guidance from the first of the Great Commandments, especially together with such passages as 1 John 5:3. One example of the type of religious ethics I mean to oppose is well explicated in Adams (1987), chaps. 7, 9.

10. See Sen (1985) and Garcia (1986b).

11. See, especially, the essays cited in note 2.

12. For complications on this point see Bratman (1985; 1987).

13. For a criticism of the stronger thesis that one can never be obligated to do something one cannot, see Sinnott-Armstrong (1984).

14. See Aquinas's intricate discussion of his distinction between *omissio* and *transgressio* in *ST* IIaIIae q.79 a.2, a.3, a.4.

15. My view is 'intentionalist' in that I hold that my doing something or my not doing is right or wrong according to and because of its connection to my adopting or rejecting certain intentions. Abelard seems to have held the stronger thesis that the (im)morality of actions is *reducible* to that of the agent's intentions.

16. Brand (1984), chap. 2.

17. Bennett (1981, 97).

18. See Stocker (1973).

19. For this dispute see Abelard and also McInerny (1982, 84–89).

20. I recall once hearing the Christian phenomenologist von Hildebrand stressing that all love is essentially a *volitional,* not an emotional, phenomenon. See also Aquinas, *ST* IIaIIae q.24 a.1.

21. I draw especially on Anscombe (1957), Davidson (1980), and White (1985, chap. 6).

22. See Davis (1984).

23. I hope to defend this view in more detail in two papers now in progress, to be entitled "The Irreducibility of the Will" and "The Intentional and the Intended."

24. For particulary careful discussions along these lines, see Audi (1986) and Harman (1986).

25. The best discussion of this point is in Bratman (1987).

26. Davis (1984), Bratman (1987).

27. I am assuming here that one need not expect that one will do what one intends to do. This has been disputed in Audi (1986) and other places. My view is argued for in the papers cited above in note 23 and agrees with the position taken in Davidson (1980) and White (1985).

28. On forward- and backward-looking accounts of the justification of behavior, see Garcia (forthcoming).

29. On positive and negative duties, see Kant (1785, *A* 421 and note), Foot (1978; 1985a; 1985b).

30. Aquinas, *SCG* III ch.9; *ST* IIaIIae q.79 a4.

31. For purposes of exposition I shall speak as if decisions were always in the background of one's behavior. Those who find such talk objectionable can rephrase my claims in some more complicated way.

32. For an unusually sophisticated account of the difference between these two cases, see Bennett (1981). Bennett correctly notes that both bombers may be glad *when* they find out the civilians are dead—Terror Bomber because it means that the populace will be demoralized, Tactical Bomber because it means that the bombs exploded on target, destroying the factory which was his target. However, he misses the obvious point that Terror Bomber is glad *that* the civilians are dead, since he needs their deaths, while Tactical Bomber is not. To the latter, the civilians' deaths are *signs* of something good, while Terror bomber must treat them as themselves good, i.e., as goals, objects of desire and preference.

33. The general line of argument I pursue here was suggested to me in reflection on Boyle and Sullivan (1977). Their interest there is to show that not all one expects to do in acting need even be part of what one intends to do.

34. Aquinas, *SCG* III ch.9; *ST* IIaIIae q.79 a.4.

35. Nozick (1981, 497f).
36. Nagel (1986, chap. 9).
37. For some examples, see Glover (1977, chap. 3) and Rachels (1986).
38. Foot makes a related suggestion in Foot (1985b, 35f).
39. Scheffler (1982, esp. chap. 4, 5).
40. This line of argument was suggested to me by a somewhat different argument in Regan (1983, 300f).
41. This way of talking is criticized cogently in Taurek (1977).
42. Here I follow Anscombe (1967). My whole approach here is influenced by this essay.
43. See the comparable principles discussed in Regan (1983, chap. 8).
44. Foot (1985a).
45. Donagan (1977); Kagan (1987).
46. Finnis (1983); Grisez (1983).
47. Nozick (1974).
48. Quotations in this paragraph are from the first published sketch of Nagel's account in "Subjective/Objective" (1979). The view is developed more fully in his late Tanner Lectures and in Nagel (1986) but not in such a way as to allay the concerns I have raised.
49. For our purposes we can construe a moral dilemma as a situation in which, no matter what an agent does, her behavior is immoral, morally wrong or forbidden, in violation of her moral obligations. Many of the major pieces on moral dilemmas are collected in Gowans (1987).
50. Nagel ("War and Massacre," pp. 73f. in Nagel 1979). In conversation with me, Philip Quinn advocated a similar view.
51. Since writing this I have learned that a case is made against admitting moral dilemmas into Christian ethics in Santurri (1987) and that MacIntyre, now a self-described Christian, expresses second thoughts about his earlier acceptance of dilemmas. See MacIntyre (1988, esp. chap. 11).
52. I heard Robert Adams commend such a view in remarks made at the NEH Summer Institute on the Philosophy of Religion at Bellingham, Washington in 1986.
53. My work on this project was supported by grants from the Ford Foundation's Postdoctoral Fellowships for Minorities program and from The Institute for Scholarship in the Liberal Arts at the University of Notre Dame. I am grateful to audiences at Virginia Common-

wealth University, Georgetown University's Kennedy Institute of Ethics, and the 1985 NEH Summer Institute at the University of Notre Dame's Medieval Institute for beneficial comments on some of the material presented herein.

BIBLIOGRAPHY

Abelard, Peter. *Peter Abelard's Ethics*. Trans. D. E. Luscombe. Oxford: Oxford University Press, 1971.

Adams, Robert. 1987. *The Virtue of Faith*. Oxford: Oxford University Press.

Anscombe, G. E. M. 1957. *Intention*. Ithaca, N.Y.: Cornell University Press.

——. 1967. "Who Is Wronged?" *Oxford Review 5*.

Audi, Robert. 1986. "Intending, Intentional Action, and Desire." In *Ways of Desire*. Ed. J. Marks. Chicago: Precedent Publishing.

Bennett, Jonathan. 1981. "Morality and Consequences." In *Tanner Lectures*, vol. 2. Ed. S. McMurin, 47–116. Salt Lake City: University of Utah Press.

Boyle, Joseph, and Thomas Sullivan. 1977. "The Diffusiveness of Intention Principle: A Counter-Example." *Philosophical Studies* 77: 357–360.

Brand, Myles. 1984. *Intending and Acting*. Cambridge, Mass.: MIT Press.

Bratman, Michael. 1985. "Davidson's Theory of Intention." In *Actions and Events*. Ed. E. LePore and B. McLaughlin, 14–28. Oxford: Basil Blackwell.

——. 1987. *Intention, Plans, and Practical Reason*. Cambridge, Mass.: Harvard University Press.

Brentano, Franz. 1889. *The Origin of Our Knowledge of Right and Wrong*. Trans. R. Chisholm. New York: Routledge & Kegan Paul, 1969.

——. 1952. *The Foundation and Construction of Ethics*. Trans. E. H. Schneewind. New York: Humanities.

Chisholm, Roderick. 1986. *Brentano and Intrinsic Value*. Cambridge: Cambridge University Press.

Curran, Charles. 1985. *Directions in Fundamental Moral Theology*. Notre Dame, Ind.: University of Notre Dame Press.

Davidson, Donald. 1980. "Intending." In *Essays on Actions and Events*, 84–102. Oxford: Oxford University Press.

Davis, Wayne. 1984. "A Causal Theory of Intending." *American Philosophical Quarterly* 21: 43–54.

Donagan, Alan. 1977. *The Theory of Morality*. Chicago: University of Chicago Press.

Ewing, A. C. 1939. "A Suggested Non-Naturalistic Analysis of Good." *Mind* 48: 1–22.

Findlay, John. 1963. *Meinong's Theory of Objects and Values*. 2d ed. Oxford: Oxford University Press.

Finnis, John. 1983. *Fundamentals of Ethics*. Washington, D.C.: Georgetown University Press.

Foot, P. R. 1978. "Euthanasia." In *Virtues and Vices*, 33–61. Berkeley, Calif.: University of California Press.

———. 1985a. "Utilitarianism and the Virtues." *Mind* 94: 197–209.

———. 1985b. "Morality, Action and Outcome." In *Morality and Objectivity*. Ed. T. Honderich, 23–38. London: Routledge & Kegan Paul.

Frankena, William. 1980. "Three Questions About Morality." *Monist* 63: 4–68.

Garcia, J. L. A. 1985. "Morals, Roles, and Reasons for Action." *Critica* 17: 29–43.

———. 1986a. "'Morally Ought' Rethought." *Journal of Value Inquiry* 20: 83–94.

———. 1986b. "Evaluator Relativity and the Theory of Value." *Mind* 95: 242–245.

———. 1987. "Goods and Evils." *Philosophy and Phenomenological Research* 47: 385–412.

———. Forthcoming. "The Right and the Good." *Philosophia*.

Gass, William. 1957. "The Case of the Obliging Stranger." *Philosophical Review* 66: 193–204.

Gilligan, Carol. 1982. *In a Different Voice*. Cambridge, Mass.: Harvard University Press.

Glover, Jonathan. 1977. *Causing Deaths and Saving Lives*. New York: Penguin.

Gowans, Christopher (ed.). 1987. *Moral Dilemmas*. New York: Oxford University Press.

Grisez, Germain. 1983. *Christian Moral Principles*. Chicago: Franciscan Herald Press.

Harman, Gilbert. 1986. "Willing and Intending." In *Philosophical Grounds of Rationality*. Ed. R. Grandy, 363–380. Oxford: Oxford University Press.

Held, Virginia. 1988. "Report on Feminist Moral Theory." *Newsletter on Feminism and Philosophy*. April: 11–13.

Kagan, Shelly. 1987. "Donagan on the Sins of Consequentialism." *Canadian Journal of Philosophy* 17: 643–654.

Kant. 1785. *Groundwork of the Metaphysics of Morals*. Trans. H. J. Paton. New York: Harper and Row, 1964.

Kekes, John. 1984. "Moral Sensitivity." *Philosophy* 59: 3–19.

MacIntyre, Alasdair. 1988. *Whose Justice? Which Rationality?* Notre Dame, Ind.: University of Notre Dame Press.

McAlister, Linda (ed.). 1976. *The Philosophy of Brentano*. London: Duckworth.

McInerny, Ralph. 1982. *Ethica Thomistica*. Washington, D.C.: Catholic University of America Press.

Meinong, Alexius. 1917. *On Emotional Presentation*. Trans. M-L. S. Kalsi. Evanston, Ill.: Northwestern University Press, 1972.

Nagel, Thomas. 1979. *Mortal Questions*. Cambridge: Cambridge University Press.

———. 1986. *The View from Nowhere*. Oxford: Oxford University Press.

Nozick, Robert. 1974. *Anarchy, State, and Utopia*. New York: Basic Books.

———. 1981. *Philosophical Explanations*. Cambridge, Mass.: Harvard University Press.

Rachels, James. 1986. *The End of Life*. New York: Oxford University Press.

Regan, Tom. 1983. *The Case for Animal Rights*. Berkeley, Calif.: University of California Press.

Santurri, Edmund. 1987. *Perplexity in the Moral Life*. Charlottesville, Va.: University Press of Virginia.

Scheffler, Samuel. 1982. *The Rejection of Consequentialism*. Oxford: Oxford University Press.

Sen, Amartya. 1985. "Well-Being, Agency, and Freedom." *Journal of Philosophy* 82: 169–221.

Sinnott-Armstrong, Walter. 1984. "'Ought' Conversationally Implies 'Can'." *Philosophical Review* 93: 249–261.

Stocker, Michael. 1973. "Act and Agent Evaluations." *Review of Metaphysics* 27: 42–61.

Taurek, John. 1977. "Should the Number Count?" *Philosophy and Public Affairs* 6: 293–316.

Thomson, Judith. 1986. *Rights, Restitution, and Risk*. Cambridge, Mass.: Harvard University Press.

White, A. R. 1985. *Grounds of Liability*. Oxford: Oxford University Press.

Taking St. Paul Seriously:
Sin as an Epistemological Category

Merold Westphal

I want to suggest in this essay that for Christian philosophers sin should be an essential epistemological category and to suggest something of what that might mean.

By sin I mean neither sins nor the tendency to commit sins but the fundamental project of which both sins and the tendency to commit them are expressions. With the Augustinian tradition I find this project best described as pride, the self-assertion which usurps a role in life not proper to me, depriving God and neighbor of their rightful places as, respectively, my absolute superior and my equal. Since the self which pridefully asserts itself beyond its proper limits is as easily corporate as personal, sin is as much a matter of chauvinism as of egoism in the individual sense. *We* are as capable of inordinate self-assertion as *I* am.

By epistemology I mean reflection on the nature and limits of human knowledge. While epistemology has often been thought of as primarily a matter of logic, distinguishing deductive from inductive inference and indentifying in each case the kinds of inferences and the degrees of confidence which are appropriate, I prefer to think of epistemology as a matter of psychology (the nature of human knowledge) and ethics (the limits of human knowledge). The (social) psychological side is then the description of how we actually form and change our beliefs, while the ethical side is the normative task of identifying what (kinds of) beliefs we are entitled to hold. It is not hard to see that logic, as the theory of what inferences we are entitled to make and with what level of confidence, is but a subdivision of epistemological ethics, specifying an important subset of epistemic rights and duties. This way of putting it shifts attention from beliefs to believings, or, to put it linguistically, reminds us that syntax and semantics are always subordinate to pragmatics. This, in turn, makes it more natural to speak of sin as an epistemological category.

To speak this way is to suggest that when we "do" epistemology, Christian philosophers should listen carefully to what their theologian colleagues (sometimes) say about the noetic effects of sin. This locution is most likely to be found among Calvinist theologians trying to explain what they mean by total depravity (that terrible T of TULIP). By total depravity they do not mean that we are as evil as we could possibly be. (Which of us, for example, could claim to have come up with an original sin?) They mean rather that depravity is total in its extent, that no part of us has escaped the corruption of the fall; that, in particular, the intellect and not just the will has been distorted by sin and no longer functions as it was intended to in creation.

In the opening chapters of his *Institutes of the Christian Religion*, Calvin develops this theme with reference to our knowledge of God (and thereby of ourselves). In spite of a "sense of Deity" that is "indelibly engraven" within us as a "natural instinct" and a corresponding "seed of religion" that is "divinely sown in all," we do not naturally come to a proper knowledge of God.[1] The reason is that through this sense and this seed we come to feel a truth "which [we] are desirous not to know" with the result that "the knowledge of God [is] stifled or corrupted" within us.[2] We end up blind through our own pride, stubbornness, and perversity.[3]

Three aspects of Calvin's discussion should be highlighted here. First, he explicitly gives to this problem the same universality that he gives to sin in general. All of us are involved.[4] Second, this is not simply a matter of ignorance or weakness. To emphasize our responsibility, Calvin insists that we "intentionally stupify" ourselves and have "deliberately turned [our] thoughts away from God."[5] Finally, the result is not so much a spiritual vacuum as idolatry. We suppress God's truth by substituting figments of our own imagination to worship and serve.[6]

Not long ago a freshman at a college of Calvinist heritage wrote, "Since Jesus Christ was born before the Protestant Reformation, he was raised as a Roman Catholic." I want to suggest a somewhat more ecumenical approach to the notion of sin as an epistemological category. For while it may be distinctive of Calvinism, it is by no means unique to that tradition. The notion that sin distorts our thinking is absolutely central to Luther, for whom Reason can thereby be an ally of the flesh in its struggle against the Spirit.[7] In his critique of logocentrism, the human logos is the truly satanic enemy of the Divine Logos, for it opposes the gospel while disguised as an angel of light (cf. 1 Cor. 11:14). It is in this Lutheran framework that Kierkegaard gives us perhaps the most sustained modern reflection on sin as an epistemological category.[8]

What makes this notion truly ecumenical, however, is its pre-Reformation roots in Augustine,[9] who belongs to the entire western church, and ultimately in Paul, who belongs to the entire Christian church and who is the point of departure for Augustine, Luther, Calvin, and Kierkegaard. That part of Paul's theology which Karl Barth summarizes simply as "The Night,"[10] gives explicitly epistemological meaning to his claim that "all have sinned and fall short of the glory of God" (Rom. 3:23 RSV). He writes

> For the wrath of God is revealed from heaven against all ungodliness and wickedness of men who by their wickedness suppress the truth. For what can be known about God is plain to them.... So they are without excuse; for although they knew God they did not honor him as God or give thanks to him, but they became futile in their thinking and their senseless minds were darkened. Claiming to be wise, they became fools, and exchanged the glory of the immortal God for images resembling mortal man or birds or animals or reptiles. Therefore God gave them up . . . because they exchanged the truth about God for a lie and worshipped and served the creature rather than the Creator, who is blessed forever! Amen. (Romans 1:18–24 RSV)

What would it mean for contemporary Christian philosophers to make this Pauline notion that as sinners we "suppress the truth" a primary theme in our epistemological reflection? For purposes of convenience in the present context, I shall speak of doing this as "taking Paul seriously."

I want to suggest, first of all, that it would mean reading the history of philosophy differently from the way we normally do, and this in two respects. One of the changes would be generic, the other specific. The generic change would consist, quite simply, in a greater sensitivity to and interest in the career of the Pauline motif in the philosophical tradition. Since it occurs in a wide variety of contexts, religious and secular, empiricist and rationalist, materialist and idealist, and so forth, we cannot expect it always to appear in Pauline packaging, explicitly evoking the concept of sin. But it should not be difficult to recognize when philosophers in various vocabularies suggest that desires and practices which in Christian terms are sinful play a constitutively distorting role in human belief formation and retention, personal and corporate. The following examples are meant to be illustrative rather than systematic, and to intimate the diversity of contexts in which sin in fact functions as an epistemological category.

(a) To take Paul seriously would mean to meditate on what Augustine suggests in the *Confessions* about the origin of language rather than dismissing it as rhetorical excess or as merely incidental. I refer to the passage with which Wittgenstein opens the *Philosophical Investigations*, but not to the problem of ostensive definition. Rather, what becomes foreground against the Pauline background is the way Augustine links language at the very end of the quotation, not to truth but to desire. Just before the sentences Wittgenstein quotes, Augustine tells us that he learned to speak "so that people would do what I wanted" or "so that my wishes should be obeyed."[11] In the context of Augustine's understanding of human desire as sinfully proud, this linkage of language to desire is explosive. In the context of contemporary understandings of the linguisticality of human understanding, it becomes as deeply disturbing as any postmodern genealogy or deconstruction of reason.[12]

(b) To take Paul seriously would mean to notice and explore the "Calvinist" moments in Hobbes. Herbert W. Schneider, for example, tells us that the *Leviathan* is "based on Calvinist psychology,"[13] though he does not say just what he has in mind. No doubt he has in mind the unflattering account of human motivations we find in Hobbes, and just perhaps he is thinking about the noetic effects of these motivations. The titles of the last two chapters are of interest in this regard. Chapter 46, "Of Darkness from Vain Philosophy, and Fabulous Traditions," expresses what is to become a standard Enlightenment worry about the power of irrational "knowledge"; beyond this, chapter 47, "Of the Benefit proceeding from such Darkness and to whom it accrueth," raises the "Calvinist" (or "Augustinian" or "Pauline") question whether superstition is just a matter of innocent blindness or rather of motivated irrationality.[14] His deep fears of either Calvinist or Roman Catholic theocracy lead him to notice, long before Marx or Foucault or liberation theology, the political power and social advantages that come with monopolies on truth. In this way he learns to ask not just what support various beliefs have, but also what functions they play, that is, what practices they legitimize. This shifts attention from the justification of belief to justification by belief. (Ironically, the rise of liberation theology shows that Hobbes's fears are as well grounded in our own century as ever they were in his own. The historic link between Roman Catholicism and domination in Latin America and the even more shameless role of Dutch Calvinism in supporting apartheid in South Africa are the focal points for two major traditions of liberation theology. The means by which both seek to rescue their respective traditions from long-standing linkage to oppression is the serious employment of sin as an epistemological category in the mode of Hobbes).[15]

Equally significant for the present topic is his discussion, in chapter 11, of the process by which, in good "Calvinist" fashion, we end up worshipping idols, by which fearful humans "are inclined to suppose, and feign themselves, several kinds of powers invisible; and to stand in awe of their own imaginations; and in time of distress to invoke them; as also in the time of an expected good success, to give them thanks; making the creatures of their own fancy, their gods."[16] Like Calvin, Hobbes notes the distortion of rationality by desire especially in the religious realm, and he goes on to formulate a more general theorem, noting "that the doctrine of right and wrong, is perpetually disputed, both by the pen and the sword: whereas the doctrine of lines, and figures, is not so; because men care not, in that subject, what be truth, as a thing that crosses no man's ambition, profit or lust. For I doubt not, but if it had been a thing contrary to any man's right of dominion, or to the interest of men that have dominion, *that the three angles of a triangle, should be equal to two angles of a square;* that doctrine should have been, if not disputed, yet by the burning of all books of geometry, suppressed, as far as he whom it concerned was able" (his italics).

This I take to be a formulation of what one of my teachers used to call the Law of Inverse Rationality. By this he meant that the ability of human thought to be undistorted by sinful desire is inversely proportional to the existential import of the subject matter. We can be reasonably rational at the periphery of our interests, where opportunities for prideful self-assertion are limited. But the closer the topic to the core of our being, the greater the tendency to subordinate truth to other values. This has the clear implication that sin's role as an epistemological category will be especially significant in the areas of ethics and politics, theology and metaphysics.

(c) Kant and Fichte surely thought so, and to take Paul seriously would mean to listen carefully to their concerns in the areas of ethics and metaphysics, respectively. Kant writes,

> Man feels within himself a powerful counterweight to all the commands of duty . . . this counterweight consists of his needs and inclinations. . . . Now reason irremissibly commands its precepts, without thereby promising the inclinations anything. . . . Hereby arises a natural dialectic, i.e., a propensity to quibble with these strict laws of duty, to cast doubt upon their validity, or at least upon their purity and strictness, and to make them, where possible, more compatible with our wishes and inclinations. Thereby are such laws corrupted in their very foundation. . . . [17]

In the debates between Kant and his critics, between formalism and nonformalism, between intuitionism and naturalism or prescriptivism, and between deontology and teleology or consequentialism, this problem of the corruption of conscience by desire has for the most part been ignored. Should it not be the proper task of Christian philosophers to challenge the assumption that ethics can responsibly continue in this manner?

Fichte is concerned with the fundamental metaphysical choice between idealism, the philosophy of freedom and the independence of the self, and dogmatism, the philosophy of materialist fatalism and the independence of the thing. Recognizing that on this kind of issue we are not dispassionate, disinterested, pure reason, he asks, "What is it, then, that motivates a reasonable man to declare his preference for one over the other?"[18] By shifting the question of the realm of inclination and interest, he hopes to give a practical argument for idealism where the theoretical debate is inconclusive. He will show that people adopt dogmatism for (practically) bad reasons.

> What sort of philosophy one chooses depends, therefore, on what sort of man one is. . . . A person indolent by nature or dulled and distorted by mental servitude, learned luxury, and vanity will never raise himself to the level of idealism. We can show the dogmatist the inadequacy and incoherence of his system . . . but we cannot convince him, because he is incapable of calmly receiving and coolly assessing a theory which he absolutely cannot endure. . . . Our science expects few converts, therefore, among those *already formed;* if it may have any hopes at all, they are set, rather, upon the young whose innate power has not yet foundered in the indolence of our age.[19]

While this reference to the indolence of the age sounds more like Rousseau than Hobbes (or Calvin or Kant), the way in which both Kant and Fichte exempt themselves from their own accounts of reason's corruption is of more importance in the present context. The Pauline recognition of our tendency to "suppress the truth" helps Fichte dispatch the dogmatist to epistemological hell, but it completely abandons him (or he it) when it is a question of his own idealism. Does the fact that he is not guilty of the dogmatist's indolence (whether it be "by nature" or "of our age") guarantee his own purity? Are we not even permitted to ask whether he is motivated to prefer idealism by resentment, will to power, or a Pharisaical need to be holier than others?

Kant's exemption is, if anything, more generous. It is because of the corruption of morals described above that "ordinary human reason [is] forced to go outside its sphere and take a step into the field of practical philosophy."[20] In other words, *die gemeine Menschenvernunft* is no *blosse gesunde Vernunft,* but needs to be rescued from its corruptibility by philosophical reflection, whose credentials as *blosse gesunde Vernunft* are apparently not to be asked for. Here it is not adherence to the right philosophy, idealism, but the mere adoption of the philosophical standpoint that makes one incorruptible. This is why the discussion takes place in a section entitled "Transition from the Ordinary Rational Knowledge of Morality to the Philosophical."[21]

If we are taking Paul seriously we will not be surprised to find that the discovery of reason's fallenness is naturally accompanied by Lord-I-thank-Thee-that-I-am-not-like-them exemptions issued to those capable of discovering transcendental depravity in others. But we will not be fooled, either, into thinking that we can honestly use this discovery to set ourselves righteously apart from those unlike us. Against Kant we will not find it self-evident that the passage from unreflective to reflective rationality constitutes our sanctification; and against Fichte we will not assume that adherence to a morally uplifting theory makes our reason pure. We will rather be inclined (heaven help us) to listen sympathetically to Derrida when he suggests that texts are symptoms, and we will not exempt idealist (or even theistic) texts from the kind of scrutiny this implies. We will even take Derrida seriously when he describes philosophy itself as a history of "motivated repression" and invites us to explore "what this history has been able to dissimulate or forbid."[22]

*　　*　　*

There are many more stops on this tour through the history of philosophy, including Bacon and Hume, Marx and Mannheim, Schopenhauer and Nietzsche, Feuerbach and Freud, Foucault and Derrida, Rawls and Habermas, Hare and MacIntyre, and, of course, Kierkegaard. To switch metaphors, the history of philosophy is a mine filled with raw materials for a deepened understanding of the Pauline motif. The task of bringing these comprehensively and systematically to light should be high, it seems to me, on the agenda of Christian philosophers. It is the generic task to which I referred at the outset. The specific task, to which I now turn, is one thematically focused part of the larger task, namely the interpretation of the rise and fall of foundationalism. I offer three suggestions about what it would mean to take Paul seriously in interpreting this event.

(a) The first of these concerns the rise of foundationalism. In its Greek origins it is concerned to replace *doxa* with *episteme*. In its modern maturity it specifies *doxa* as tradition, authority, and superstition, while modelling *episteme* not only on mathematics but also on mathematical physics. The role of physics as a paradigm opens the door to empiricist-positivist versions of foundationalism, keeping it from being nothing but an expression of sense-intellect and mind-body dualism. The specification of *doxa* as tradition, authority, and superstition, which concerns us here, opens the door to diagnosing *doxa* not just as finitude, disinterested and innocent though limited, but also in Pauline fashion, as sin. Seen this way, foundationalism is not only the quest for certainty, but equally the quest for purity. In other words, the Enlightenment ideal of pure reason envisages human thought not only as unconstrained by the limits of perspective, but also uncontaminated by the stain of perversity. Floating between these poles of perspective and perversity, the concept of prejudice become ambiguous.

If it is the specification of *doxa* as tradition, authority, and superstition that makes this possible, this is because tradition and superstition are linked to authority, not just in the epistemological but also in the political sense. The link between knowledge and power, discussed above in relation to Hobbes, discloses and expresses the more general link between knowledge and desire, discussed above in relation to Augustine, Kant, and Fichte. In both cases it becomes clear that disinterested finitude is not our only problem.

Hume is as clear about this as is Hobbes.[23] The foundation is laid in the *Treatise* with its understanding of the link between reason and the passions. But it is in *The Natural History of Religion* that the distorting role of devious passions becomes fully explicit. There Hume inquires into the passions, in particular the hopes and fears, which give rise to belief in gods and to practices of prayer and sacrifice. He identifies these, in contrast to "speculative curiosity" and "the pure love of truth" and in conjunction with our profound ignorance of the causes of events, as "the anxious concern for happiness, the dread of future misery, the terror of death, the thirst of revenge, the appetite for food and other necessities."[24] Given the utterly self-centered character of these passions and the complete absence of the moral sentiments from their number, it is not surprising that Hume finds the resultant religious beliefs anything but pure. On the one hand they take the form of shameless flattery of the gods in the effort to enlist their power for our interests.[25] On the other hand they function to legitimize immoral behavior. Idolatrous worship, here defined as religion grounded in the passions of self-assertion, "is liable to this great inconvenience, that any practice or opinion, however barbarous or corrupted, may be authorized by it." Thus, "the greatest crimes have been found, in many instances, compatible with a superstitious piety and devotion." We are forced to ask, "What so pure as some of the morals, included in some theological systems? What so corrupt as some of the practices, to which these systems give rise?"[26]

In the light of these texts it becomes clear that Hume, the father of positivistic foundationalism, seeks to affirm science while eliminating metaphysics in order to free us not just from beliefs whose function is only to mask our ignorance, but also from beliefs whose function is both to mask and to serve our immoral desires. I believe that what is fully self-conscious in the foundationalist projects of Hobbes and Hume is present in all foundationalism, even if it is not fully explicit. Beyond the finitude of human understanding, foundationalism is the more or less conscious awareness of the noetic effects of sin and the attempt to neutralize these effects.[27]

This dawning awareness can surely be affirmed by those who would take Paul seriously. But the foundationalist attempt to remedy our transcendental depravity can only be problematic unless we are Pelagians. For it is, in effect, the claim that sin can be cured by our own unaided efforts, that epistemological sanctification requires nothing more than the epistemological asceticism of sound method, whether that method be syllogistic, Euclidian, experimental, transcendental, or whatever. Those who try to take Paul seriously from within an Augustinian framework will find foundationalism to be what Augustine found Platonism to be, presumption (pride) where confession (humility) is called for.[28] The irony is that this pride is the response to a more or less conscious awareness of the problematic character of human pride.

(b) My second suggestion about interpreting foundationalism concerns its demise. Two strategies (by no means mutually exclusive) have been adopted for showing the failure of the foundationalist project, now widely acknowledged. One takes the form of *modus tollens*. If foundationalism is true, then such and such beliefs must be abandoned as irrational. But such and such beliefs are rational (more obviously so than any theory which repudiates them). Hence foundationalism is not true. The other strategy consists in urging the plausibility of an alternative model of knowledge. Heidegger, Gadamer, Merleau-Ponty, and others have argued the essentially situated character of all cognition and the corresponding inescapability of the hermeneutical circle or prejudice. Wittgenstein and Peirce have pointed in the same direction with their distinctive denials of immediate cognition. Kuhn, Feyerabend, Hanson, Hesse, and others have argued against the possibility of theory-free data and for what might be called the hermeneutical understanding of natural science.

What these important traditions have in common is the recognition that what is first in the order of knowing lacks the self-evidence which would make it self-grounding. The earth rests on the elephant who stands on the turtle who has no place to stand. In retrospect it can be said that it was Kant who let the cat out of the bag (thereby leaving the turtle to float in mid-air). Having noted that the *a priori* yields universality and necessity, he also noted the contingency of the *a priori*. "This peculiarity of our understanding, that it can produce *a priori* unity of apperception solely by means of the categories, and only by such and so many, is as little capable of further explanation as why we have just these and no other functions of judgment, or why space and time are the only forms of our possible intuition."[29] Since the constitutive role of the *a priori* is not affected by this contingency, and since this contingency means that the *a priori* itself is neither necessary nor necessarily universal, attention is directed to those *a priori* elements which yield universal and necessary results only for those who happen to employ those elements. For example, racial bias is an *a priori* that makes it universally and necessarily true that members of the despised race are inferior, but only for those who see the world through the lenses of racial bias. The Kantian concession combined with the growing awareness of the contingency of our *a prioris*, or, to be more precise, of the "historical singularity" of our *a prioris*, makes it increasingly clear that foundationalism rests on the sustained forgetfulness of the situated nature of our perception and thought and the (historically contingent) assumption that we can attain "the view from nowhere."[30]

What all this has to do with taking Paul seriously is simply this. As long as we operate in some foundationalist framework sin does not need to be an epistemological category. Or, to be more precise, sin appears and disappears from the epistemological scene at the same moment. For the foundationalist project is simultaneously the (more or less conscious) recognition of the problem of judgment distorted by devious desire and the solution to that problem. In that project method becomes the means, not of grace, but of our own self-purification. But from the moment we recognize the contingent particularity of our *a prioris* and the consequent ineluctability of the hermeneutical circle, this escape from the human condition becomes unavailable. The inescapable subjectivity of understanding leaves knowledge permanently vulnerable to distorted desire. Of course, it does not follow that we will begin to take Paul seriously. The door has been opened, but we need not go through it. The collapse of foundationalism offers new opportunity for making sin a significant epistemological variable. But this is no more inevitable for post-foundational reflection than it was for foundationalism. For it is entirely possible to find in the ashes of foundationalism only finitude and not sinfulness, to discover preunderstandings that are perspectival but not perverse. This is just what has happened for many, if not most, of those who have played major roles in the undermining of foundationalism.[31]

(c) My third suggestion is that "Reformed" or "Calvinist" epistemology belongs in this camp, that while it shows the failure of foundationalism with exceptional clarity, the alternative it proposes does not take advantage of the new opportunity to make sin an essential epistemological category.[32] If this is true it is, of course, ironical. For Calvin is in the front rank of those who take Paul seriously, and it would be strange if epistemological reflection that associates itself with his name should fail to do so. But that is what I shall try to show to be the case.

In addition to the specific invocation of Calvin, there are other features of "Reformed" epistemology that seem to prepare the way for taking Paul seriously. First, its primary focus is religious knowledge, the primary locus of the noetic effects of sin for Calvin as for Paul (in keeping with the Law of Inverse Rationality). Second, it gives to epistemology the ethical framework mentioned at the beginning of this essay. It speaks freely of epistemic rights and duties.[33] Third, in opposition to foundationalism it recognizes the pervasiveness of prejudice (in Gadamer's sense), the "historical singularity" (Foucault) of the criteria (*a prioris*, control beliefs) at work in shaping the beliefs of various communities.[34] Finally, it is explicitly aware that belief is not always innocent.

Yet for all this it seems that the issue is mentioned only to be, if not entirely repressed, at least restricted to a mere cameo role. In Plantinga's account, for example, the familiar Reformed suspicion of natural theology is an attempt to express the claim that we do not need arguments for the existence of God because belief in God is properly basic. Without fully realizing it, Calvin (along with Bavinck, Kuyper, and Barth) has anticipated the foundationalist-evidentialist objection to theistic belief and given the outlines of an alternative account of religious knowledge. I want to suggest that this is right as far as it goes, but that it falls short of capturing what Calvin is driving at.

Plantinga quotes Calvin's claim that "there is within the human mind, and indeed by natural instinct, an awareness of divinity," that "God himself has implanted in all men a certain understanding of his divine majesty."[35] While citing other passages in which Calvin makes creation an epistemological category, but not those in which he does the same with the fall,[36] Plantinga writes

> Calvin's claim, then, is that God has created us in such a way that we have a strong tendency or inclination toward belief in him. This tendency has been in part overlaid or suppressed by sin. Were it not for the existence of sin in the world, human beings would believe in God to the same degree and with the same nat-

ural spontaneity that we believe in the existence of other persons, an external world, or the past. This is the natural human condition; it is because of our presently unnatural sinful condition that many of us find belief in God difficult or absurd. The fact is, Calvin thinks, one who does not believe in God is in an epistemically substandard position. . . . Although this disposition to believe in God is partially suppressed, it is, nonetheless universally present.[37]

Calvin would have put that last part rather differently, I suspect. In order to remind us that none of us come *naturally* to a proper knowledge of God, he would have said that while the tendency to believe is present, it is nevertheless suppressed, reversing Plantinga's order and emphasis. And in order to remind us that *none* of us comes naturally to a proper knowledge of God, he would have said that while the tendency to believe is universally present, it is *universally*, and not just partially, suppressed. Both terms are ambiguous and might miss his meaning. Universal suppression might be construed as degree rather than extension, suggesting that creation is entirely obliterated rather than that none of us is exempt from the distorting effects of sin. Partial suppression might be construed as extension rather than degree, suggesting that some of us are exempt rather than that our natural tendency to believe in God has been distorted but not obliterated. I do not doubt that Calvin would rather risk overstating the damage by speaking of universal suppression than risk suggesting that some are exempt from the noetic effects of sin by speaking of a partial suppression.

But the latter implication is just what we find in Plantinga. The most natural reading of the passage quoted above is that sin is at work in the beliefs of unbelievers but not in those of believers.[38] This is the same exemption for oneself and one's belief community which we found in Kant and Fichte. If this is Calvin's proper meaning, then we shall have to ask how seriously he himself takes Paul. But since he joins Paul in such a strong emphasis on the universality of sin, and since he sees the noetic effects of sin not so much in atheism and agnosticism as in idolatrous distortion of the divine nature, it is unlikely that this is his deepest intention. In any case, for believers to draw a line between themselves and unbelievers and to find the noetic

effects of sin only on the other side of that line is closer to epistemological Phariseeism than it is to taking Paul seriously. For
unbelief is not the only way of suppressing the truth about God.
It is only the most honest.

It might be argued at this point that it is unbelief in God
per se that is "in an epistemically substandard position," while
belief *per se* is innocent of distortions due to sin. But there are
two problems with adopting this strategy. First, there are no
such things as beliefs *per se*. There are only the actual beliefs of
actual persons and communities. Second, Reformed epistemology
has already committed itself to consideration of these actual beliefs. Its ethics of belief is explicitly person and situation relative.
What is properly basic and, more generally, rational or irrational, is the believing or not believing of concrete persons in specific situations. Correct beliefs may be irrational, and false
beliefs rational.

But in this case, even if belief in God is correct, the believer's beliefs are no more immune from the noetic effects of sin
than the unbeliever's. The motives leading to belief and the function belief plays in the believer's life may be sinful. Or sinful se-
lectivity may lead to creation of God in the believer's image (as
when God is very concerned about sexual immorality but not
about racism, or vice versa). This sinful belief can be compared
with the innocent unbelief of the unbeliever whose unbelief is
properly basic (as in the case of the young child whose loving
parents tell her there is no God). Properly to speak of the partial
suppression of our natural, instinctive belief in God is not to
suggest that only unbelievers are subject to the noetic effects of
sin; it is rather to claim that in each of us, believer and unbeliever alike, distortions due to depravity are present but less than
total.

Wolterstorff agrees with Plantinga that belief in God can be
properly basic, that it can be rational even if it has no foundations, that is, even if it is not derived from other beliefs which
provide evidence for it. But he seeks to show this somewhat differently, by giving a general account of rational belief. His principle is as follows: "A person S is rational in his eluctable and
innocently produced belief Bp if and only if S believes p, and it is
not the case that S has adequate reason to cease from believing
p."[39] For the sake of precision Wolterstorff gives more complex

versions of this principle, but for present purposes his common-sense formula is more to the point. It is that our beliefs and belief dispositions are innocent until proved guilty rather than guilty until proved innocent.[40]

It will be noticed from the formal statement of the innocence principle that there are two exceptions. It does not apply to ineluctable beliefs, those about which we neither can do nor could have done anything to bring it about that we believe differently. Nor does it apply to beliefs not innocently produced. This is the exception that Wolterstorff stresses and that is important in the present discussion. Over against the innocent belief dispositions he finds described in Thomas Reid, he mentions "those rather ignoble belief dispositions of which Marx and Freud have made so much: our disposition to believe what gives us a sense of security, our disposition to believe what serves to perpetuate our positions of economic privilege, our disposition to adopt clusters of beliefs which function as ideologies and rationalizations to conceal from our conscious awareness the ignobility of those other dispositions, and so on." These are exempted from the innocence principle, since "it seems evident that the outcomes of a noninnocent disposition should not be accorded the honor of innocence until their guilt has been proved."[41]

It does indeed. It also seems evident that the acknowledged presence of sinful belief dispositions deserves more attention in the reflections of Christian philosophers than is suggested by the following. "The Christian, though, will have a reason for not thus railing, for accepting our native and naturally developed noetic dispositions as trustworthy. He believes that we have been made thus by a good Creator. . . . It is true that he may well acknowledge that some of our dispositions are signs of our fallenness, not part of our pristine nature, so that they are unreliable. The dispositions of which Marx and Freud made so much are examples. But the Christian will trust that the unreliability of such as these will show up."[42]

This does not seem to me to be a good example of taking Paul seriously. In this epistemology creation does a full day's work, while the fall is only asked to put in a cameo appearance. It is rather different with Paul. For him creation does not serve to assure us that we naturally have innocent beliefs. Rather, he appeals to our sinful suppression of the truth about God to insist that we do not, and he invokes creation to illuminate, not the innocence of our truth but the culpability of our untruth. Wolterstorff might have taken Paul more seriously if his epistemological ethics had taken a clue from his own social ethics. Can one imagine him writing, for example, with reference to apartheid or the oppression of the Palestinians, that "the Christian will trust that the evil of such practices will show up"? And leaving it at that? Is it not rather the task of the Christian thinker in both cases to help expose the evil and to explore options for doing something about it?

If we wish to move in that direction epistemologically, the references to Marx and Freud can be helpful in several ways. First, since their analysis of ignoble and noninnocent belief dispositions in the area of religion is directed toward the believing soul, it can hardly remain as obvious as it seemed in Plantinga's case that the boundary between innocent and noninnocent noetic acts and habits corresponds to the boundary between believer and unbeliever. Sin as an epistemological category cannot be, as Fichte and Plantinga, Marx and Freud seem to want it to be, merely a device for discrediting one's opponents. To take Paul seriously is to take seriously the universality of sin. Only if perfectionism is true could even a few believing souls be noetically uncontaminated. And it would be exceeding strange for a "Reformed" epistemology suddenly to turn perfectionist.

It is clear that Wolterstorff wants to draw a line between innocent and noninnocent beliefs, even if he cannot, having invoked Marx and Freud, draw it between belief in God and unbelief. But if one takes Paul seriously about the universality of sin and sees that for him "all our [noetically] righteous deeds are like a polluted garment" (Isa. 64.6 RSV), how is the distinction to be maintained at all? How is it possible to take Calvin and Marx and Freud as seriously as Wolterstorff seems to and still talk with Thomas Reid about noetic innocence? Or, in other words, why should we think that there are any innocently produced beliefs (at least about God) to which Wolterstorff's principle of rationality could apply?

Here the mention of Marx and Freud is important in a second way. We have already noted that Calvin talks as if the noetic effects of sin are fully conscious, intentional, and deliberate. Sometimes Wolterstorff seems to talk the same way, in spite of his references to Marx and Freud, and perhaps this is why he thinks his principle has application. He writes, for example, "The exception [to the innocence principle] to which I alluded was this: Suppose that someone has undertaken to alter some native belief disposition or to cultivate some new belief disposition, for perverse reasons, or for reasons having nothing to do with getting in touch with reality. The extent to which such undertakings, *such resolutions,* can be successful seems to me severely limited. But no doubt they sometimes have their effect."[43] If we could restrict depravity to those undertakings conscious enough to be described as resolutions, perhaps we could retain an area of noetic innocence. But everything we have learned from Marx and Freud (not to mention Augustine and Sartre) about self-deception suggests that we are most skillful at doing things without resolving to do them and thus without noticing that we are doing them precisely when we are doing something shameful.

If, then, we cannot preserve a domain of innocent beliefs either by restricting the noetic effects of sin to the unbeliever or by restricting them to conscious resolutions to suppress the truth, wouldn't taking Paul seriously mean abandoning the idea that we naturally have innocent beliefs or belief dispositions and adopting the principle that our beliefs are guilty until proved innocent (at least in the areas where the Law of Inverse Rationality suggests that belief is most vulnerable to desire, including, of course, religion)? Isn't this in fact Calvin's own conclusion, his critique of natural theology being but a subordinate moment in a larger argument denying that we can have any trustworthy knowledge of God, direct or inferential, apart from the divine gift of the Word and the Spirit?

In suggesting that we replace Wolterstorff's innocence principle with a more genuinely Pauline guilt principle—doesn't the latter sound more genuinely "Reformed" in any case?—I am not suggesting a return to foundationalism. Over and above the irreparable damage done to foundationalism by the arguments of Plantinga, Wolterstorff, and many others, such a return would be doubly inappropriate. For, in the first place, nothing in the

Pauline notion of suppressing the truth suggests that the problem is a lack of evidence or self-evidence. In fact, as we shall shortly see, correct beliefs can be as useful in suppressing the truth as incorrect ones. Secondly, as we have already seen, foundational-ism itself is partly to be understood as a sinfully arrogant attempt at methodological self-purification, void of contrition, confession, or dependence upon divine grace.

Neither is the guilt principle meant to suggest an epistemology which contents itself with a wholesale condemnation of natural beliefs in areas where self-interest is present. This would be the equal but opposite complacency to that of the innocence principle, and I believe that Foucault is right in finding such a wholesale approach "arbitrary and boring."[44] This is not to deny that there is something universal or wholesale about the guilt principle. It is only to say that we become complacent, arbitrary, and boring when we take the wholesale claim as our concluding doctrine rather than as the point of departure for a retail practice of seeking to expose the variety of particular ways in which we suppress the truth and to find ways to counteract these tendencies within ourselves, individually and corporately.

At the point where we undertake these tasks we see the point of mining the history of philosophy for a deepened understanding of the Pauline motif. This is an important source of the conceptual tools for exposing the techniques by which we suppress the truth in such areas as ethics, politics, metaphysics, and theology.

Here Marx and Freud can be helpful once again, if only for the purpose of illustration. Marx's theory of ideology teaches us to ask not just *what* is believed but also *how* it is believed. Here, as with Hobbes above, the *how* question is a question about social function, about the role beliefs play in shaping and justifying public practices.[45] We suppress the truth when our ethics, politics, metaphysics, or theology serves to justify ungodly practices of exploitation or domination whether based on race, ethnicity, nationality, class, gender, or whatever. If we assume that Christian orthodoxy consists primarily of correct beliefs in theology proper, Christology, soteriology, and so forth, and we notice the frequent and easy marriage of orthodoxy with various forms of exploitation and domination, we will begin to realize that correct beliefs can be just as useful in suppressing the truth as falsehood.

Freud's theory of illusory beliefs as those based on wish-fulfillment helps us to see this in a different way. He suggests that we believe in God because it is nice to have a heavenly father. But he knows that not just any father will do. So we come to believe that "over each one of us there watches a benevolent Providence which is *only seemingly stern* and which will not suffer us to become a plaything of the overmighty and pitiless forces of nature."[46] This is the theological version of what Kant describes above in ethics, where by doubt and quibble we manage to make the moral law "more compatible with our wishes and inclinations." There is surely more than one way to produce a comfortable ethics or theology. One of the best is prudent selection. We stock our ethics with prohibitions of vices to which we are not tempted or for which we have not the courage. And we edit out of our sacred texts (in one or more of the many ways this is possible, including simply neglect) any stories or teachings which imply a genuine sternness to benevolent Providence. We end up with a collection of moral principles and theological doctrines which may be as correct as human beliefs can ever be, and precisely with this collection of truths we suppress the truth. We turn the moral law into flattery and God into a wimp.

Like Foucault, who turns from a Nietzschean theory of the relation of knowledge and power to the detailed examination of concrete practices, the Christian philosopher who takes Paul seriously will be led to a critical examination of the relation of belief and practice in our various Christian communities far more detailed and specific than anything I have attempted here.[47] As we do this we will have something new to say to our theologian colleagues by way of challenging them to join us in this project.

I want to conclude by briefly addressing several objections to such a project, in ascending order of seriousness. Objection: Such a project is too negative. It will not make people feel good about themselves. Reply: There is no shortage of politicians and possibility thinkers to flatter the public and to make us feel good about ourselves, provided we stop thinking.

Objection: Such a project is not really philosophical. It is not what philosophers do. The task of philosophy is to provide arguments which show whose beliefs are right and whose wrong. Reply: Most philosophers do not engage in the project I have described. But there are some, such as Marx, Nietzsche, and Foucault (admittedly not everyone's favorite philosophers) who do, and in any case, need the Christian philosopher be restricted to what is professionally fashionable? Much of the history of philosophy cries out for such a project, and the Christian church is desperately in need of it.

Objection: Your own objection to foundationalism as a sinful attempt at self-sanctification seems to undercut the project you recommend. Does it not presuppose that through reflection we can cleanse ourselves of the noetic presence of sin? Reply: No. It is surely possible to undertake the project in a spirit of Pelagian self-sufficiency. But it is not necessary to do so. We can recognize that reflective thought is just as vulnerable to the distortions of devious desire (for example, finding sin at work in the thinking of others but not in our own) as is prereflective thought. This will lead us to the recognition that grace and truth are inseparable at every level, and that we are as dependent upon God's help in this project of noetic cleansing as in any other mode of sanctification. To coin a cliché, we shall have to work as if everything depends on us and pray as if everything depends on God.

In his American lectures Karl Barth said that theology must be done on one's knees. Perhaps this is true for philosophy as well. Perhaps the notion of Christian philosophy makes sense after all, not in terms of its propositional *what* but in terms of its prayerful *how*. The prayer I have in mind will have many forms, no doubt. But its content will always be the same.

> Nothing in my hand I bring, Simply to Thy cross I cling;
> Naked, come to Thee for dress, Helpless look to Thee for grace;
> Foul, I to the fountain fly; Wash me, Savior, or I die.[48]

NOTES

1. I quote the *Institutes* from the Henry Beveridge translation (London: James Clarke & Co., Ltd., 1957) rather than from the more widely used Ford Lewis Battles translation (Philadelphia: Westminster,

1960) because it seems to me more forceful. The references here are to 1.3.1, 1.3.3, and 1.4.1. Since the primary biblical inspiration for the crucial passages in the *Institutes* is clearly the first chapter of Romans, a comparison of Calvin's commentary is useful. There he speaks of our attempts to "suppress or obscure" God's truth. *The Epistles of Paul to the Romans and Thessalonians,* trans. Ross Mackenzie, vol. 8 of *Calvin's New Testament Commentaries,* ed. Thomas F. Torrance and David W. Torrance, 12 vols. (St. Andrews Press, Edinburgh, and Oliver and Boyd, Edinburgh; reprint, Grand Rapids, Mich.: Eerdmans, 1979–84), 30. (Henceforth *Romans.*)

2. *Institutes* 1.3.2 and 1.4.title.

3. *Institutes* 1.4.1 and *Romans,* 31.

4. This is clear enough in the *Institutes,* but is perhaps more explicit in *Romans,* 30 and 33.

5. *Institutes* 1.4.2. and *Romans,* 37.

6. *Institutes* 1.4.3, 1.5.11–15, 1.6.1–3, and *Romans,* 36.

7. For a brief sketch of Luther on this point, see my *Kierkegaard's Critique of Reason and Society* (Macon, Ga.: Mercer University Press, 1987), 106–108.

8. The most important Kierkegaard texts in this regard are *Philosophical Fragments* and the writings of Anti-Climacus, *The Sickness Unto Death* and *Training in Christianity.* For discussion of these as related texts, see *Kierkegaard's Critique,* chaps. 2, 6, and 7.

9. For samples in Augustine, see his analysis of the motives and function of his long-standing Manichaean belief, *Confessions* 4.5; 5.10; 7.3; 8.10; 9.4; his analysis of the bad faith by which this was possible, 8.7; and the discussion in the next paragraph but one of this essay.

10. Karl Barth, *The Epistle to the Romans,* trans. Edwyn C. Hoskyns (London: Oxford, 1968), 42–54.

11. *Confessions* 1.8. These are the Warner and Pine-Coffin translations, respectively (New York: New American Library, 1963) and (Hammondsworth, England: Penguin, 1961).

12. For other Augustinian contributions to the development of the Pauline motif, see note 9 above. For a sample of the postmodernism to which I refer, see Foucault's essay, "Nietzsche, Genealogy, History," *The Foucault Reader,* ed. Paul Rabinow (New York: Pantheon, 1984). There he joins Nietzsche in a genealogy that looks for the *Herkunft* and *Entstehung* of every *Ursprung,* and thereby discovers chance, accident, and error in reason's lineage.

13. In the Editor's Introduction to *Leviathan,* Parts I and II, (Macmillan: New York: 1958), ix. Why he limits his suggestion to parts II and III is not clear.

14. *Motivated Irrationality* is the title of a useful book by David Pears in this connection (Oxford: Clarendon Press, 1984).

15. In this connection see "The Challenge of Liberation Theology," a paper from the Theology Commission of the Reformed Church in America, *The Acts and Proceedings of the 180th Regular Session of the General Synod, Reformed Church in America,* vol. 66 (1986), 301–321. If Hobbes can be said to practice a "Calvinist psychology," the reverse is just as true. As long as it is not said to be the whole story about religious belief, Calvin will also call our attention to the visible link between religious belief and political domination; see *Institutes* 1.3.2.

16. In this setting Hobbes finds the difference between religion and superstition to reflect simply the difference between our gods and their gods.

17. Immanuel Kant, *Grounding for the Metaphysics of Moral,* trans. James W. Ellington (Indianapolis: Hackett, 1981), 405. N.B. I give Academy Edition pages.

18. Fichte, *Science of Knowledge (Wissenschaftslehre) with the First and Second Introductions,* trans. Peter Heath and John Lachs (New York: Appleton-Century-Crofts, 1970), 14. In this English translation the *First Introduction* and the *Second Introduction,* both published in 1797, are included with the 1794 edition of the main text. The passages I cite are from the *First Introduction.*

19. *First Introduction,* 16.

20. *Grounding,* 405.

21. In the Preface Kant suggests that the corruption of morals is to be overcome, more precisely, by the metaphysics of morals (p. 390). Since this occurs in the section entitled "Transition from Popular Moral Philosophy to a Metaphysics of Morals," the implication here seems to be that it is Kant's moral philosophy and not philosophy as such that is exempt from corruption.

22. Jacques Derrida, *Positions,* trans. Alan Bass (Chicago: University of Chicago Press, 1981), 6–7.

23. Hume's relation to foundationalism is ambiguous because he is skeptical in two distinct ways. In his "Sceptical Doubts concerning the Operations of the Understanding" and his "Sceptical Solution of these Doubts" (sections 4 and 5 of *An Enquiry Concerning Human Understanding*), he gives an anti-foundationalist account of empirical knowledge. But in the book-burning scene with which he concludes "Of the Academical or Sceptical Philosophy" (section 12), he becomes the father of positivist foundationalism. His skepticism toward science differs from his skepticism toward metaphysics in that the former does

not discredit science as a reasonable enterprise, while the latter does so discredit metaphysics. In the larger picture, sections 4 and 5 become qualifying footnotes in a theory which affirms that science rests upon empirical foundations in a way that metaphysics does not.

24. David Hume, *The Natural History of Religion*, ed. H. E. Root (Stanford, Calif.: Stanford University Press, 1957), 26–32.

25. Ibid., 43 and 65–67.

26. Ibid., 48, 72, 76. For a discussion which links these passages in Hume to the religion critique of Marx, Nietzsche, and Freud, see my "Taking Suspicion Seriously: The Religious Uses of Modern Atheism," *Faith and Philosophy* 4 (1987): 26–42.

27. There is a hint of this even in Descartes. In the Third Meditation he asks why he is convinced that ideas resemble objects, and answers, "Well, I seem to be taught that way by nature." But he judges that this is insufficient warrant.

> When I say that I have been taught so by nature, I understand only that I am driven by a spontaneous impulse to believing this position, and not that some light of nature shows me it is true. These two positions are at considerable odds with one another. For whatever this light of nature shows me . . . cannot in any way be doubtful. . . . As for natural impulses, I have very often judged myself to have been driven by them to the poorer choice, when it was a question of choosing a good; I do not see why I should trust them any more in other matters. (Quoted from the Cress translation, [Indianapolis: Hackett, 1979], 25–26).

While not as explicit as Plato or Kant, Descartes here evokes the opposition between reason and passion or inclination in the moral domain and the negative effect of the latter on our beliefs.

28. *Confessions* 7.20.

29. *Critique of Pure Reason* B 145–46.

30. The latter phrase is the title of a book by Thomas Nagel. The former appears in Foucault's Preface to *The History of Sexuality*, vol. 2, in *The Foucault Reader*, 333–339. A helpful account of the historical nominalism implied in Foucault's phrase can be found in John Rajchman, *Michel Foucault: The Freedom of Philosophy* (New York: Columbia University Press, 1985), 50–60. Nagel and Foucault, as different from each other as they are, are both concerned to undermine foundationalism.

31. I have argued this with respect to Heidegger and Merleau-Ponty, respectively, in "Socrates Between Descartes and Jeremiah" and "Situation and Suspicion in the Thought of Merleau-Ponty: The Ques-

tion of Phenomenology and Politics." For a more general discussion of the difference between the hermeneutics of finitude and the hermeneutics of suspicion, see my "Phenomenology and Religious Truth." All three essays forthcoming.

32. I have in mind here especially the essays of the editors in *Faith and Rationality: Reason and Belief in God,* ed. Alvin Plantinga and Nicholas Wolterstorff (Notre Dame, Ind.: University of Notre Dame Press, 1983). Important background for these essays is found in Alvin Plantinga, *God and Other Minds: A Study of the Rational Justification of Belief in God* (Ithica, N.Y.: Cornell University Press, 1967) and Nicholas Wolterstorff, *Reason within the Bounds of Religion,* 2d ed. rev. (Grand Rapids, Mich.: Eerdmans, 1984). Plantinga develops the *modus tollens* critique of foundationalism, while Wolterstorff develops the alternative model of knowledge strategy.

33. See Plantinga, "Reason and Belief in God," in *Faith and Rationality,* 30–39, 48, 52, 71–75, and 83–84; and Wolterstorff, "Can Belief in God Be Rational If It Has No Foundations?" in *Faith and Rationality,* 142–58. Subsequent references are to these essays unless otherwise noted.

34. In doing so, however, it refuses to draw the conclusion of relativistic historicism or nihilistic postmodernism that the concepts of truth and rationality must be abandoned. See Plantinga, 77–78, and Wolterstorff, 4–5 and 155. This refusal places "Reformed" epistemology in the company of many in both the "continental" and "Anglo-American" philosophical traditions who are seeking to find a middle way between absolutisic objectivism of foundationalism and the nihilistic subjectivism typified by the recent work of Richard Rorty.

35. Quoted from *Institutes* 1.3.1. in Plantinga, 65–66.

36. The supporting passages are from 1.5.1 and 1.5.2. Thus Plantinga skips over 1.4, a major locus for sin as an epistemological category, and stops short of Calvin's continued development of the theme in 1.5.4–15. Note the emphasis on creation and the silence on sin in this summary of Plantinga's own view. "Belief in the existence of God is in the same boat as belief in other minds, the past, and perceptual objects; in each case God has so constructed us that in the right circumstances we form the belief in question. But then the belief that there is such a person as God is as much among the deliverances of reason as those other beliefs" (90).

37. Plantinga, 66.

38. Since in the passage from Calvin which Plantinga quotes (p. 66) the belief in question is "that *there is some God,*" it appears that even the most generic believer is home free.

39. Wolterstorff, 164.

40. Ibid., p. 163. Following Thomas Reid, Wolterstorff distinguishes "credulity dispositions" from "reasoning dispositions," the former producing beliefs immediately, that is, non-inferentially, while the latter produces beliefs by deriving them from other beliefs. He also classifies dispositions by origin, distinguishing innate from acquired dispositions and subdividing the latter into those acquired by classical and operant conditioning. See pp. 149–153. If I understand him correctly, (1) this produces a 3 by 2 grid with six different types of belief disposition, (2) the innocence principle applies to all six types, and (3) it applies to beliefs as well as to belief dispositions.

41. Wolterstorff, 149 and 163.

42. Ibid., 174.

43. Ibid., 163, my italics. The subsequent account of culpably revised dispositions reinforces the sense that loss of innocence is quite fully conscious. "(It is to be remembered here that many of our belief dispositions *get* revised by conditioning; we do not *undertake* to revise them.) If one undertakes to revise it for some other reason, and succeeds, then the disposition, with respect to the points of revision, is no longer innocent with respect to rationality. It has been *culpably revised*. . . . The innocent-until-proved-guilty principle which I have affirmed for beliefs must be understood as applying just to those not produced by culpably revised dispositions" (p. 164, his italics).

44. "Shall we try reason? To my mind nothing would be more sterile . . . because such a trial would trap us into playing the arbitrary and boring part of either the rationalist or the irrationalist" (Foucault, "The Subject and Power," Afterword to Hubert L. Dreyfus and Paul Rabinow, *Michel Foucault: Beyond Structuralism and Hermeneutics* [Chicago: University of Chicago Press, 1982–83], 210). The equivalence of the two complacencies lies in the fact that both are in practice content to "trust that the unreliability of such [belief dispositions] as these will show up."

45. Wolterstorff distinguishes the *what* from the *how* question on page 156. But there the *how* question only concerns the degree of firmness of belief rather than function and does not, so far as I can see, contribute to taking Paul seriously. When Kierkegaard poses the *how* question in terms of objectivity vs. subjectivity (in *Concluding Unscientific Postscript*), he poses, as does Marx, a question of function. Its purpose is to uncover a mode of suppressing the very truth one proudly proclaims.

46. Sigmund Freud, *The Future of an Illusion* in *The Standard Edition of the Complete Psychological Works of Sigmund Freud*, ed.

and trans. James Strachey *et al.* (London: Hogarth Press, 1953–74), 21:19. My italics.

47. Marx is as good a model as Foucault. His philosophical theorizing leads to the critique of political economy which culminates in *Capital.*

48. From "Rock of Ages, Cleft for Me" by Augustus Toplady.